£11.95

FRONT COVER: Marown

PHOTOGRAPHS: Mark Cranham - cranhamphoto.com; John Grossick - grossick.co.uk; Tim Holt - timholt@talktalk.net; www.healyracing.ie; Nigel Kirby - www.nigelkirbyphotography.com

ISBN: 978-1-872437-76-7

Contents

Welcome
PAUL FERGUSON

EVERY National Hunt season is eagerly awaited – certainly from my point of view – but, perhaps, more so than ever, jumps fans are eager for the serious stuff to return, given the premature ending to the latest campaign.

Obviously, there was far more important things happening around the world during the spring than National Hunt racing, but it returned in July, and we were fortunate enough to enjoy some fairly competitive stuff for the time of year. However, the 2020-2021 season 'proper' is almost upon us, and Jumpers To Follow once again aims to whet the appetite.

Before moving on to what lies ahead, I would like to congratulate both Brian Hughes (Champion Jockey) and Jonjo O'Neill Jnr (Champion Conditional) on their achievements from last season. Both return to form part of this year's *A View From The Saddle* section, which now consists of 10 jockeys. This year's new additions are Adrian Heskin, retained rider for the McNeill Family who have plenty to look forward to this season, and Ben Jones, who quickly made a name for himself last winter, with his Ladbrokes Trophy success aboard De Rasher Counter thrusting him into the spotlight. Ben is attached to the Philip Hobbs yard, whilst also having a strong link with Emma Lavelle, and both riders are welcome additions.

I would like to thank all 10 jockeys – the others being Johnny Burke, Jamie Codd, Aidan Coleman, Jerry McGrath, Nick Scholfield and Harry Skelton – for their time and effort. All of them seemed happy to talk through the summer, clearly starved of action, and have, therefore, nominated plenty of horses for the notebook.

Most (some more so than others) have included an un-raced horse or two, and I have myself this year – in the *Around The Yards* section – tried to include a clutch of nicely-bred youngsters, who have yet to see a racecourse. The thinking behind this being that there will have been a lot of young horses denied a run in a spring bumper, due to the Covid-19 outbreak, and the subsequent suspension of racing.

The lack of end-of-season bumpers has also contributed towards the fact that, for the first

time in the 14 years of Jumpers To Follow, I have included a couple of Point-to-Point winners (yet to race under Rules) and a juvenile hurdler among my *40 Leading Prospects*. The first section of the book once again focuses on the horses I am most looking forward to following this winter, and as ever, the list consists of horses who are far from being fully exposed. Three horses retain their place from last year – with Shishkin probably the most unoriginal selection of them all – but I cannot wait to see him jump a fence, and think that he could go right to the top of the chasing tree. As always, a large proportion of my selections will be either running in novice hurdles, or switching to fences, with a few handicappers thrown in for good measure.

Another new addition this year is an interview with Richard Thompson, son of the owners of Cheveley Park Stud. Given their ever-increasing string of National Hunt horses, I thought it a good time to speak with Richard, who kindly runs through their horses for the season ahead. Their squad is once again headed by Envoi Allen and the unbeaten six-year-old is set to go novice chasing this term.

This year's Foreword has been written by Jane Mangan, who first appeared in the pages of Jumpers To Follow way back in 2013. The former jockey is now one of the most knowledgeable pundits on TV and it is great to have her back.

Thank you to both Richard and Jane for their contribution, and also to the many trainers (or their representatives) and owners – of whom there are too many to name in person – who have answered my many questions. Thanks also to my colleagues at Weatherbys (in particular Paul Wright), who have again done a great job with the design of the book; regular readers might notice a slightly new look. And, thanks to everyone else – including the photographers – who have helped make this year's publication possible.

Finally, thank you to each and every one of you, for purchasing a copy of Jumpers To Follow 2020-2021. Your continued support is greatly appreciated and I sincerely hope you enjoy this year's edition.

Best of luck for a successful season,

Paul

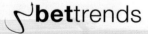

Foreword
JANE MANGAN

A COMMON interest has the ability to bring people together for a purpose, and often in achieving that purpose, friendships are born. Paul Ferguson was a mere pen pal of mine until thirty minutes before the 2020 Arkle Chase at Cheltenham, yet when we met for the first time it was as if we were old mates.

In an effort to predict the future, let's take a look back. The year was 2013, I was juggling riding as an amateur with my college studies when a guy I had never heard of popped into my Twitter DM's. Now before your mind races to conclusions, Paul Ferguson was, and still is a happily married man!

This is not a Cinderella story, instead one of opportunity. Paul asked if I would be interested in contributing to his Jumpers To Follow book for the coming season, indicating that having ridden some smart bumper horses, I might have a unique insight into the Irish contingent.

Honestly, I was dubious. Lots of books get published but few are actually worth consideration. Paul must have sensed my hesitation as he popped the previous year's book in the post immediately. A few days later and after some light reading, I knew I wanted to be part of this story.

Fast forward seven years, I've swapped riding races for discussing them and like myself, Weatherbys recognised Paul's talent too! This little anecdote is a testament to a common passion that can unite regardless of geography or any other barriers for that matter.

As always, this edition is full of exclusive insights from industry professionals along with some juicy big priced Pointers that are only beginning their careers.

What I always find most interesting in Jumpers To Follow is how the best in each category progress up the ladder (or not!). For instance, I put up Very Wood as a horse to follow after he won his bumper at the Punchestown Festival. While he did go on to win a Grade 1 as a novice hurdler, it was the Albert Bartlett over three miles – I'd have had good money on that he was fast enough for the Supreme.

Horses are humans on four legs. All different personalities and mindsets. Some want it more than others and are willing to try harder than most to get their head in front. Luck is an essential ingredient and blood plays an important role, too. That's what makes our sport so encapsulating – there is no formula to success.

Yes, one can hedge bets and play it safe with the tried and trusted but there are exceptions to every rule. The Moore family have unearthed an ace in their pack with Goshen, while Joe Donnelly has arguably the best quality to quantity ratio of any owner in the game.

When news broke last summer of Gigginstown's phased out departure and that Paul and Clare Rooney would be concentrating on the Flat, fear set in amongst breeders, pin-hookers and Point-to-Point handlers. Who will take their place?

However, if we rewind just a decade to when Jim Lewis was in Joe Donnelly's position and Clive Smith owned the chaser of any lifetime; colours come and go, but the game remains the same.

In recent months, Sean Mulryan, Kenny Alexander, Brian Acheson, Cheveley Park Stud and more have picked up the mantle. Why? I'm sure they enjoy owning and watching their horses run, but also, the product of horse racing, and it's entertainment and satisfaction value is immeasurable.

If you are reading this book, chances are you and I have a mutual bond. The industry of horse racing is multi-dimensional and has more layers than this book has pages. We're all entitled to our opinions, and at one stage or another, horses will make us all look stupid. The main thing to remember is that unlike the enigma, nobody has ever cracked the horse racing code.

Information is currency, some more valuable than others. Identifying the right source of information is paramount, and if you are reading this book then well done, you've taken that all important first step

Whether you're a breeder, owner, trainer, rider, groom, or simply an admirer, there is something for everyone in Paul Ferguson's Jumpers To Follow.

Best of luck for the season,

Jane

SILVER FOREVER - THE GREY IS ONE TO FOLLOW IN THE MARES' DIVISION

Leading
PROSPECTS

AJERO

5yo Red Jazz – Eoz (Sadler's Wells)

Trainer
Kim Bailey
Owner
Mrs Julie Martin and David R Martin

Optimum Conditions
2m on decent ground
Career Form Figures
3-

GIVEN his pedigree, it should come as no surprise that Ajero has been purchased by the owners of Charbel and is now in training with Kim Bailey. A half-brother to the 2018 Peterborough Chase winner, the five-year-old made an eye-catching racecourse debut, when third in a bumper at Thurles.

Held-up, Ajero refused to settle for Jamie Codd, but still latched himself onto the tail of the main group – travelling well – leaving the back straight. Despite never really looking like he would get on terms with the front pair, he ran on well in the closing stages to record a most promising start to his career, and the form of the race was later advertised when the runner-up won at Leopardstown and the fourth at Navan.

Albeit a little more experienced (had run three times, winning twice before finishing fourth in the Grade 1 at Punchestown), Charbel had also shaped with considerable promise for Thomas Mullins and owner Sandra McCarthy before enjoying a fruitful first season over hurdles, and Ajero is taken to follow suit. If he learns to relax, he could well develop into a smart performer and should be capable of winning a bumper on reappearance, if Bailey opts to start down that route. To date, Red Jazz is yet to sire a National Hunt winner, but Ajero should soon change that.

APPRECIATE IT

6yo Jeremy – Sainte Baronne (Saint des Saints)

Trainer
W P Mullins
Owner
Miss M A Masterson

Optimum Conditions
2m4f+ on easy ground
Career Form Figures
31/3112-

RUNNER-UP to stable-mate Ferny Hollow in the Weatherbys Champion Bumper at Cheltenham, Appreciate It had earlier won two Leopardstown bumpers, and looks a high-class prospect for the novice hurdle division this season.

Only third on his debut under Rules at Fairyhouse – at a time when the Mullins horses were needing the run – he made all and stayed on strongly to win over 2m4f at the Christmas fixture. Dropping back to the minimum trip proved no inconvenience at the Dublin Racing Festival, where he won the Grade 2 in taking fashion

Ridden a shade more patiently at Cheltenham, the imposing six-year-old joined issue coming down the hill and lead the field on the turn for home, seeing off all bar his often headstrong stable-companion, who came from a long way off the pace. It was still a fine effort and one that promises so much more once going up in distance over obstacles.

A winner at the second time of asking in the Point-to-Point sphere, he had finished third behind Envoi Allen on debut, and it could be that he follows a similar path to him this season, taking in the Grade 1 Lawlor's of Naas Novice Hurdle, en route to Cheltenham, where the Ballymore would seem the most likely target at this early stage.

BALLYADAM

5yo Fame And Glory – Grass Tips (Bob Back)

Trainer
Gordon Elliott
Owner
Cheveley Park Stud

Optimum Conditions
2m+ on decent ground
Career Form Figures
131-

CHEVELEY Park Stud have a lot to look forward to this season, with Champion Bumper winner Ferny Hollow spearheading a strong team of novice hurdlers.

Willie Mullins' headstrong performer could easily develop into a high-class novice this season, but the same can be said of Ballyadam, who cost the leading owners a lot of money (£330,000) on the back of an easy sole Point-to-Point success at Portrush.

He made his debut for current connections in a bumper at Navan in February, before which he was himself the subject of ante-post support for the Champion Bumper at Cheltenham. Having pulled hard early, the son of Fame And Glory could finish only third on heavy ground, and although it appeared as though his bubble was burst somewhat, it was a promising start on reflection. The race worked out well, too, with the winner finishing seventh at Cheltenham and the runner-up winning at Down Royal.

Ballyadam made no mistake next time, in a weaker race and on better ground, at Downpatrick. Again sent off at prohibitive odds, the five-year-old settled better and was ridden more prominently. He travelled with purpose, and cruised clear from the two pole, to win by 18 lengths. Despite that victory coming over 2m1½f, he looks to have the gears to be fully effective over the minimum trip.

BEAR GHYLLS

5yo Arcadio – Inch Princess (Oscar)

Trainer
Nicky Martin
Owner
Bradley Partnership

Optimum Conditions
2m+ on any ground
Career Form Figures
1-

SOMERSET-BASED trainer Nicky Martin – who has also has horses in training with Charlie Longsdon and her neighbouring Philip Hobbs – does well with the small string she has at her disposal, with the likes of Colonel Custard, Sykes and The Two Amigos a trio who have served her well in recent seasons.

Martin only saddled three winners during the 2019-20 season, with Can You Believe It winning a handicap hurdle at Newton Abbot last August and Mole Trap winning a mares' handicap hurdle at Hereford in December. However, without doubt, her most interesting winner was Bear Ghylls, who won a Warwick bumper by 19 lengths in early-March.

Sent off at 33-1, the son of Arcadio was kept wide throughout, but was never too far from the pace. Having travelled with purpose, he hit the front still going well on the side of the course, and was already well clear as he straightened for home. Despite looking distinctly green, he continued to forge further ahead, running out a thoroughly convincing winner.

With the top three in the betting under-performing, the form has to be treated with a degree of caution, but I'm prepared to think that Bear Ghylls possesses a fair amount of ability and he looks to have a bright future. His pedigree suggests that he won't mind going up in trip and should also handle better ground.

BOB OLINGER

5yo Sholokhov – Zenaide (Zaffaran)

Trainer
Henry de Bromhead
Owner
Robcour

Optimum Conditions
2m4f+ on easy ground
Career Form Figures
11-

SOME high-class horses have won the Point-to-Point bumper at Gowran in early-March – namely First Lieutenant, Yorkhill and Minella Melody – and Bob Olinger ran out a hugely impressive winner of this year's renewal.

A 15-length winner of a maiden Point for Pat Doyle the previous November, he made all at Gowran to score by an easy 10 lengths. Held together in front, he quickened away inside the final furlong to score with any amount in hand.

Visually, it was one of the most taking performances of the season in the bumper division, and it is worth noting that his usually reserved trainer mentioned both Aintree and Punchestown as possible options in his post-race interview. Obviously neither meeting took place, but it highlights the regard in which this horse is held. That bumper success came over 2m2f, so I would expect him to start off over an intermediate trip as a hurdler.

Brian Acheson (Robcour) has tasted plenty of success as an owner already, with the victories of Poker Party (Kerry National) and Chris's Dream (Troytown & Red Mills Chase) his biggest to date, but Bob Olinger looks to have the potential to promote his now well-known silks in an ever greater light. He could easily be a Graded class novice hurdler, and longer-term, will make an exciting chaser.

BOOTHILL

5yo Presenting – Oyster Pipit (Accordion)

Trainer
Harry Fry
Owner
Brian & Sandy Lambert

Optimum Conditions
2m+ on decent ground
Career Form Figures
221-

RUNNER-UP in a couple of Irish Points, Boothill still fetched £125,000 when going through the sales ring at Cheltenham last November, and that appeared to be, potentially, money well spent when the five-year-old made a winning debut for Harry Fry in a Kempton bumper.

Keen throughout, the son of Presenting was never too far from the pace, and he swept three-wide into the home straight. Around a length up with a couple of furlongs to run, he responded well to Johnny Burke's urgings, and duly drew clear to score by more than four lengths. The runner-up had earlier chased home Third Time Lucki (went on to finish fourth in the Champion Bumper) on debut, so the form looks reasonable, and the concluding race on Betway Chase day is often well-contested, with Riverside Theatre a notable winner back in 2008.

Prior to joining his current connections, Boothill twice ran to a decent level in Ireland, on both occa-sions chasing home a good prospect from the Colin Bowe stable. Given how keenly he raced at Kempton, it is likely that he will start off over the minimum trip, before going up in distance once he learns to relax. His pedigree suggests that he might always be best on a decent surface, and he is another for whom both Aintree and Punchestown were mentioned.

BRINKLEY

5yo Martaline – Royale Majesty (Nikos)

Trainer
David Pipe
Owner
Brocade Racing

Optimum Conditions
2m4f+ on soft ground
Career Form Figures
7/31-

SADLY for Garth and Anne Broom, Native River was ruled out of this year's Gold Cup shortly after his third win Newbury's Denman Chase. The owners did see their colourful silks carried to Cheltenham success earlier in the season, however, courtesy of Harry Senior, and Brinkley made a winning debut in the colours of Brocade Racing at Newbury in late-February.

Formerly in the care of Liz Doyle, the grey had shaped with promise in the four-year-old bumper at last year's Punchestown Festival, and even more so, when third behind Blue Sari and The Bosses Oscar in a maiden hurdle at the same track.

Although there were a couple of notable disappointments at Newbury, it was hard not to be impressed. Prominent throughout, he jumped well and stayed on really strongly in the closing stages to score by 15 lengths.

Whilst he looks all over a future 3m chaser, he is only five so is likely to remain over hurdles for now, and he looks potentially well-handicapped on an opening mark of 130. Given that he remains a novice until the end of November, there ought to be plenty of options for Brinkley, however Haydock's valuable Betfair Stayers' Handicap Hurdle – a race that David Pipe has won with Grands Crus, Dynaste and Gevrey Chambertin – could be the ideal early season target.

CAPTAIN GUINNESS

5yo Arakan – Presenting d'Azy (Presenting)

Trainer
Henry de Bromhead
Owner
Declan Landy

Optimum Conditions
2m – 2m4f+ on easy ground
Career Form Figures
12B-

GIVEN that he only stepped foot on a racecourse for the first time in mid-December, Captain Guinness made giant strides last season and might well have been involved in the finish of the Supreme Novices' Hurdle, had he not been brought down two out.

Sent off 20-1 for a maiden hurdle at Navan, he travelled really well into contention, and picked up stylishly in the closing stages, looking as though he would have won even if the oods-on favourite hadn't fallen at the final flight. He confirmed the promise by giving the more experienced Andy Dufresne a fright in the Grade 2 Moscow Flyer, where he raced enthusiastically on the front end.

I actually thought his inexperience might catch him out in the Supreme, but he went through the race nicely, and was still moving sweetly when badly hampered three out. Back on the bridle, he had nowhere to go when Elixir d'Ainay fell in front of him.

After just three starts, there is a chance that he will remain over hurdles, but he is a lengthy individual who looks to have the scope for chasing. His trainer doesn't usually hesitate in sending his horses over fences, and he would certainly be an exciting recruit to the novice chase division. I would expect him to follow a similar path to that taken by stable-mate Notebook last season.

CHANTRY HOUSE

6yo Yeats – The Last Bank (Phardante)

Trainer
Nicky Henderson
Owner
John P McManus

Optimum Conditions
2m4f+ on any ground
Career Form Figures
U/11/113-

THE first of three of last year's *Leading Prospects* to retain their place, Chantry House did little wrong in three starts over hurdles, and given his physique, he should take high rank in the novice chase division. A cosy winner at Cheltenham last December – where he had Stolen Silver (Grade 2 winner next time) and Pileon (won his next two before finishing second in the Martin Pipe) in behind – the son of Yeats followed up in effortless fashion at Newbury.

Despite the sharp rise in class, he ran a sound race to finish third in the Supreme at Cheltenham. A mistake at the top of hill put him on the back foot, and from there on, he could never really get on terms. He did stay on well, again suggesting that he will improve for stepping up in distance, and had Aintree taken place, I'm sure the Mersey Novices' Hurdle would have been considered.

An Irish Points winner on his second start, he was still leading when coming down four out on debut, in a maiden which also was contested by Monkfish (winner), Fury Road and Fiddlerontheroof.

Intermediate trips could prove ideal this season, with Newbury's Grade 2 Berkshire Novices' Chase a possible starting point. The Scilly Isles is another likely target, whilst the Marsh could end up being the race for him at Cheltenham.

COCONUT SPLASH

5yo Stowaway – Presenting Chaos (Presenting)

Trainer
Evan Williams
Owner
Mr & Mrs William Rucker

Optimum Conditions
2m+ on easy ground
Career Form Figures
1/2F1-

THOSE of you who read this year's Cheltenham Festival Betting Guide might remember that Coconut Splash was a horse I was hoping to see in a handicap hurdle in the spring, possibly at Aintree. That obviously didn't transpire, but he remains a horse of some potential, and one who could be well-treated on a mark of 131.

The winner of a four-year-old maiden Point for Cormac Doyle, the chestnut made his debut for Evan Williams in a maiden hurdle at Aintree, where he was beaten by the narrowest of margins. Having travelled really well, he was collared by another of this year's *Leading Prospects*, Imperial Alcazar, who along with the third, franked the form.

Coconut Splash dropped back to the minimum trip for his final two outings, starting at Newbury, where he held every chance when falling at the last. He then justified favouritism a shade cosily at Wetherby, where he beat Bean In Trouble, who won off 122 next time.

Although he will make a lovely chaser in time, being only five I expect he will return in a handicap hurdle, and stepping back up to 2m4f should bring about further improvement. Chepstow's Silver Trophy is a possible starting point, after which there should be plenty of options over an intermediate trip, and he can land a nice prize this season.

DO WANNA KNOW

6yo Frammassone – Mille Et Une Nuits (Ecologist)

Trainer
Charlie Longsdon
Owner
Girls Allowed

Optimum Conditions
2m4f+ on any ground
Career Form Figures
2/1F1-

SADDLING Loose Chips to win at the age of 14 must have been a personal highlight for trainer Charlie Longsdon during the 2019-20 campaign, during which he looked to have introduced a nice long-term prospect in the shape of Do Wanna Know, who won twice in novice hurdles.

Runner-up to Punchestown Festival bumper winner Longhouse Poet (placed in Grade 1 company last term) in his sole Irish Point – where he came from off the pace and jumped particularly well – he was picked up for £50,000 last February, and he made the perfect start for his new connections. Prominent throughout, he travelled with purpose and jumped fluently (especially at the last, when it was needed) en route to winning a competitive-looking novice event at Huntingdon.

The runner-up advertised the form by winning his next two before finishing third in the re-routed EBF Final (off 131), whilst Do Wanna Know was in the process of running another big race, when coming down two out at Newbury. He still held every chance at the time, and following a short break, returned to winning ways, albeit in a two-runner race at Catterick.

Rated 125, this imposing six-year-old looks potentially well-treated and would be of significant interest if heading straight over fences. However, given his low-mileage, there is a chance that he could head down the handicap hurdle route.

EASY AS THAT

5yo Sans Frontieres – Bell Storm (Glacial Storm)

Trainer
Venetia Williams
Owner
Kate & Andrew Brooks

Optimum Conditions
2m+ on soft ground
Career Form Figures
11-

THE 27 winners who carried the silks or Kate and Andrew Brooks during the 2019-20 season included a Cheltenham Festival winner (Simply The Betts), Kingmaker winner Rouge Vif, and Itchy Feet, who provided the owners with their first winner at Grade 1 level when landing Sandown's Scilly Isles Novices' Chase.

The likes of Saint Calvados and Skandiburg also provided them with Saturday winners, whilst dual bumper winner Easy As That marked himself down as a potentially smart sort, when scoring at Ffos Las and, under a 7lbs penalty, at Musselburgh.

Having made most to make a winning debut on heavy ground in South Wales, the son of Sans Frontieres was even more impressive, when sent north to Scotland. Again, making most of the running, the five-year-old appeared to have the opposition in trouble at the top of the home straight, and wasn't hard pressed to stride right away, eventually crossing the line with 13 lengths to spare.

To date, Easy As That has raced exclusively on testing ground and given how well he handled it on both occasions, might always need deep ground to show his best. He looks a nice prospect for the novice hurdle division, and given that his dam is a half-sister to high-class staying hurdler Time For Rupert, he should have no problem in stepping up in distance in due course.

ELVIS MAIL

6yo Great Pretender – Queenly Mail (Medaaly)

Trainer
N W Alexander
Owner
The Ladies Who

Optimum Conditions
2m on any ground
Career Form Figures
443/41231/181-

TWICE a winner over hurdles during his novice campaign, Elvis Mail continued his ascent through the ranks last winter, winning twice from three starts in handicap company. Reappearing off a mark of 132, he produced a smart performance to make a winning return at Ayr, where he came from last to first to win with plenty in hand.

Sent south for the first time in his career, things didn't go to plan in Newbury's Gerry Feilden, where he failed to land a blow in a race won by subsequent Champion Hurdle winner, Epatante.

Returning to action – at his favourite track, Kelso – after a six-week break, Elvis Mail returned to winning ways in workmanlike fashion. Despite not travelling as smoothly as is often the case, he came back on the bridle in between the final two flights, and showed a good attitude to give a subsequent winner 18lbs. That was his third win from four hurdles starts at the Borders track.

When he returns, the 137-rated hurdler will embark on a novice chase campaign, and he ought to enjoy another fruitful campaign. If he reaches a similar level – and there is no reason why he shouldn't – over fences, something like the Red Rum at Aintree could be an ideal spring target, as a strong pace seems to bring the best out in the six-year-old.

FIGAROC

5yo Masterstroke – Oxyna (High Yield)

Trainer
W P Mullins
Owner
Mrs S Ricci

Optimum Conditions
Unknown
Career Form Figures
2-

THE winner of the Group 2 Grand Prix de Deauville when trained by Andre Fabre, Masterstroke has yet to make a real impact at stud, but Figaroc ran a race full of promise on his sole start in France, and could well be one of the horses who highlights him as a sire.

Runner-up at Compiegne last May, the five-year-old travelled with purpose and jumped well in the main. He looked all over the winner approaching the final hurdle, but was run out of it late on, perhaps finding the 2m2f trip stretching his stamina somewhat, having raced a shade keenly early on. The winner (twice) and the third have won over fences since, whilst there were a couple of subsequent hurdles winners also in behind, so the form looks fairly strong.

Bought privately, Figaroc is now in training with Willie Mullins, and although we didn't get to see him last season, the five-year-old is expected to return to action in the autumn. Mullins has taken the patient approach with several French imports in the past, and the fact that he remains a novice for the upcoming season is a bonus. A half-brother to Energie Blue (winner over hurdles and fences), Figaroc could well prove best over the minimum trip, and he is bred to handle better ground than he encountered on debut.

FLIGHT DECK

6yo Getaway – Rate Of Knots (Saddlers' Hall)

Trainer
Jonjo O'Neill
Owner
John P McManus

Optimum Conditions
2m4f+ on any ground
Career Form Figures
600/1-

RUNNER-UP in the valuable mares' novices' chase final at Newbury, Rate Of Knots featured as a *Leading Prospect* in this publication, and some 11 years later, her second foal Flight Deck follows suit.

Representing the same connections of Jonjo O'Neill and JP McManus, Flight Deck was only seen once last season, when running out a convincing winner of a handicap hurdle at Newbury. Clearly appreciating the longer trip, the son of Getaway was ridden with utmost confidence, and was produced with a well-timed run inside the final furlong, shedding his maiden tag off a mark of 114.

The race worked out well, with the runner-up and fourth both winning next time, and given the ease with which he won, a 7lbs rise should not prove beyond Flight Deck when he reappears, with the conditional jockeys' race (0-125 over 2m5f) at Cheltenham's November meeting a possible early-season target. JP McManus has actually owned five of the past six winners of that particular contest, so it would certainly be interesting if the six-year-old was handed an entry, although there ought to be plenty of options open to him, especially as he remains a novice until the end of November. Flight Deck appeals as a horse who is capable of progressing through handicaps, and it is hoped that he lands a valuable prize at some point.

GARS DE SCEAUX

4yo Saddler Maker – Replique (April Night)

Trainer
Gordon Elliott
Owner
John P McManus

Optimum Conditions
2m+ on easy ground
Career Form Figures
1-

FOR the first time in the 14 years of Jumpers To Follow, I have included a couple of Point-to-Point winners (who have yet to race under Rules) among my 40 *Leading Prospects*. The first of those is Gars de Sceaux, who created a lasting impression when winning a four-year-old maiden at Borris House for Denis Murphy.

Ridden by Jamie Codd, the grey travelled kindly in behind the leaders, and despite getting in tight three out, quickly made up ground, to join Magic Tricks on the run to two out. Having looked all set to take command at that point, he made what looked quite a serious error (although Jamie Codd states in *A View From The Saddle* that it probably looked worse than it actually was), but quickly regained equilibrium, and was a length up when winging the final fence. Despite the short run-in, he drew six lengths clear of the runner-up, and he would have won by much further, but for that mistake two out.

A big, good-looking son of Saddler Maker, his dam is from the family of Bristol de Mai, and he was purchased privately – as was the runner-up – by JP McManus, to join Gordon Elliott. Given his pedigree, he could easily go hurdling this season, but I suspect that he will be contesting bumpers, and he looks a fine long-term prospect.

GRAN LUNA

4yo Spanish Moon – Coppena (Balko)

Trainer
Nicky Henderson
Owner
Surrey Racing (GL)

Optimum Conditions
2m+ on easy ground
Career Form Figures
1-

THE first of four bumper winning mares to feature amongst this year's 40 *Leading Prospects*, Gran Luna made a winning racecourse debut in what looked a strong event, on the same Newbury card on which Brinkley and Flight Deck had earlier won.

Buried in mid-field, the Spanish Moon filly was ridden with plenty of confidence by Nico de Boinville, who didn't have to get at all serious with her at any stage. Having eased her way to the front, she didn't do an awful lot when there, suggesting that she would come on considerably for the experience.

A slowly-run contest, Gran Luna had too much speed for the runner-up, although it is also worth remembering that she is bred to appreciate an extra half-mile herself. Nicky Henderson stated after the race that she would be aimed at the valuable sales bumper back at Newbury the following month, suggesting that she is held in fairly high regard at Seven Barrows. Henderson won that contest in 2014 with Gaitway, two years after My Tent Or Yours finished runner-up for the stable.

When she returns, Gran Luna has the option of heading to Cheltenham for the Listed mares' bumper in November, or going straight over hurdles. If the latter is chosen, her trainer might have one eye on the Listed novices' hurdle at Newbury's Winter Carnival.

HOI POLLOI

5yo Shantou – Backtothekingsnest (King's Theatre)

Trainer
Emma Lavelle
Owner
Nicholas Mustoe

Optimum Conditions
2m+ on decent ground
Career Form Figures
1-

FOLLOWING the victories of Runswick Bay and Red Rookie – who would go on to make it two-from-two under Rules at Uttoxeter on Midlands Grand National day – Emma Lavelle made it three debutant bumper winners in just two-and-a-half weeks, when Hoi Polloi won division one of a Kempton bumper in early-February.

Given the lack of pace, it wasn't surprising that the field was still well-bunched as they turned for home, and having made ground onto the heels of the leaders, Hoi Polloi looked to have nowhere to go. The Shantou gelding looked pretty green when first asked to pick up, and after failing to find a gap, was forced to switch around horses, finding himself on the inside with less than a quarter-mile to run. The penny soon dropped, however, and having seen daylight as the leaders passed through the wings of the final flight, he picked up stylishly to run out a decisive winner.

Given how the race unfolded, it could well be that there were a few hard luck stories in behind, but there was no denying the impressive finishing speed showed by the winner, who looks a nice prospect for novice hurdles. An expensive purchase as a store, he is bred to stay a bit further in time, but clearly isn't short of pace and is, therefore, likely to start over the minimum trip.

IMPERIAL ALCAZAR

6yo Vinnie Roe – Maddy's Supreme (Supreme Leader)

Trainer
Fergal O'Brien
Owner
Imperial Racing Partnership 2016

Optimum Conditions
2m4f+ on soft ground
Career Form Figures
423/1221-

UNABLE to win a bumper the season before last, Imperial Alcazar appealed as a horse who would improve as he stepped up in distance over obstacles, and he duly made up into a smart novice hurdler last season.

Having stayed on strongly to beat Coconut Splash at Aintree (looked booked for third jumping the last), he was far from fluent when runner-up under a penalty at Newcastle. Again, this race would work out well, and Imperial Alcazar stepped up in grade on New Year's Day, in a race in which he was second past the post, but awarded the race after Protektorat (later reinstated, following an appeal) was disqualified. The eventual outcome might not have pleased his connections, but there was no denying the promise in the run, with him again appearing green throughout. Welsh Saint (3rd) won a Pertemps Qualifier next time, before which Imperial Alcazar had returned to winning ways at Leicester.

He looks to be crying out for 3m and should take a big step forward in staying novice chases this winter. He will need to jump more fluently, but ought to pay fences more respect, and he is one of the more exciting staying novices in England. Before going chasing, there is a chance that he could reappear in the Betfair Stayers' Handicap Hurdle at Haydock, from an appealing mark of 140.

JETAWAY JOEY

5yo Getaway – Present Your Own (Presenting)

Trainer
Olly Murphy
Owner
Mrs Barbara Hester

Optimum Conditions
2m4f+ on soft ground
Career Form Figures
21-

RUNNER-UP in what turned out to be a fair race at Market Rasen on debut, Jetaway Joey was green in the prelims, and duly stepped forward to win a Fontwell bumper with something to spare.

Having lost his position slightly, he was only fifth leaving the back straight at Market Rasen, but stayed on down the middle of the course to finish an encouraging second. The winner ran well in a Listed race next time and shaped well for a long way on hurdles debut, whilst the third (bumper) and fourth (maiden hurdle) went on to win.

Given three months off, Jetaway Joey himself went one better next time, when he travelled a lot more sweetly in the hands of Aidan Coleman. Never too far from the speed, he was still on the bridle when taking over, and kept on really well to score by a comfortable three lengths.

Given both his physique and his pedigree, it bodes well that he was able to win a bumper around Fontwell, and he ought to take a big step forward when going up in distance and encountering a more galloping track. A full-brother to Getaway John (winner of two heavy ground bumpers and a 2m7f maiden hurdle for Gordon Elliott), this good-looking five-year-old could be a very nice long-term staying prospect.

KALOOKI

6yo Martaline – Karuma (Surumu)

Trainer
Philip Hobbs
Owner
Andrew L Cohen

Optimum Conditions
2m5f+ on soft ground
Career Form Figures
0325/4112-

PHILIP Hobbs looks to have a smart bunch of youngsters for the novice chase division this season, with Pileon and St Barts both appealing as horses who will do well over fences. However, I've opted to side with Kalooki as the *Leading Prospect* from the stable, in the hope that he wins his share of races during the middle of the winter, when the mud is flying.

Having caught the eye without winning in bumpers, he duly improved for going hurdling, winning at Ludlow and Wetherby, after an encouraging debut in a decent race at Warwick. He didn't jump particularly fluently on that occasion, but made up plenty of late ground.

Relishing the stiffer test of stamina, he made all to win by a 17 lengths on each of his next two starts, before running well in defeat in Grade 2 company at Haydock. He travelled best in the Prestige, but was outstayed by the more-experienced Ramses de Teillee, after he made a mess of the final flight.

Now rated 141, the valuable Betfair Stayers' Handicap Hurdle would be an option on reappearance (a race his half-brother Kruzhlinin won for the stable in 2016), but I suspect that he will be sent straight over fences, and although occasionally cumbersome over hurdles, he appeals as the type to take to chasing.

KESKONRISK

5yo No Risk At All – La Courtille (Risk Seeker)

Trainer
Joseph Patrick O'Brien
Owner
Claudio Michael Grech

Optimum Conditions
2m+ on any ground
Career Form Figures
1-

WHEN Grech and Parkin decided to sell their horses in May 2019 – in a dispersal which included the record-breaking sale of Interconnected – it was difficult to envisage the owners returning so soon. However, it seems that they are ready to have another crack at National Hunt racing (independently) and one half of the partnership, in particular, has spent big in recent months, with Mike Grech employing Henrietta Knight to recruit him a new string of horses.

Just over a month after the former trainer paid £450,000 on his behalf to secure Irish Point-to-Point winner Gallyhill (now in training with Nicky Henderson), she came out on top in a bidding war to secure Fairyhouse bumper winner Keskonrisk, who cost a mere £370,000.

The son of No Risk At All – sire of Champion Hurdle winner Epatante – is a half-brother to Paul Nicholls' Kingwell Hurdle winner Grand Sancy, and he looked an exciting prospect when winning on his sole start for Timmy Hyde on New Year's Day.

Having been held-up early, the five-year-old took up the running down the far side and dictated matters from the front. Striding out well, he took a breather with around half-a-mile to run, then lengthened away stylishly from the two pole. The runner-up advertised the form when winning at Thurles, and Keskonrisk is a novice hurdler of considerable potential.

LARGY DEBUT

5yo Shirocco – Debut (Presenting)

Trainer
Henry de Bromhead
Owner
C Jones

Optimum Conditions
2m+ on easy ground
Career Form Figures
13-

AS well as having smart novice chase prospect Cedarwood Road (see *Across The Sea*) to look forward to, owner Chris Jones looks to have another potentially smart five-year-old on his hands, in the shape of Largy Debut, who won a maiden Point at Oldtown by 13 lengths.

Having travelled strongly, he took up the running on the bridle, and drew right away to score impressively. Still in the care of Stuart Crawford, the Shirocco gelding made his debut under Rules just a month later, and he was heavily-supported to land a bumper at Navan.

Quite keen in the early part of the race, he travelled like the best horse, and looked as though he would pick up the leaders in the closing stages. Switched to the inner, he was unable to quicken inside the final furlong, perhaps due to the testing ground, but more likely due to how freely he had raced. It was still a hugely encouraging effort, however, and one that bodes well for the future, plus it might well have been a fair race, as the winner looks a nice stayer in the making.

When Largy Debut returns, he should be more than capable of winning a bumper, although he is probably more likely to head straight over hurdles. Now in training with Henry de Bromhead, he has the pace to start over the minimum trip.

MAROWN

6yo Milan – Rosie Suspect (Presenting)

Trainer
Nicky Richards
Owner
Trevor Hemmings

Optimum Conditions
2m4f+ on soft ground
Career Form Figures
1/11-

THE winner of his only bumper in March of last year, Marown returned from almost 10 months off to make a winning debut over hurdles at Ayr on 2nd January. Ridden prominently throughout, not too many horses got into the race, and as a result, Marown and Sirwilliamwallace (won next time) got into a protracted battle up the straight. Nicky Richards' six-year-old showed a fine attitude and was comfortably on top in the closing stages, despite the lack of match practice.

The son of Milan returned to the Scottish track to maintain his unbeaten record in early-March, when he conceded 6lbs to one-time smart chaser Aloomomo. Again, Marown was doing his best work late on, suggesting that he will have no problem in stepping up to 3m at some stage.

Rated 130, he could easily make an impact in handicap hurdles, however, given the shape he makes over his hurdles, he looks the type who will improve again once sent chasing. His form doesn't amount to a great deal at this stage, but he looks a lovely long-term prospect and a typical Trevor Hemmings type, in that we probably won't see the best of him until he is contesting staying events over fences. To date, Marown has raced exclusively on testing ground, and he remains one of the brighter prospects in the North.

MONKFISH

6yo Stowaway – Martovic (Old Vic)

Trainer
W P Mullins
Owner
Mrs S Ricci

Optimum Conditions
3m+ on easy ground
Career Form Figures
P1/2/2111-

THE winner of a strong maiden Point, Monkfish finished runner-up in a bumper at last year's Punchestown Festival, and again finished second on his hurdles debut. Like many from the Mullins stable, he benefited from his reappearance and duly got off the mark at Fairyhouse, relishing the step up in trip (2m7f).

Having followed up over a similar distance at Thurles, he completed the hat-trick in the Albert Bartlett at Cheltenham. Despite racing too freely and making a serious mistake down the far side, Monkfish was still able to come out on top, in a fantastic four-way finish. Leading into the straight, he appeared a sitting duck for those in behind, and having dropped to third after the final flight, had to dig deep to get back up and win by a neck.

Monkfish is sure to head straight over fences on his return and the Neville Hotels Novice Chase over Christmas appeals as an obvious mid-season target. A thorough stayer, Willie Mullins will want to keep him and The Big Getaway apart for as long as possible, and it is likely that Patrick will be eyeing one up for the National Hunt Chase. Whilst the RSA would seem the more obvious long-term target, I wouldn't be shocked if Monkfish were aimed at the amateur riders' race.

MUCKAMORE

6yo Sholokhov – Gales Return (Bob's Return)

Trainer
Nigel Twiston-Davies
Owner
Noel Fehily Racing Syndicate

Optimum Conditions
2m4m+ on soft ground
Career Form Figures
2/1221-

SINCE retiring from the saddle, former Jumpers To Follow contributor Noel Fehily has set up his pre-training yard, and amongst other things, has also formed a racing syndicate, which started extremely well.

Pride Of Lecale (a *Leading Prospect* in this book four years ago) gave Noel Fehily Racing the best possible start – with their very first runner successful at Market Rasen – whilst Goodbye Dancer (winner at Cheltenham), Shall We Go Now (winner after almost two years off) and I'd Better Go Now (another to win on his first start for the owners) all added to last season's tally.

Muckamore was another winner for the syndicate – when justifying skinny odds at Taunton – and he now rates a good prospect for fences, with an opening handicap mark of 125 looking potentially lenient.

Runner-up at both Leicester (behind another *Leading Prospect* Imperial Alcazar) and Ludlow, he jumped well in two Irish Points, winning on his second start, which came on the back of a year off. He certainly has the build of a chaser, and beginning the season at the right end of the handicap, it will be disappointing if he can't (at least) win a couple of novice handicaps.

Clearly well-suited by soft ground, he could prove best at around 2m4f – 2m5f, when ridden positively, and he could develop into a smart handicapper in time.

NADA TO PRADA

5yo Kayf Tara – Ambrosia's Promise (Minster Son)

Trainer
Michael Scudamore
Owner
Mrs Lynne Maclennan

Optimum Conditions
2m+ on soft ground
Career Form Figures
11-

TRAINER Michael Scudamore wouldn't boast the strongest of records in bumpers and his two winners in that division last season came within 10 minutes of one another on 21st February. Let Me Entertain U completed the across-the-card double at Exeter, shortly after Nada To Prada had made a successful Rules debut in a mares' event at Warwick.

The daughter of Kayf Tara had won her Point-to-Point less than seven weeks earlier and, in the meantime, had gone through the sales ring at Cheltenham. To say she did a lot in under two months is an understatement, and she impressed with the ease with which she hit the front at Warwick. Still on the bridle, she cruised into the lead on the home bend, and having shot clear, appeared to be idling in front, so the official margin might not do her justice.

The runner-up gave the form a boost when filling the same spot in a Listed contest at Kempton, whilst the third had earlier finished much closer to Anythingforlove, who was capable of winning again under a penalty. Despite the small field, it looked a truly run race, so the form could be useful. Bred to appreciate further in time, the form of her Point success also reads well, with four of the next five home winning before the end of the season.

NICKOLSON

6yo No Risk At All – Incorrigible (Septieme Ciel)

Trainer
Olly Murphy
Owner
Tim Syder

Optimum Conditions
2m+ on any ground
Career Form Figures
1/12-

ANOTHER of last year's *Leading Prospects*, we only got to see Nickolson twice, and he remains open to considerable improvement this winter. The winner of an Ayr bumper the previous season, he made a pleasing start over hurdles, scoring comfortably at Wincanton.

Kept off the track for almost five months, he was keen when returning at Warwick and probably got racing too far from home, pulling his way to the front halfway down the side of the track. Still looking the likely winner turning in, he began to tire and a mistake at the last ensured that his perfect record came to an end. Given the time off and how strongly he had raced, it is easy to forgive this defeat, plus he was conceding 6lbs to a horse of some potential.

When he returns, Nickolson will be heading into handicap company off a mark of 135, and although that could look stiff enough on the face of it, he has the scope to take a big step forward. Whilst races such as the Greatwood, Gerry Feilden and Betfair Exchange Trophy would make some appeal, it might be that he benefits from starting off at a lower level, as he still looked quite green at Warwick. However, at some stage, there could be a big prize to be won with him.

PAROS

3yo Masterstroke – Soft Blue (Green Tune)

Trainer
Nicky Henderson
Owner
Middleham Park Racing

Optimum Conditions
Unknown
Career Form Figures
1

ANOTHER first for the *Leading Prospects* this year, as Paros becomes the first juvenile hurdler to feature in this section of Jumpers To Follow. A winner on his sole start in France, when trained by Gabriel Leenders, the chestnut was purchased by Middleham Park Racing, and is now in training with Nicky Henderson.

Sent off favourite for a three-year-old hurdle at Dieppe in May, Paros made most of the running, having taken it up with a huge leap at the second. Ears pricked, he jumped well in the main (slightly big at times), and only had to be pushed out to win comfortably.

The form of his win has already worked out well, with the runner-up winning at Clairefontaine, before finishing runner-up in the Grade 3 Prix Aguado at Auteuil, where he finished much closer to the winner than he had done in a Listed event at Compiegne. The third home also won impressively next time out, despite giving away ground by shifting left, so the form looks strong.

The ground was described as a soft at Dieppe, and Masterstroke handled some dig in the ground, so he should be fine with winter ground when he makes his British debut. Nicky Henderson has won the Triumph Hurdle a record seven times, and it is hoped that Paros develops into a leading contender for the 2021 renewal.

PETIBONOME

4yo Al Namix – Olafane (Le Balafre)

Trainer
Henry de Bromhead
Owner
Robcour

Optimum Conditions
2m+ on easy ground
Career Form Figures
F1D-

BRIAN Acheson (Robcour) has been busy adding to his string of horses, and Petibonome looks an exciting addition to his ever-expanding squad. Having taken a heavy fall on debut for Pat Doyle – in what was the first four-year-old maiden of the season – he returned just five weeks later, when crossing the line in splendid isolation at Lismore.

The son of Al Namix was disqualified for taking the wrong course (raced the wrong side of a bale in between the final two fences), but that did not detract from the visual impression that he had created. Allowed to stride on following a good jump two out, he eased clear on the bridle, and even allowing for him getting in tight at the last, he quickened clear to win by 12 lengths. Rather like Gars de Sceaux, he would have won by even further, but for that late mistake.

Although his full-brother failed to deliver on the track for Paul Nicholls and the McNeill Family, I thoroughly expect Petibonome to make a name for himself under Rules. From the family of the useful Tanerko Emery, he is not too dissimilar in looks to several of Al Namix's high-profile progeny. I would expect him to start in a bumper, and like many by the same sire, he looks to possess plenty of pace.

QUEENS BROOK

5yo Shirocco – Awesome Miracle (Supreme Leader)

Trainer
Gordon Elliott
Owner
Noel Moran/Mrs Valerie Moran

Optimum Conditions
2m4f+ on easy ground
Career Form Figures
3/113-

A WINNER at the second time of asking in the Point-to-Point sphere, Queens Brook created a deep impression on her debut for Gordon Elliott, when winning a bumper at Gowran Park by 21 lengths.

The daughter of Shirocco settled well just in behind the speed, and made steady progress inside the final mile. Just about in front on the turn for home, Jamie Codd elected to grab the stands' side rail, and once asked to put the race to bed, she began to draw further and further clear in the manner of a high-class mare.

Allowed to take on the boys in the Champion Bumper at Cheltenham, she acquitted herself really well and finished a hugely honourable third. Kept fairly wide throughout, she held every chance at the foot of the hill, and although she couldn't fend off the Willie Mullins-trained pair, she ran a huge race in third.

The ground was atrocious the day she won at Gowran, and given her stamina laden pedigree, she is likely to relish stepping up in trip once sent jumping. A half-sister to Shotgun Paddy (winner of the Classic Chase and beaten just a neck in the National Hunt Chase), Queens Brook will come into her own over 2m4f or beyond in time. The Grade 1 event for mares at Fairyhouse over Easter could be the ideal spring target.

ROSE OF ARCADIA

5yo Arcadio – Rosie Lea (Supreme Leader)

Trainer
Colin Tizzard
Owner
Cheveley Park Stud

Optimum Conditions
2m+ on soft ground
Career Form Figures
11-

THE silks of Cheveley Park Stud are becoming increasingly more familiar under the National Hunt code, and for a second successive season, they enjoyed a Cheltenham Festival double in March, with Ferny Hollow providing them with back-to-back wins in the Weatherbys Champion Bumper, and Envoi Allen landing the Ballymore.

On the eve of this year's festival, Rose Of Arcadia made a successful debut for Cheveley Park, in a bumper at Taunton. The first horse they have had in the care of Colin Tizzard, the five-year-old had made all to beat Shirocco's Dream (won next time and is now also in training with Tizzard) in a maiden Point, and she again made her own running to score comfortably.

Racing with plenty of zest, she had the race sewn up at the top of the home straight, before easing away to score with plenty in hand. The form might not amount to a great deal, but visually it was impressive, and she rates a nice prospect for mares' novice hurdles.

Bred to stay further, she is likely to begin over the minimum trip given her racing style, and although she has raced exclusively on testing ground to date, there is no reason to believe that Rose Of Arcadia won't be as effective under less demanding conditions. She looks to possess plenty of size and scope for jumping.

SAINT ROI

5yo Coastal Path – Sainte Vigne (Saint des Saints)

Trainer
W P Mullins
Owner
John P McManus

Optimum Conditions
2m+ on easy ground
Career Form Figures
3/511-

GOLD Cup day was one to remember for Willie Mullins, who saddled the first four winners. Burning Victory may have been fortunate in the Triumph, but there was no luck involved with Saint Roi's smooth victory in the County Hurdle, on what was just his fourth start over hurdles.

Third in a Listed race at Auteuil, he made his Irish debut almost 15 months later, when disappointing at Clonmel. Not fluent, he jumped better when winning at Tramore on New Year's Day. He won easily and initiated a double on the card for Mullins and Paul Townend, with Gold Cup winner Al Boum Photo making a winning return later in the afternoon. At that stage, it seemed unlikely that both horses would again win on the same card in March.

Clearly having improved considerably in the interim, the five-year-old took his chance in the County, and he duly justified strong market support. Ridden patiently, he made eye-catching ground coming down the hill, and cruised to the front. He picked up stylishly to win in the manner of a horse capable of much better, and I think we would have seen him in Grade 1 company had Punchestown gone ahead.

A scopey son of Coastal Path, he could make up into a high-class novice chaser, if sent straight over fences, although given how the County Hurdle form worked out over the summer, he might be given the chance to see how far he can go as a hurdler.

SHISHKIN

6yo Sholokhov – Labarynth (Exit To Nowhere)

Trainer
Nicky Henderson
Owner
Mrs J Donnelly

Optimum Conditions
2m+ on any ground
Career Form Figures
3/11/F111-

LIKE stable-mate Chantry House, Shishkin featured among last year's *Leading Prospects* and although his inclusion is a much more obvious one this time around, the imposing six-year-old looks to have everything required to reach the very top as a chaser.

An impressive Kempton bumper winner the previous spring, Shishkin was an early faller on his reappearance, in a maiden hurdle at Newbury, but returned to the Berkshire track to score in emphatic fashion just a month later.

Despite stepping up to 2m3½f to land Huntingdon's Listed Sidney Banks Novices' Hurdle, Nicky Henderson was adamant that he would run in the Supreme at Cheltenham (despite the owners having plenty of options in the division) and he landed the festival curtain-raiser, despite not everything going to plan.

An untimely mistake down the back could have proven costly, but despite being forced wide coming down the hill, he finished extremely strongly to beat Abacadabras by a head, with the pair well clear of the aforementioned Chantry House.

Strong at the line in all of his races to date, he will no doubt stay further in time, but there appears no need to go up in trip again at this stage, and providing his trainer with a seventh win in the Arkle is probably the main objective this season. His debut over fences is eagerly awaited.

SILVER FOREVER

6yo Jeremy – Silver Prayer (Roselier)

Trainer
Paul Nicholls
Owner
Colm Donlon

Optimum Conditions
2m4f+ on soft ground
Career Form Figures
1/1312/1131-

AN impressive Point-to-Point winner in Ireland, it wasn't surprising to see Silver Forever improve on her good bumper form when sent hurdling last season. Twice placed in Listed bumpers, the grey made a decisive winning debut over obstacles at Chepstow.

Again jumping well, she successfully dropped in trip to beat Floressa at Newbury, before the runner-up reversed the form in Listed company at the same track, when Silver Forever was unable to draw the finishing sting out of her. The second and fourth advertised that form by finishing runner-up in Grade 1s, and Silver Forever looked ready for a step back up in distance.

That duly came at Sandown, when she successfully stepped out of novice company to win a Listed event impressively. The combination of softer ground, longer trip, and stiffer finish all contributed to a stylish performance. Again, the form would work out well thanks to Indefatigable.

Silver Forever met with a setback and didn't run again, but is due to return in the autumn, when chasing is an option. A wide-margin Points winner (beat the smart Annie Mc), it is likely that she will reappear over hurdles to begin with, and given how strongly she finished at Sandown, the 3m mares' event at Kempton in late-November could be ideal. Ascot's Grade 2 would be another option in the New Year.

SIZABLE SAM

5yo Black Sam Bellamy – Halo Flora (Alflora)

Trainer
Jeremy Scott
Owner
The Hopefuls & Kelvin-Hughes

Optimum Conditions
2m+ on decent ground
Career Form Figures
21-

FOLLOWING a hugely encouraging second on his racecourse debut at Wincanton, Sizable Sam confirmed the promise, when going one place better in 16-runner event at Warwick. Handy throughout on debut, the white-faced chestnut battled on tenaciously when challenged by the eventual winner and was only beaten a short-head at the line.

The third home advertised the form by winning easily at Ludlow, whilst Jeremy Scott's five-year-old made no mistake at Warwick. Ridden with a shade more restraint, he was only fifth into the straight, but picked up really well when the split came, and he stayed on in determined fashion to score. As is often the case with progeny of Black Sam Bellamy, Sizable Sam again displayed a fine attitude.

His final target for the season would have been the valuable sales bumper at Newbury, for which he held a five-day entry, before racing was first suspended.

Both his running style and pedigree – on the dam's side, at least – suggest that he will appreciate going up in distance over hurdles, and he looks a fine long-term prospect, who is sure to be well-placed by his shrewd trainer. He will sport new colours when he returns, as he was purchased by a syndicate – in which leading owner Richard Kelvin-Hughes is involved – during the closed season.

SOARING GLORY

5yo Fame And Glory – Hapeney (Saddlers' Hall)

Trainer
Jonjo O'Neill
Owner
P Hickey

Optimum Conditions
2m on decent ground
Career Form Figures
112-

ANOTHER who won a Warwick bumper, Soaring Glory was successful on his racecourse debut, where he showed a fine turn of foot to beat Truckers Pass, a horse who had caught my eye when finishing runner-up in an Irish Point. Ridden confidently, the son of Fame And Glory picked up well in the closing stages, and the pair pulled nicely clear.

Despite facing much softer ground, Soaring Glory made it two-from-two at Ascot, winning even more impressively. He travelled like a dream on this occasion, and appeared to have too much pace for Kid Commando, who had won by 18 lengths on his previous start and went on to win a Plumpton maiden hurdle before finishing third in the Dovecote.

Although Soaring Glory confirmed the form with the runner-up (and the third) when they met again in Listed company, he was unable to maintain his unbeaten record. Having again travelled smoothly, it could be that the heavy ground blunted his speed.

The winner failed to advertise the form in the Champion Bumper, but Soaring Glory remains a bright prospect for novice hurdles, when facing a sounder surface will surely see him in a better light. Clearly blessed with a fine turn of foot, I expect him to be campaigned over the minimum trip, and he is a half-brother to dual Grade 3 winner Three Stars.

THE BIG BREAKAWAY

5yo Getaway – Princess Mairead (Blueprint)

Trainer
Colin Tizzard
Owner
Eric Jones, Geoff Nicholas, John Romans

Optimum Conditions
2m4f+ on easy ground
Career Form Figures
1/114-

AN expensive purchase from last year's sale at the Punchestown Festival (€360,000), The Big Breakaway looked a serious prospect when winning a maiden hurdle at Chepstow and a novice at Newbury.

The chestnut ran out a facile winner on debut, drawing right away in the final quarter-mile, having sauntered through the race. The runner-up won at the same track later in the season before finishing second in a handicap off 130, whilst the penalty proved no barrier for The Big Breakaway, who followed up in similarly impressive fashion.

The third and fourth both won their only subsequent starts, to give that form some substance, whilst the winner was forced to miss his festival prep in the Grade 2 on trials day, having met with a small setback. That meant that he headed to the festival with little experience and without a run in almost three months. He didn't really travel with the same fluency, but still kept on for fourth in the Ballymore, finishing best of the English-trained runners.

It is also worth noting that the front three were all a year older, and this wide-margin Points winner could take a significant step forward once sent chasing. He also looks to be crying out for 3m, so could easily develop into the leading staying novice this side of the Irish Sea.

THE BIG GETAWAY

6yo Getaway – Saddlers Dawn (Saddlers' Hall)

Trainer
W P Mullins
Owner
Mrs J Donnelly

Optimum Conditions
2m4f+ on any ground
Career Form Figures
1/22/1413-

THE yellow and black silks of Joe and Marie Donnelly were twice carried into the winners' enclosure at Cheltenham in March – with Shishkin successful in the Supreme Novices' Hurdle and Al Boum Photo winning his second Gold Cup – whilst The Big Getaway ran a big race, finishing third behind Envoi Allen in the Ballymore.

A huge, imposing, sort who had won his sole Point by 30 lengths, the six-year-old failed to win in two bumpers the previous spring, but won in a canter on his return. Quickly sent jumping, he lost all momentum with a bad mistake at the last on debut, but soon got off the mark, beating a next-time-out winner by 17 lengths at Naas.

Having taken over with more than a circuit to run at the festival, he got into a lovely rhythm and jumped fluently. Beaten for speed on the run to the last, this was his first start in graded company, and it was a performance which promised much for the future.

Given both his size and how he jumps – both over hurdles and in his Point – he could easily improve again once sent chasing, and the RSA is his likely festival target. Given that last season's form came over intermediate trips, I would expect to see him campaigned over 2m4f-2m5f to begin with, before going up in distance in the spring.

THIRD TIME LUCKI

5yo Arcadio – Definite Valley (Definite Article)

Trainer
Dan Skelton
Owner
Mike and Eileen Newbould

Optimum Conditions
2m+ on any ground
Career Form Figures
2/3114-

AN eye-catching third, two smooth victories, and a fourth placing in the Champion Bumper, Third Time Lucki really put together a solid campaign last term.

Prior to joining his current connections, the son of Arcadio had finished runner-up in an open maiden for Francesca Nimmo, and he came from way off the pace to finish third at Ascot, on his first start under Rules. Ridden with plenty of patience, he travelled really well into the straight, only coming off the bridle in the final couple of furlongs.

Despite not being able to reel in the front pair, it was a hugely encouraging effort, and he scored with a minimum of fuss at Market Rasen next time. It was a similar result at Huntingdon under a penalty, too, where he again came from the back of the field to win impressively.

Ridden similarly at Cheltenham, he travelled sweetly to the foot of the hill, then kept on in determined fashion to finish fourth, clear best of the British-trained runners.

Given how he likes to be ridden, big fields and truly-run races are likely to bring the best out in Third Time Lucki, although there has been no indication that he will fail to settle in smaller fields, and he rates a really good prospect for novice hurdles.

ENVOI ALLEN – THE UNBEATEN SIX-YEAR-OLD IS SET TO EMBARK ON A NOVICE CHASE CAMPAIGN

Across
THE SEA

ALFA MIX

5yo Fair Mix – Alora Money (Alflora)

Trainer
Gavin Cromwell
Owner
John P McManus

Optimum Conditions
2m4f+ on easy ground
Career Form Figures
F0/96415127-

A FALLER two out in his Point (still held every chance), Alfa Mix made his debut behind Front View at last year's Punchestown Festival, finishing down the field in a bumper which has been well covered in this year's publication.

After running reasonably well for a long way at Bellewstown, Alfa Mix improved for going hurdling and got off the mark at Tramore in October. Not beaten far in a Punchestown novice, he was then switched to handicap company, appreciating stepping up to 2m4f at Navan. He travelled really well over the longer trip and was probably value for a shade more than the winning margin.

Following a 9lbs rise, he returned to the same track and beat all bar Kilfenora, with the pair 18 lengths clear. That was enough to persuade JP McManus to buy Alfa Mix, who made his debut in the green and gold in the Coral Cup. Only seventh, he ran better than the bare result, racing up with the pace, and only fading after the last.

Still only five, he looks to have the scope to improve again for going chasing, and is very much one to note in the novice division over intermediate distances. Gavin Cromwell is also set to send high-class hurdler **Darver Star** chasing, and he could well develop into a genuine Arkle contender.

ASTERION FORLONGE

6yo Coastal Path – Belle du Brizais (Turgeon)

Trainer
W P Mullins
Owner
Mrs J Donnelly

Optimum Conditions
2m+ on any ground
Career Form Figures
1/1114-

DESPITE causing chaos by jumping out to his right, Asterion Forlonge still finished fourth in what appeared to be a very strong renewal of the Supreme Novices' Hurdle in March, and – provided that those jumping issues can be ironed out – he remains a very bright prospect.

Sent off favourite to win the opener at the festival, his tendency to drift to his right became alarmingly more dramatic travelling down the hill, and after causing severe interference three out, he took out two of his rivals at the second last. Despite this waywardness, he still managed to finish less than three lengths off Chantry House in fourth.

Earlier in the campaign, he had won a bumper at Thurles, a maiden hurdle – by an impressive 10 lengths – at Navan, and the Grade 1 Chanelle Pharma Novice Hurdle, at the Dublin Racing Festival. At both Navan and Leopardstown he shifted to his right at times, and he even hung slightly to his right when winning his Point at Oldtown (right-handed track) for Pat Doyle (strong form beating several subsequent winners).

Given that background, I would expect him to head straight over fences this season, when he might be best served racing right-handed. Stepping up in distance by half-a-mile should bring about further improvement, and he could easily develop into a high-class novice, despite those obvious flaws.

CEDARWOOD ROAD

5yo Stowaway – Valleyboggan (Saddlers' Hall)

Trainer
Gearoid O'Loughlin
Owner
C Jones

Optimum Conditions
2m on any ground
Career Form Figures
9/611-

GEAROID O'LOUGHLIN and Chris Jones enjoyed a fine couple of weeks during March, with the Ulster National victory of Space Cadet coming just 12 days after Cedarwood Road won a Listed novice hurdle at Naas.

Like one of this year's *Leading Prospects*, Brinkley, (and the aforementioned Alfa Mix) Cedarwood Road made his racecourse debut in the four-year-old bumper at last year's Punchestown Festival, where he ran on encouragingly into ninth.

The son of Stowaway again shaped with promise when sixth in a maiden hurdle at Fairyhouse, before winning the opening race of Leopardstown's Christmas meeting. Ridden closer to the pace, he travelled beautifully for Davy Russell, and had the race in safe-keeping as the field bypassed the final flight. He gave Jungle Junction an 11-length beating and this confirmed his improvement, as that rival had finished more than 20 lengths in front of him at Punchestown. He again travelled smoothly at Naas, and showed a fine turn of foot to run down Beacon Edge after the last, with old adversary Jungle Junction back in fourth.

Chris Jones has owned some fine 2m chasers in the past, including Grand Annual winner Tiger Cry and, of course, Arkle and Champion Chase winner Klairon Davis. Whilst it is far too early for any such comparisons, Cedarwood Road is a fine-looking, athletic individual, who could easily be a Graded-class novice.

DELVINO

5yo Dylan Thomas – Alliata (Southern Halo)

Trainer
Dermot A McLoughlin
Owner
Mrs P J Conway

Optimum Conditions
2m+ on soft ground
Career Form Figures
21-

A HALF-SISTER to the same connections' Avellino, Delvino made a bright start to her career at Navan in February, and soon went one better at Down Royal, the following month.

Pitched in against the boys, the daughter of Dylan Thomas was ridden with plenty of patience, but eased her way into the lead early in the home straight. Looking the likely winner when going for home two furlongs out, she showed signs of greenness when challenged, but kept going in a likeable fashion to record a highly encouraging second. The winner went on to finish seventh in the Champion Bumper, whilst third home Ballyadam won in a canter at Downpatrick, so the form looks useful.

Sent off odds-on to go one place better against her own sex at Down Royal, Delvino made no mistake, keeping on well in the closing stages. Both runs came on heavy ground and it would be interesting to see how she fares under slightly less-demanding conditions. Dermot McLoughlin has the option of testing her in Listed company before embarking on her hurdling career, with Gowran's Muckelmeg Mares Flat Race a possible starting point.

These connections have had some smart mares in recent seasons – including **Santa Rossa** who should also win races over hurdles this season – and Delvino, who should stay further once sent hurdling, looks another bright prospect.

DIOL KER

6yo Martaline – Stiren Bleue (Pistolet Bleu)

Trainer
Noel Meade
Owner
Gigginstown House Stud

Optimum Conditions
2m4f+ on easy ground
Career Form Figures
2F1/532/1-

A HORSE whose career to date has been a little stop-start, but there is no denying the potential that Diol Ker has, and he could begin to fulfil that potential as a novice chaser this winter.

He kept good company in his first couple of Point-to-Points, chasing home Sams Profile (twice placed at Grade 1 level as a novice hurdler) on debut when Monkfish was pulled-up in behind, he then matched strides with The Big Getaway, until taking a horrible fall three out. He justified favouritism on his third and final start between the flags, staying on stoutly to record a facile success in April 2018.

Switched from Pat Doyle to Noel Meade, he ran well in a bumper behind Envoi Allen, and would have made a winning start over hurdles at Leopardstown, but for stumbling after the final flight. Given one more run that season (runner-up at Navan), he was then given time, and made a winning return at Fairyhouse in November, beating subsequent Albert Bartlett winner Monkfish and Escaria Ten (won his next two).

We didn't get to see Diol Ker again, but he held entries at Cheltenham (until the five-day stage) and is expected back in the autumn. Given the strength of his form, and the fact that he promises to be even better over 3m and over fences, there should be plenty to look forward to in the months ahead.

EKLAT DE RIRE

6yo Saddex – Rochdale (Video Rock)

Trainer
Henry de Bromhead
Owner
P Davies

Optimum Conditions
2m4f – 3m on soft ground
Career Form Figures
121-

A MAIDEN Point winner at Dromahane last November, Eklat de Rire finished runner-up on his debut under Rules at Punchestown in February, before going one place better, in taking fashion, at Thurles the following month.

Stepped up to 2m7f, the son of Saddex – who had chased home the 125-rated (I.H.R.B. rating) Foxy Jacks at Punchestown – made all, and jumped with aplomb, when scoring under Rachael Blackmore. Having dictated matters, the six-year-old had the opposition beaten leaving the back straight, so would probably have little trouble in dropping back in distance, if ridden similarly. He drew clear in the closing stages, and came right out of his rider's hands at the final flight, suggesting that his future most certainly lies over fences.

Eligible for novice hurdles in the early part of the season, it will then be interesting to see how the handicapper assesses him, although it is unlikely that we will see the best of Eklat de Rire until he goes chasing. Nevertheless, his progress over hurdles should be monitored closely, in the meantime.

He also measured his obstacles nicely when winning his maiden for Liz Doyle, so he could develop into a really nice chaser in time, and he is certainly in the right stable to utilise what looks to be a very natural jumping technique.

ENVOI ALLEN

6yo Muhtathir – Reaction (Saints des Saints)

Trainer
Gordon Elliott
Owner
Cheveley Park Stud

Optimum Conditions
2m4f on any ground
Career Form Figures
1/1111/1111-

THE only reason that Envoi Allen doesn't again feature as one of this season's *Leading Prospects* is that he is highly unlikely to represent value at any stage during the coming months, but he remains just about the brightest young prospect in the National Hunt game.

The six-year-old remains unbeaten following his four-from-four novice hurdle campaign last season, culminating with victory over stable-mate Easywork in the Ballymore at Cheltenham. The highlight of the performance was the change of gear on the run to the final hurdle, and despite the fact that he is bred to appreciate going up in distance, I have little doubt that he could easily drop back to 2m and be equally as effective.

He showed in the Royal Bond at Fairyhouse – where he beat Supreme runner-up Abacadabras and Champion Hurdle third Darver Star – that he has the pace for 2m at the top level.

It is worth noting that his Point-to-Point win came over 2m4f, so the Ballymore (2m5f) is as far as he has gone at this stage, and it could be that the Marsh ends up being the race for him at Cheltenham, with the Drinmore and Flogas Grade 1 options on home soil, over intermediate trips. Richard Thompson does, however, suggest elsewhere in this year's publication that he will step up in distance, something that Jamie Codd also hints at (see *A View From The Saddle*).

FAROUK D'ALENE

5yo Racinger – Mascotte d'Alene (Ragmar)

Trainer
Gordon Elliott
Owner
Gigginstown House Stud

Optimum Conditions
2m4f+ on easy ground
Career Form Figures
1/11-

GIGGINSTOWN House Stud looked to have a nice crop of bumper horses last season, one of them being Farouk d'Alene, who won at Down Royal and Naas.

A wide-margin winner of a Point when trained by Donnchadh Doyle, the five-year-old made a winning start under Rules at Down Royal over Christmas, making all to win by 17 lengths under Jamie Codd. As he had done in his Point-to-Point, he dictated from the front, and saw off his rivals one-by-one.

Despite facing just four opponents, he faced a stiffer test at Naas, where he got a lead from Vinnie Is Busy to the final quarter-mile. Challenged by a fellow Gigginstown runner in the shape of Fire Attack, he kept on in tenacious fashion to the land the spoils on the line, providing the powerful owners with a seventh win in the race, in the past 10 years.

Given the way he went through both his Point-to-Point and his first bumper at Down Royal, he gives the strong impression that he will improve for a trip over hurdles, and he could be seen at his best between 2m4f and 3m.

Runner-up at Naas **Fire Attack** also looks a nice prospect, having beaten Julies Stowaway (beat Delvino and Ballyadam at Navan next time) at Limerick, and the full-brother to Western Ryder should also be winning races over hurdles for Gigginstown.

FERNY HOLLOW

5yo Westerner – Mirazur (Good Thyne)

Trainer
W P Mullins
Owner
Cheveley Park Stud

Optimum Conditions
2m+ on easy ground
Career Form Figures
1/2211-

FOLLOWING his 15-length romp over 2m4f at Knockanard, Ferny Hollow was just about top of my list of winning Pointers at this time last year, so it was slightly disappointing that he was beaten on his first two starts under Rules.

Prominent throughout on both occasions, he was far too keen and didn't see out either race. Dropped right out on his third start at Fairyhouse – where he wore a first-time hood – he settled better and breezed home, at the main expense of On Eagles Wings, who won at Limerick next time.

Just 17 days later, Ferny Hollow was given a top-class ride to beat stable-mate Appreciate It in the Weatherbys Champion Bumper, coming from last-to-first. Appearing to relish the stronger gallop and bigger field, he made his challenge up the straight, and had plenty left on the run to the line. He will need to relax if he is to fulfil his potential, but he seems to be improving in that respect, and he should take high rank among the Irish novice hurdlers this season.

I was actually concerned about his temperament ahead of the festival, but he showed that he can cope with the occasion, and even if he struggles to settle in small-field contests earlier in the season, he should appreciate racing at championship pace come next March.

FURY ROAD

6yo Stowaway – Molly Duffy (Oscar)

Trainer
Gordon Elliott
Owner
Gigginstown House Stud

Optimum Conditions
3m on soft ground
Career Form Figures
41/513/11143-

As well as saddling Envoi Allen to win the Ballymore, Gordon Elliott was responsible for a placed horse in each of the three novice hurdles at Cheltenham. Abacadabras was beaten a short-head in the Supreme, Easywork chased home his stable-mate, and Fury Road finished a narrow third behind Monkfish in the Albert Bartlett.

All three carried the silks of Gigginstown and like his conqueror on Gold Cup day, Fury Road looks a smart staying novice chase prospect. He actually finished fourth behind Monkfish in a maiden Point, before winning easily at Dromahane, and following an adequate bumper campaign, he flourished over longer trips as a novice hurdler.

After a wide-margin win at Down Royal, he provided his connections with a third win in the space of four years in the Monksfield Novice Hurdle (Death Duty and Samcro the other pair) before winning a Grade 2 at Limerick over Christmas.

Only fourth behind Latest Exhibition at the Dublin Racing Festival, he appreciated the stronger gallop at Cheltenham and closed the gap with the winner. Fury Road stayed well and looks another player in what promises to be a deep division in Ireland.

The aforementioned **Easywork** is less-exposed, and also produced a career-best at the festival. He, too, should make an impact in novice chases, over an intermediate distance.

GYPSY ISLAND

6yo Jeremy – Thieving Gypsy (Presenting)

Trainer
Peter Fahey
Owner
John P McManus

Optimum Conditions
2m+ on decent ground
Career Form Figures
12111/

A *LEADING PROSPECT* in last year's edition of Jumpers To Follow, it was announced last November that Gypsy Island would sadly miss the whole season, having suffered a small fracture. Given the ease with which she had won a Listed bumper at Fairyhouse and a Grade 3 at the Punchestown Festival, she had looked a top-class prospect for the mares' novice hurdle division.

Expected to return to action this season, she remains a very bright prospect, with her form having worked out extremely well whilst she was side-lined. Having beaten Yukon Lil and Colreevy (finished fourth and fifth in the Dawn Run at Cheltenham) with ease at Fairyhouse, she beat Grade 3 novice hurdle winners Daylight Katie and Minella Melody at Punchestown, where Jeremys Flame and Heaven Help Us (both finished runner-up in Grade 1s against the boys last season) were down the field.

Even going back to her maiden hurdle second, it was none other than Arkle heroine Put The Kettle On who lowered her colours at Navan, when she gave the winner too much rope. That defeat proved to be a blessing-in-disguise, as she reverted to bumpers to great effect, and if retaining all of her ability, she could make a big impact as a novice hurdler. Whilst the Dawn Run would appeal as the obvious target, she has the class to take on the geldings.

LATEST EXHIBITION

7yo Oscar – Aura About You (Supreme Leader)

Trainer
Paul Nolan
Owner
Toberona Partnership

Optimum Conditions
2m4f+ on any ground
Career Form Figures
21/12112-

THERE was just a neck and a nose between the front three in this year's Albert Bartlett, and all three could develop into high-class staying novice chasers in Ireland. It certainly seems likely that the division will be very deep, and Latest Exhibition has every chance of making a big impact, as he did in novice hurdles last term.

After beating Thatsy (won next time and ended up contesting the County Hurdle), he got to within three lengths of Supreme second Abacadabras at Navan, before relishing the extra half-mile in the Grade 2 Navan Novice Hurdle. Despite a serious error down the back, he was still able to burst the bubble of the hitherto unbeaten Andy Dufresne in fine style.

He landed a first Grade 1 at the Dublin Racing Festival, and went down fighting at Cheltenham, where he travelled well to lead turning for home. He did nothing wrong, and ran right through the line, proving his stamina, although I would have little concern if he dropped back to 2m4f over fences. Latest Exhibition is another who looks to have the size and scope for fences, and given the apparent depth in this division, we could be in for some exciting clashes during the winter. Alternatively, if connections have a re-think, there would be plenty of options for him over hurdles, when he could develop into a Stayers' Hurdle contender.

POLITESSE

6yo Beat Hollow – Dalamine (Sillery)

Trainer
Mrs Lorna Fowler
Owner
P G Davies & Mrs A Frost & R H Fowler

Optimum Conditions
2m+ on any ground
Career Form Figures
3/211-

A HIGHLY-PROMISING mare, Politesse shaped with an abundance of promise on her sole start the season before last, when third behind Longhouse Poet and Albert Bartlett winner Monkfish in a 2m2f bumper at the Punchestown Festival.

Off the track for nine months, she again ran a race full of promise when runner-up in Grade 2 company at the Dublin Racing Festival, form which was given a small boost when The West Awaits (6th) won at Clonmel. Down in class, Politesse made no mistake next time, justifying favouritism in comfortable fashion at Thurles, and shortly after, she returned to the same track to make a winning debut over hurdles.

Never too far from the pace, she turned the screw on the run to three out, after which she always looked in control, despite being joined halfway up the straight. She again finished strongly, suggesting that she will appreciate further in time, something that her pedigree concurs with.

A half-sister to Don Poli, she has the build of a chaser, but is sure to remain over hurdles for now. Placing her might not be easy this season, but she remains a novice until the end of November, and the Grade 3 at Down Royal could be an option. Improvement should be forthcoming once upped in trip, so the Grade 2 over 2m4½f at Leopardstown over Christmas is another possible target.

UHTRED

5yo Fame And Glory – Ingred Hans (Beneficial)

Trainer
Joseph Patrick O'Brien
Owner
Gigginstown House Stud

Optimum Conditions
2m+ on any ground
Career Form Figures
1/21-

FIRE ATTACK (touched upon earlier in this section) isn't the only bright prospect for novice hurdles this season, for Joseph O'Brien and Gigginstown. O'Brien looked to boast a strong squad of bumper horses last season, and Uhtred – who had won a bumper the previous spring in the colours of his mother – ran out a taking winner in Listed company last December.

Prior to that, the son of Fame And Glory had finished runner-up to stable-mate Front View in a four-year-old maiden hurdle at Cork. Angled out to challenge at Navan, he quickened up stylishly to put the race to bed. The fourth and fifth would win maiden hurdles next time, whilst the form of his debut win was well-advertised by Chuvelo, who won two bumpers for Donald McCain. He looks sure to win a maiden hurdle in the early part of the season, before he steps up in class.

Another from the O'Brien/Gigginstown academy to note is **Forged In Fire**, who beat Champion Bumper winner Ferny Hollow at Leopardstown over Christmas. A Presenting half-brother to Stellar Notion, he was pushed along down the side of the track, but really picked up in the straight, and left the impression that he would come on for the experience. We didn't get to see him again, but the form worked out very well (if taken literally), and he is yet another highly promising five-year-old.

BRIAN ELLISON
RACING CLUB

◆ ◆ ◆ ◆ ◆

The Brian Ellison Racing Club is an exclusive membership-only club formed by Brian and Claire in 2017. For a one-off annual payment of £249.99 members can enjoy a taste of ownership and experience the thrills and emotions involved, without having to pay the, sometimes substantial, fees normally associated with racehorse ownership.

Members will become one of the connections of a minimum of five horses trained by Brian, all of which will carry the club's black and white diamond colours.

As Brian trains both flat and national hunt horses, members are guaranteed racing year round. Application for race day owners' badges when the club has a horse running and entitlement to discounted badges when available, the opportunity to meet the trainer, team and horses during exclusive members-only stable visits are just a few of the perks offered with this membership.

MALYSTIC - ONE TO NOTE IN 2M HANDICAP HURDLES FROM THE PETER NIVEN STABLE

Around
THE YARDS

Nick Alexander

EBONY JEWEL

FAR too keen when beaten on his first two starts over hurdles, Ebony Jewel set a more sensible gallop when winning at Haydock, but still needs to learn to relax if he is to fulfil the potential that she showed in bumpers the previous season. He didn't do too much wrong when just beaten at Kelso, but was already struggling when taking a heavy-looking fall in the Grade 2 Premier Novices' Hurdle at the same track. If he has matured over the summer, the six-year-old would certainly make some appeal in handicap company off a mark of 126, whilst there is also the option of going chasing.

GINGER MAIL

GIVEN the premature ending to the 2019-20 season (and the likelihood that plenty of horses will have missed opportunities to run in a spring bumper), I thought that I would try to include several un-raced horses in this year's publication, and the first is Ginger Mail, a half-brother to *Leading Prospect* and stable-mate Elvis Mail. A four-year-old grey by Derby and Arc winner Sinndar, he is likely to start in a bumper, and will carry the silks of owner Mrs Judy Douglas Miller, who has enjoyed success with Road To Gold in recent seasons. Nick Alexander doesn't boast a particularly strong record in bumpers, so it will bode well for his future should Ginger Mail shape well in that sphere, before going hurdling.

WAKOOL

I WAS fortunate enough to watch this four-year-old in one of his early schooling sessions at the beginning of last season, and the Motivator gelding made steady progress in three starts over hurdles. Keen on debut, he wasn't fluent but finished a fair fourth, before returning to Musselburgh and going one place better. Ridden closer to the pace this time, he made a serious error down the far side, but still travelled up well before tiring from two out. The grey appreciated the stronger gallop in a 17-runner novices' handicap at Doncaster on his third start, and finished his race off well to win by a half-length. The front pair pulled 17 lengths clear and a 5lbs rise seems more than fair; if he can brush up his hurdling, he could be in for a good campaign.

Sam Allwood

AQUILA SKY

HAVING run twice for Harry Fry, Aquila Sky was picked up for just £5,500 in January, and he caught many an eye – including that of the Doncaster Stewards – when fourth on his first start for Sam Allwood. Anchored in last, he refused to settle in the first half of the race, but began to make progress down the far side. Having latched himself on to the back of the main group, he moved well to two out, and given how hard he had pulled early, it was surprising that he ran on all the way to the line. On his two starts for Fry, he was far too keen (wore a hood) in a Newbury bumper and also in a maiden hurdle at Ludlow (2m5f), so it was understandable that he was ridden with restraint. It will be interesting to see if he can learn to relax, as he clearly has an engine, and perhaps handicaps will help in that regard.

Caroline Bailey

BOLDMERE

A USEFUL hurdler when trained by Graeme McPherson (novice winner at Market Rasen), Boldmere improved significantly for going chasing last season, following his switch to Caroline Bailey. He jumped left (violently at times) on debut at Huntingdon, and although not as markedly, still shifted that way when winning at Leicester off a mark of 123. The combination of switching to a left-handed track and going up to 3m brought about plenty of improvement at Doncaster, where he readily defied a 10lbs rise, and teed up a crack at Wetherby's Towton Novices' Chase. He had the Grade 2 at his mercy when falling at the last, and although he will need to defy another rise when he returns (now rated 145), he will be of interest in 3m handicaps on left-handed tracks.

Kim Bailey

ESPOIR DE ROMAY

IMPRESSED when beating West Cork (won his next two before finishing second in the Dovecote Novices' Hurdle) at Warwick, and also when winning a handicap at Wincanton, on both occasions making most in uncomplicated fashion. Unable to dominate in the Martin Pipe, he ran well until the home bend, and can be expected to bounce back to winning ways if switched to fences this season. Currently rated 142, the novices' handicap at Cheltenham – a race that the stable won last season with Imperial Aura – could be a suitable option, if rated similarly come next spring, and 2m4f (or thereabouts) seems to be his trip.

GETAWEAPON

A FIVE-YEAR-OLD mare by Getaway who has yet to race for the Kim Bailey stable, Getaweapon created a really good impression when winning a Point-to-Point bumper for Christopher Barber in March of last year. She showed a good turn of foot when making a race-winning move on the home bend, before drawing right away to score by 10 lengths. The form reads well, too, with Tango Charlie (2nd) winning a Point before finishing fifth in a competitive Leopardstown bumper for Mags Mullins, while Tile Tapper (3rd) won an Exeter bumper on New Year's Day for Jimmy Frost. Although she failed to make it to the track last term, Getaweapon is expected to return in the autumn and looks to possess the ability to win a mares' bumper before going hurdling. She will sport the silks of John Perris, a long-standing owner of the yard, who has enjoyed Graded race success with Emily Gray and Rocky's Treasure in the past.

JAVA POINT

RAN well in a couple of bumpers and two novice hurdles without winning last season, this former winning Irish Pointer will be of interest when heading into handicap company from an opening mark of 119. Having chased home Allart at Ludlow, he followed home another of Nicky Henderson's Supreme runners when finishing fourth to Chantry House at Newbury, where he kept on well once headed two out. Fortunate when winning his Point (left in front by a final fence faller), he stayed on particularly well that day, suggesting he will improve once going up in distance.

LORD APPARELLI

FAILED to win in two bumpers last term, but there was promise in both runs. Fourth behind Soaring Glory at Ascot on debut, he went on to chase home Mount Segur at Ludlow, with the pair nicely clear. Probably capable of winning a bumper, there are races to be won with Lord Apparelli – who is a full-brother to stable-mate Prince Llewelyn – over hurdles, especially if settling a little better this season.

SHANTOU EXPRESS

SHOWED a fine turn of foot when winning a bumper at Stratford on his reappearance last October, where he beat Highway One O Two (won all three starts over hurdles subsequently, including the Grade 2 Dovecote), Shantou Express went on to finish third behind Israel Champ and Soaring Glory in a Listed event at Ascot, on unsuitably heavy ground. Conditions never really came right for him after that, but he remains a smart prospect for novice hurdles on decent ground. A full-brother to Nicky Henderson's Champagne Mystery, he is one to note in the early part of the season.

THE EDGAR WALLACE

A HALF-BROTHER to Black Hercules, The Edgar Wallace won at the third attempt in bumpers, justifying favouritism at Hereford, where he made all and stayed on strongly. His earlier placed efforts entitled him to win in the style that he did, and he appeals as the type who will appreciate a greater test of stamina once sent jumping. In contrast to Shantou Express, soft ground doesn't seem to pose any problems to the five-year-old, who was an expensive store back in 2018 (€140,000).

Jack Barber

FLYING SARA

ONLY seen once last season, Flying Sara created a good impression when winning a bumper at Taunton, and the runner-up won at Ascot later in the campaign. A full-sister to Samarquand (won a bumper and an introductory hurdle for Harry Fry), she was prominent throughout under Nick Scholfield, and took up the running after cornering particularly well on the sharp turn for home. A five-year-old by Malinas, she lengthened right away in the final couple of furlongs, and it was a highly promising start to her career.

David Bridgwater

COMOTION

A RECORD of three winners from 142 runners would suggest that David Bridgwater isn't a trainer who focuses on the bumper division, so it is noteworthy when one of his string catches the eye, and Comotion did it twice at Warwick last term. Fourth on debut (in what looked a rough race) behind Here Comes McCoy in a newcomers' event, he came from a long way back, passing plenty of horses up the home straight. Again ridden patiently, he reversed form with Wildfire Warrior when third behind Sizable Sam, when he once again finished strongly. A half-brother to Soul Emotion (twice a winner for Nicky Henderson) and Slowmotion (Grade 2 winner over hurdles and Grade 3 winner over fences), he is bred to do well as a hurdler and won't mind an extra half-mile in time. He looks a nice prospect and might go under the radar somewhat.

ENRICHISSANT

OFF the mark at the third time of asking over fences – when winning by 18 lengths at Huntingdon in February – Enrichissant will have a 12lbs rise to contend with when he returns. The lightly-raced six-year-old won with plenty in hand, however, and he clearly relishes the Cambridgeshire course, as his sole hurdles win came at the same track. The son of Speedmaster has always threatened to develop into a nice horse and, perhaps, chasing will be where he excels.

THE CONDITIONAL

MADE giant strides in staying handicap chases last season, winning at Cheltenham in October and returning there to land the Ultima at the festival (first festival winner for his trainer), where he travelled notably well for Brendan Powell. Despite making an error two out, he picked up really well and stayed on strongly up the hill, always keeping the runner-up at bay. The Grand National is an option this season, whilst Newbury's Ladbrokes Trophy – a race in which he finished runner-up last year – is a possible early-season target.

Jennie Candlish

CHEDDLETON

FOLLOWING a promising debut at Wetherby, Cheddleton was a wide-margin winner at Bangor on his second start over hurdles, before following up in determined fashion at Kelso. Third in the Grade 2 at the same track, he kept on well in the closing stages over a new trip (2m2f) suggesting that he will have no problem staying further in time. In order to get the longer trip, he will need to learn to relax in the early part of his races, but he is a horse who remains full of potential, and although an initial handicap mark of 135 would seem stiff enough, he has the scope to progress further now that he goes chasing. A good-looking son of Shirocco, he seems at home on testing ground, so is one to monitor closely in the novice chase division throughout the mid-winter.

MINT CONDITION

THIRD in a Warwick bumper on his debut for Jennie Candlish, Mint Condition went on to run three times over hurdles without winning, but appeals as the type to do well when entering handicap company, from an opening mark of 115. Fourth on his only start in an Irish Point, he will make a chaser in due course, but should be capable of winning over hurdles beforehand, and he is worth another chance over a longer trip.

Rebecca Curtis

MINELLA BOBO

A *LEADING PROSPECT* in last year's book, we sadly didn't get to see Minella Bobo in action, but it is hoped that he returns to the track this autumn. A progressive staying novice hurdler the season before last, he looked potentially well-handicapped on a mark of 126 this time last year, and his form continued to work out well throughout last season. Sixth on his debut for Rebecca Curtis, he wasn't far off the likes of Edwardstone, Allart and Imperial Alcazar that day, and after two encouraging efforts over hurdles, he won a weak race by a wide-margin at Stratford. He beat Liosduin Bhearna (now rated 139) in his Irish Point, and with the prospect of further improvement over fences, it is very much hoped that he returns to action this term. He is one to catch in a novices' handicap chase over a staying trip.

Keith Dalgleish

PRINCE KAYF

CAUSED a minor shock when winning The French Furze Novices' Hurdle at Newcastle (next three home all won later in the season), Prince Kayf didn't do much wrong when just beaten by Overthetop at the same track in early-January. We didn't see the six-year-old again after that, but from a mark of 128, he looks potentially well-treated for when he does reappear. It should be remembered that he beat Kiltealy Briggs (rated 136) and Shishkin (rated 159) in a maiden Point at Inch as a four-year-old. He could be another for novice handicap chases to begin with.

Stuart Edmunds

QUEENOHEARTS

ANOTHER who missed the whole of last season and yet another who has the size and scope to do well if sent chasing. A winner at Listed level in bumpers and a Grade 2 winner over hurdles, she relishes deep ground, and is certainly one to have onside mid-winter. There is a good programme for mares over hurdles nowadays, but given her age (seven), her connections might want to press on with her chasing career, and stepping her up to 3m will open up further opportunities. She is very likeable, and has a proper jumps pedigree, being by Flemensfirth and out of an Old Vic mare.

Brian Ellison

THE KING OF MAY

HAVING missed the previous season, he won twice from three starts over fences last season, starting at Carlisle, where he jumped well and beat Henry VIII winner Esprit du Large. He then disappointed at Newcastle (perhaps, the ground being too soft) before bouncing back at Sedgefield, where he stayed on strongly to score off a mark of 131. Up another 3lbs, he looks the type to improve for better ground, and should also relish a strongly-run race, so a better quality handicap might bring about further improvement.

TUPELO MISSISSIPPI

CAUGHT on the line in his sole Irish Point (had jumped well and stayed on strongly, before the winner swept by him late on), Tupelo Mississippi again shaped like a stayer when only fourth on his first start for Brian Ellison and Phil Martin, in a Wetherby bumper. Ridden more positively on the all-weather at Newcastle, he galloped on strongly under a determined Danny Cook drive, and recorded a first career success. At the two furlong pole, a winning distance of 13 lengths didn't seem at all likely, but he powered away in the closing stages, again suggesting that he is all about stamina. The Yeats five-year-old again responded kindly, when following up under a penalty, also at Newcastle (turf) where he beat the promising Onward Route, with the pair a long way clear. The soft ground probably brought his stamina to the fore, and he rates a decent prospect for novice hurdles over 2m4f or beyond.

WINDSOR AVENUE

LOOKED an exciting novice chaser when winning impressively at both Sedgefield and Carlisle, he then disappointed at Doncaster (reported to have scoped dirty after the race) before falling in a Grade 2 at Haydock. He was still in contention at the time, and if he can recapture his early-season form, there could be a big race in him this year. The eight-year-old goes well fresh, so something like the Old Roan at Aintree – a race the same connections won with Forest Bihan last year – might be a good option. Owner Phil Martin also won the 2013 renewal with Conquisto, and 2m4f appears to be his ideal trip at present.

Still lightly-raced for his age, he clearly wasn't himself at Doncaster, where he weakened quickly. Given how he likes to get on with things, being ridden aggressively from the front over 2m4f – 2m5f might prove ideal.

Jimmy Frost

TILE TAPPER

THIRD behind Getaweapon (now in training with Kim Bailey) in a Point-to-Point bumper on good ground, Tile Tapper ran well on soft ground in a couple of bumpers at Exeter last winter. Sent off at 100-1 on debut, he finished fourth in a race which worked out well (third and fifth also won before the season was out), coming from well off the pace to finish strongly. Visibility was poor when he won at the same track on New Year's Day, lowering the colours of market leader Truckers Pass, with Hooligan (winner over hurdles next time) back in fifth. Ridden closer to the pace, he was in fourth as the field disappeared into the gloom at the top of the home straight, but he emerged from the mist in front, again finishing strongly. He already looks to be crying out for a step up in trip, but clearly has plenty of ability, and should do well over hurdles this winter.

Harry Fry

GET IN THE QUEUE

IMPRESSIVE in winning three bumpers the season before last, Get In The Queue featured as a *Leading Prospect* in last year's book, but injury kept him off the track. Since then, owners Paul and Clare Rooney have decided to focus solely on the Flat, so their National Hunt stock was sold. I'm sure Harry Fry didn't have to work too hard to persuade another of his leading owners, Masterson Holdings Limited, to purchase the son of Mount Nelson, who beat a strong field by upwards of 16 lengths at Exeter on his second start. Provided he retains that ability, he remains a very bright prospect for the season ahead.

Interestingly, given their link with the former jockey, the same owners have named a horse **Fehily** and he is also in training with Fry. Being by Asian Heights, he wouldn't have the most appealing of pedigrees (although his dam is a sister to the ill-fated Cuddles McGraw – a winning chaser for Fergal O'Brien), but he is noteworthy all the same, given the name.

KING ROLAND

ANOTHER who sports the silks of Masterson Holdings Limited and another who was unbeaten in bumpers the season before last, winning at Uttoxeter and Ffos Las. Runner-up in a maiden hurdle at Newbury, he got off the mark in a weaker race at Exeter (another gloomy day when visibility was very poor) scoring by 19 lengths, over 2m2½f. Stepped up in both grade and distance, he was sent off favourite for the Classic Novices' Hurdle on trials day, and he travelled like the winner for most of the race. Still going well when hitting the lead on the approach to the last, his effort levelled out on the run-in, and he was beaten by Harry Senior, a performance which clearly left his trainer disappointed. Having stated in an interview shortly after that he was far from certain to run at the festival, it could be that he would have been saved for Aintree, a track which probably would have suited this strong-travelling six-year-old. Rated 140, a strongly-run handicap would likely play to his strengths, and it could be that he drops in trip for the Greatwood on his return. Alternatively, this wide-margin Point-to-Point winner (when trained by Sophie Lacey) has the option of heading down the novice chase route.

PHOENIX WAY

ANOTHER of last season's *Leading Prospects*, Phoenix Way made a pleasing return to action at Huntingdon in January, winning a Pertemps Qualifier rather cosily, on what was his first start in just over a year. Another who eventually missed the festival, the imposing seven-year-old is clearly not the easiest to keep sound (given how little we have seen of him recently) and given his age, it is likely that he will now be sent down the novice chase route. He jumped well when winning his Point for Donnchadh Doyle and has the build for fences. If enjoying a clearer run of things, he could make up for lost time and rate higher than his current mark (140).

WINNINGSEVERYTHING

ANOTHER who was previously owned by Paul and Clare Rooney, Winningseverything won both starts over hurdles last season, looking a potentially smart sort. A bumper winner at Market Rasen the previous season, he appeared to struggle under a penalty, although in hindsight, he probably needed a stiffer test. Stepped up to 2m4½f for his hurdles debut at Southwell last October, he made virtually all to score with plenty in hand. He had most of the opposition in trouble quite a long way from home, and kept up the gallop under Sean Bowen. The third home Garry Clermont advertised that form by winning twice, whilst Winningseverything followed up, under a penalty, back at Market Rasen. In a weaker race, he again made all, and despite shifting to his left up the straight, went away to win easily once challenged. Now in the ownership of Jago and Allhusen (owners of bumper winner Pure Bliss) the six-year-old begins the campaign on a mark of 135, from which he would be of interest in a handicap hurdle over 2m4f or further. Alternatively, he has the option of going chasing, and being a half-brother to both Edmund Kean and Brave Vic, is always likely to appreciate soft ground. He should stay further, and remains completely unexposed.

Tom George

BIG BRESIL

IT was announced during May that – due to the truncated 2019/20 season – horses who lost their novice status from February onwards would remain a novice until the end of November (usually this is only applicable to horses who won in March or April, who remain a novice until the end of October) and it will help a couple of novice hurdle winners from the Tom George stable. One of those is Big Bresil, who made a winning debut over hurdles at Exeter in February, having finished runner-up in a bumper at the same track a month earlier. Runner-up to Papa Tango Charly in his sole Irish Point, the imposing son of Blue Bresil ran a sound race in his bumper, and appreciated the longer trip (2m2½f) when winning a heavy ground novice hurdle. Ridden more positively, he kept on tenaciously when challenged, again suggesting that he might be suited by going even further. He looks a staying chaser through-and-through, but the new rule will give him the opportunity to contest a couple more novice hurdles when he returns. Interestingly, Johnny Burke (*A View From The Saddle*) suggests that he could go straight over fences, despite his lack of experience.

CAPTAIN BLACKPEARL

UNABLE to win in three starts over hurdles last season, Captain Blackpearl should be capable of winning in handicap company from a mark of 114. He travelled really well when runner-up at Uttoxeter, and when fourth at Leicester, where he tired on the run to two out. Dropped back in trip at Carlisle, he finished only fourth of five, so perhaps 2m4f on less demanding ground/track will prove suitable. Given how he moved at both Uttoxeter and Leicester, there should be races to be won with him.

COUPDEBOL

WE only got to see this grey once last season, when sixth behind Son Of Camas in a competitive maiden hurdle, at Newbury's Winter Carnival. Third on his only start in France, the five-year-old crept into the race at Newbury, and wasn't too far behind the main group approaching two out, after which he faded. On this evidence, there will be races to be won with him at a lower level.

HOOLIGAN

LIKE Big Bresil, Hooligan will remain a novice through November thanks to the amended ruling, having made a winning hurdles debut in March, beating *Leading Prospect*, Nickolson. Only fifth in a bumper at Exeter on New Year's Day, he was held-up for most of the race at Warwick, and only really began to make progress from three out. Still fifth turning for home, he was into second by the time he kicked down the penultimate flight, but was on terms at the last and stayed on strongly to win. He was in receipt of 6lbs from the runner-up, who might have set things up for him, but either way it was a highly promising start, and he should appreciate going a bit further in time. I would imagine that Tom George will attempt to get him out fairly early, making use of his extended novice status.

KAKAMORA

ONE of several of last year's *Point-to-Point Graduates* who failed to make the track, Kakamora had impressed when winning at Loughanmore, where he beat Timberman (runner-up in a bumper for Nicky Henderson). Ridden positively, he jumped accurately, and might be at his best over intermediate trips once sent hurdling. His dam is a half-sister to Grade 1 winner Bitofapuzzle, and it is hoped that we get to see him in the early part of this season. Given how last season ended (forcing many horses to miss spring bumpers) it could be that there will be some very competitive races – in both bumpers and maiden/novice hurdles – during October and November, or possibly even earlier.

LETS GO CHAMP

ANOTHER who failed to race for the stable last season, the giant Lets Go Champ is a gorgeous son of Jeremy, who created a very good impression when beating Full Back (Fontwell maiden hurdle winner for Gary Moore) at Bartlemy last May. He made smooth progress to lead with a fine leap three out, and from that point had the race in safe-keeping, despite not being particularly fluent at either of the final two fences. Given his huge frame, it might not be a bad thing that he has had a lengthy break, and he remains one to be excited about for the upcoming season.

OSCAR ROBERTSON

HAVING finished mid-division in a Chepstow bumper on his first start for current connections, Oscar Robertson appreciated the step up in distance when winning a soft-ground novices' hurdle at Wetherby. Never too far away, he jumped well in the main, and stayed on strongly to score by six lengths. It wasn't the strongest of races, but he did it well. He returned to Wetherby just a few weeks later, when he shaped better than the bare result, tiring from the last, having been in a battle with the eventual winner for a long way. Given time to fill into his frame, he is expected to head straight over fences, and from a mark of 120, is certainly one to note in novice handicap chases.

SLAP DASH HARRY

A HALF-BROTHER to Honest Vic (won two handicap hurdles before finishing fifth in the Coral Cup last season, for trainer Henry Daly), he is one who did run in a bumper last season, finishing a well-beaten tenth in the end. Quite keen for most of the race, it wasn't surprising that he faded in the final half-mile, and he can leave this behind if settling better. He carried the colours of Paul and Clare Rooney, but at the time of writing was in the ownership of his trainer.

Chris Gordon

BADDESLEY

RUNNER-UP in a Plumpton bumper in April 2019, he reversed the form with the winner when making a winning reappearance at Fontwell, where he drew clear to beat a clutch of subsequent hurdles winners a shade comfortably. Only fourth under a penalty at Wincanton, he was bumped halfway up the straight before running on, perhaps finding the ground under the stands' side rail a little better. It was another encouraging run, and he can win more races once sent hurdling on decent ground.

GO WHATEVER
IMPROVED as he went up in distance over hurdles on testing ground last season, Go Whatever looked a thorough stayer when winning an Irish Point (at the fifth attempt) and can continue his progression when he returns. Given the experience he gained in Ireland, he would be of interest in staying novice handicap chases, especially in the depths of the winter when the mud is flying. A six-year-old with a fine attitude, it could be that he ends up contesting handicaps over a marathon trip and he could return to Plumpton – where he won a novice hurdle – for the Sussex National one day.

HIGHWAY ONE O TWO
A FLAG-BEARER for the Chris Gordon yard last season, Highway One O Two won all three races over hurdles, culminating in Grade 2 success in Kempton's Dovecote Novices' Hurdle. Like Go Whatever (who carries the same colours), it could be that he proves at his best on soft ground, so expect him to add to his tally once sent chasing this winter. His positive style of racing means that he won't be inconvenienced by small-fields over fences, and if he takes to it, he could well develop into a very smart novice.

LORD BADDESLEY
RUNNER-UP at Worcester on debut (came from off the pace and was beaten just a neck), Lord Baddesley would have appreciated a stronger gallop in a Kempton bumper, which was won by *Leading Prospect*, Hoi Polloi. Held-up out the back, he was unable to pick up the leaders in what turned into a sprint. Whilst I am excited by the winner, I also believe that several of those in behind could well improve on the bare form in time, and this son of Doyen falls into that category. A half-brother to Nicky Henderson's ill-fated mare Robins Reef, he looks another to note in the novice hurdle division, in the two-tone blue silks of owners Richard and Carole Cheshire.

ON THE SLOPES
COMMANCHE RED and Highway One O Two were probably the two highest-profile winners for the Chris Gordon stable last season, but the former might prove a shade difficult to place this time around, whilst On The Slopes – who finished behind

him on Boxing Day – could still be ahead of his current mark (143). Following that Kempton third, he filled the same spot behind two festival winners on trials day, then returned to Kempton to win twice, with his mark now a stone higher. A strongly-run race looks sure to suit the six-year-old, who I had in mind for the Red Rum at Aintree, before racing was suspended. There could be another big handicap in him this season, and he could reappear in the Haldon Gold Cup.

PRESS YOUR LUCK
ALTHOUGH he failed to add to Chris Gordon's tally of four bumper wins last season, Press Your Luck did shape with a bit of promise in a bumper at Kempton, which was won by *Leading Prospect*, Boothill. Too keen, it wasn't surprising that he faded late on, but he was still on the premises until the home turn, and there was definite promise in the run. It was actually slightly surprising how he went through the race, as he looked a stayer when winning his Irish Point, and once relaxing, he could have a future over hurdles.

SMURPHY ENKI
DIDN'T win in four starts in Irish Points, but he did shape with promise, and ran out a wide-margin bumper winner at Wincanton in March. Twice behind the aforementioned Boothill, he also chased home Coqolino (runner-up to another *Leading Prospect*, Bob Olinger) at Ballindenisk, and he appreciated the shorter trip on his debut under Rules. Settled well in front, the son of Blue Bresil made all, and looked to have the opposition beaten on the turn for home. He might well have been allowed a relatively uncontested lead, but he went further and further clear up the home straight, winning emphatically. The top-two in the betting finished tailed-off so it remains to be seen how the race will work out, but visually it was impressive.

TWOMINUTES TURKISH
A FIVE-YEAR-OLD by Mahler, Twominutes Turkish is from the family of Racing Demon (his dam being an un-raced half-sister to the dual Peterborough Chase winner) and he ran a race full of promise, when fifth in a Newbury bumper last November. He didn't look as comfortable on soft ground on his second start at Huntingdon, although he kept on well enough up the straight, again suggesting that he is a horse with a future. Whilst he could probably win a small bumper beforehand, the son of Mahler appeals as a horse who will improve for jumping, and he is another to note from the stable in novice hurdles.

Warren Greatrex

GO PHARISEE FLYER

A FULL-BROTHER to Fortunate Fred (shaped well in bumpers for Jamie Snowden last season) and a half-brother to Paul Nicholls' Darling Maltaix (winner of an Ascot handicap hurdle), Go Pharisee Flyer boasts a nice pedigree, and is, therefore, one to note in a bumper. As with many of the un-raced horses featured in this section, it could be that he would have run in the spring, had the season not ended prematurely.

KEMBLE'S CASCADE

SHAPED with promise in a bumper the season before last, and again at Lingfield in January, which came on the back of a wind-operation. The son of Kalanisi stayed on well from off the pace that day (not always easy to do on the all-weather track at Lingfield) and he ought to appreciate an extra half-mile once sent hurdling. He is a half-brother to Pumped Up Kicks, who was a four-time winner on good ground for Gordon Elliott and Dan Skelton. She also won her Point on good ground, so the ground could well be key to his progression.

PICARA'S PROMISE

A HALF-SISTER to *Leading Prospect* Nada To Prada, Picara's Promise is an un-raced four-year-old by Gentlewave (sire of impressive Cross-Country winner Easysland, and multiple-winners Poker Party and Erick Le Rouge, among others) so clearly boasts a good pedigree. Owned by The Spero Partnership Ltd (same owners as stable-star Emitom), she might well have made her debut in a bumper during the spring, and given her trainer's record in such races, she is very much one to note when she does make it to the track in the autumn. Given her pedigree, she ought to be even more effective once sent jumping over a longer trip, and should have no problem in coping with testing ground.

EMITOM

A *LEADING PROSPECT* last year, Emitom won the Rendlesham Hurdle at Haydock on his second start of the season, before finishing a most creditable fourth in the Stayers' Hurdle at Cheltenham. He stuck on really well that day, going someway to ease my theory that he is much better on a flat track. Rated 155 over hurdles, he is now expected to be sent chasing, and despite the fact that he hasn't always been foot-perfect over hurdles, he could well develop into a high-class novice. A good-looking six-year-old, he possesses the scope for fences, and the Kauto Star – a race the stable won in 2018 with La Bague Au Roi – would appeal as an obvious mid-term target. At his best on soft ground, he remains unexposed as a stayer, and has lost just three times in his nine career starts. He has the speed to win over 2m4f, so there ought to be plenty of options for him during the months ahead.

Oliver Greenall

A LARGE ONE PLEASE
SHAPED with promise on his racecourse debut, when third in a Chepstow bumper for Dan Skelton, he was formerly owned by the Rooney's, and is now in training with Oliver Greenall. Held-up at Chepstow, he kept on well, suggesting that he will be capable of landing something similar before going over hurdles.

EVANDER
WON twice over hurdles at Sedgefield last season, latterly stretching clear to score by seven lengths in what was no more than an ordinary event. A horse with a good attitude, this was evident when he fended off the opposition to win his Irish Point, and the five-year-old could either head down the handicap hurdle route or switch to novice chases. Given his ability to dictate in small fields, he could be very effective in northern novice chases.

VANDEMERE
THIRD behind Sporting John in a maiden Point which worked out well, Vandemere won nicely at Portrush on his second start, controlling matters from the front, and drawing away in the closing stages. Sold for £120,000 at Aintree's sale in April of last year, he failed to make it to the track for his new connections last season, but is expected to return in the autumn. Whilst he would be of interest in a bumper, he appeals as the type who will be better served by a little further over hurdles, and he is very much one to look forward to in novice hurdles. By Jeremy out of an Old Vic mare, he has a nice jumping pedigree, and is a half-brother to At Your Ease, a winner over hurdles and fences for Arthur Moore and JP McManus.

Nicky Henderson

ALLART
A FALLER at the first on his hurdles debut, Allart won a couple of minor midweek novice hurdles (Ludlow and Doncaster, both on soft) before taking his chance in the Supreme Novices' at Cheltenham. Despite the big rise in class, he acquitted himself very well and was still third on the home bend. Eventually crossing the line in fifth, he is set to remain over hurdles (unlike stable-mates Shishkin and Chantry House, who finished in front of him) and from a mark of 143, looks capable of making an impact in some of the better handicap hurdles.

Whilst he will probably stay further, he could easily kick off his campaign in the Greatwood Hurdle, with Newbury's Gerry Feilden another early-season option.

ANGELS BREATH
DESPITE not being the biggest, Angels Breath is well put together and took to fences really well, winning both starts at Ascot in impressive fashion. Very nimble, he could have easily developed into one of the top novices in England, but for picking up a serious injury when winning in December. It remains to be seen as to how long he will be sidelined for, but if he returns in the second half of the season, he clearly possesses the class to mix it in Grade 1 company. The six-year-old has had just six starts under Rules.

BIRCHDALE
A *LEADING PROSPECT* last year, Birchdale was bitterly disappointing on his chase debut behind Angels Breath at Ascot, but returned to action with a pleasing run in the Coral Cup at Cheltenham. Beaten just under 10-lengths by the same connections' Dame de Compagnie, he came from an uncompromising position, and would probably have benefited more than most from being able to run again, had the season not ended early. Now rated 145 over hurdles and fences, he has the ability to rate a fair bit higher, so could land a valuable handicap at some stage. Something like the Lanzarote Hurdle at Kempton – a race that Henderson has won three times since 2013 – could be an option in the New Year.

BOTHWELL BRIDGE
DESPITE not winning in two starts in bumpers, Bothwell Bridge showed enough to suggest he will be winning races over hurdles this season. On both occasions he looked a little outpaced by the winner, so it is likely that he will come into his own once stepping up in trip.

Among the un-raced horses at Seven Barrows, Bothwell Bridge's owner (Thomas Barr) has a Yeats four-year-old named after a small town in Scotland just north of Perth racecourse, **Blairgowrie**. A €150,000 purchase as a store (2019 Derby Sale), he has a nice pedigree, with his dam a half-sister to Frantic Tan and Irish Raptor, so he will want a trip in time.

BUZZ
REGULAR readers of my work will know that I was a fan of Buzz during his days on the Flat, and he duly made the best possible start over hurdles,

winning a maiden at Taunton and a novice at Doncaster. The form of his Taunton success was given a boost when the second won the Finesse Juvenile Hurdle on trials day, and he beat a fair yardstick at Doncaster. Sent off favourite for the Dovecote on the back of those two wins, he was beaten quite far out, suggesting that he failed to give his true running. A keen-going sort on the Flat, he will need to relax if he is to fulfil his potential over hurdles, but strongly-run handicaps might bring out the best in him. From a mark of 138, he is certainly worth another chance, and the Listed contest at Ascot (31st October) – a race the stable won with Sign Of A Victory back in 2014 – would be an option. He doesn't want the ground too soft (did handle soft on the Flat, but winter ground would likely be too testing), so I hope his connections get him out nice and early.

CHAMPAGNE PLATINUM

FAILED to win in four starts over fences last season, Champagne Platinum was sent off favourite for the Kim Muir at Cheltenham, where he stepped up markedly in distance. Sporting first-time cheek-pieces, he travelled well, and having made stealthy progress from the back of the field, looked a blatant non-stayer in the end. I suspect that Henderson will now drop him in trip, and from a mark of 137, races such as the BetVictor Gold Cup are likely options, whilst he can also revert to novice company if required.

DIAMOND RIVER

PLACED in two bumpers, Diamond River took a bump on the home turn at Warwick, and would have been better served with a stronger gallop at Kempton. Having shaped more like a stayer, he will probably need 2m4f over hurdles, and his pedigree suggests that he will need even further in time.

FLINTEUR SACRE

A FULL-BROTHER to the one and only Sprinter Sacre (as if you didn't know!), Flinteur Sacre made a promising start to his career, when coming from off the pace to finish runner-up at Newbury. He went one better next time, in what looked an ordinary event by Kempton standards (division one – which Diamond River finished second in – looked much the stronger event), where he was very impressive on the eye. A strong-traveller, he is another who will need to learn to settle if he is progress as a hurdler, but he clearly has an engine, and has the pedigree to go with it. It is unlikely that you will hear this horse mentioned this season without reference to his top-class sibling.

FUSIL RAFFLES

A GRADE 1 winner as a juvenile (beat Fakir d'Oudairies at Punchestown), he made a winning return in the Kingwell Hurdle at Wincanton, where he had to be stoked up to reel in Grand Sancy up the straight. Pulled-up in the Christmas Hurdle, he ran reasonably well until a mistake three out in the Champion, and might now be ready to switch to fences. A well-built son of Saint des Saints, he has the physique to make a chaser, and there wouldn't be many higher-rated hurdlers (150) going chasing. He has also always left the impression that he would be worth trying over an extra half-mile, so there would be lots of opportunities for him.

GIANTS TABLE

A MAIDEN Point winner for Colin Bowe in March last year, he failed to make it to the track for the Henderson stable last season, but remains a bright prospect for his owner, Lady Bamford. He was getting the better of Jeremy Pass when he came down at the last, and although he didn't really advertise the form in bumpers for Paul Nicholls, eventual runner-up Argumental won a maiden hurdle for Gigginstown. Conditions were atrocious the day he won, and given how he travelled, he would surely appreciate better ground. He is likely to head straight over hurdles.

GLYNN

LOOKED exciting when winning a maiden hurdle at Doncaster, on his only start for the stable last season. With Papa Tango Charly appearing to not run his race, the form probably isn't the strongest, but he could hardly have won any easier, cruising to the front before drawing right away from two out. He might well have gone to Aintree, but with the season ending as it did, he will be forced out of novice company after just that one start. At the time of writing, he hasn't been handed a handicap mark, but I would expect something around the 140 mark, so he will probably be aimed at the better handicaps. Prior to joining Henderson, Glynn had beaten the smart Brief Ambition (bumper winner for Fergal O'Brien) in his Point-to-Point.

KNOWN

YET to win, Known has shown promise on all of his starts, latterly when third behind stable-mate Shishkin at Newbury in January. Bred to appreciate an extra half-mile, he is one to note in novice handicap hurdles from an appealing opening mark (119). It will be disappointing if he can't exploit that rating, although there is also the option of running in a maiden hurdle, and starting off at one of the smaller tracks might prove beneficial.

MARIE'S ROCK

SHOWED a fine turn of foot when winning an introductory hurdle at Haydock, and again when maintaining her unbeaten record in impressive fashion in a Listed event at Taunton. Ruled out of the festival due to a stress-fracture, she is set to return this autumn and remains a really bright prospect. Given her pace, better ground would surely see her in better light, and the Listed mares' event at Wetherby (Charlie Hall Chase meeting) would be a possible starting point, if she were ready in time. Already rated 144, she could prove difficult to beat against her own sex over the minimum trip, with the Grade 2 Yorkshire Rose at Doncaster another likely target in the New Year. There is every chance that we have yet to see the best of her.

MISTER COFFEY

A GIANT son of Authorized, who won a bumper for Harry Whittington, before being purchased by Lady Bamford for £340,000. He made a winning debut for Henderson and his new owner in an introductory hurdle at Newbury over Christmas, where he showed a good turn of foot from the back of the last. Sent off at prohibitive odds to follow up at Huntingdon, he was far too keen in front, and found little once challenged and passed by West Cork. He will need to settle much better than this, but an opening mark of 128 looks more than fair based on raw ability. He is likely to start off in handicaps over the minimum trip and the Gerry Feilden would appeal as a suitable starting point, back at Newbury.

Henderson first won that race with Bacchanal in 1999 and saddled the 1-2-3 last year, with Epatante providing him with a seventh win in the race. His own worst enemy when last seen, it is hoped that he has matured over the summer, and returning to some better ground might also help Mister Coffey, who has the physique to make a chaser in time.

MISTER FISHER

BEST of the British when finishing fourth in the Marsh at Cheltenham, he had earlier shown a fine turn of foot when winning the Lightning Novices' Chase at Doncaster, and the pick of his form remains on flat tracks. With that in mind, the Old Roan at Aintree might be a good starting point (although that is slightly earlier than Nicky Henderson tends to have his string ready), whilst the Peterborough Chase and Kempton's Silviniaco Conti are another couple of options. At his best on decent ground, Mister Fisher is still only six and remains lightly-raced.

MY WHIRLWIND

COST £400,000 following her maiden Point success, My Whirlwind didn't make it to the track last season. Visually impressive in dreadful conditions at Ballycahane, the daughter of Stowaway was purchased by JP McManus and will be campaigned in the mares' novice hurdle division. It should be noted, however, that the form didn't work out particularly well, with the runner-up only fourth on her debut for Henderson, whilst the fourth was beaten in a handicap hurdle off 100. On a more positive note, Ruth Jefferson's Clondaw Caitlan (Grade 2 winner) was pulled-up before two out.

PIPESMOKER

ANOTHER who has yet to win, but another who shaped with considerable promise on both starts over hurdles last season. A real eye-catcher behind stable-mate and *Leading Prospect* Chantry House, staying on strongly in a slowly-run event at Cheltenham, form which now reads particularly well. He again ran on well behind Sporting John at Ascot, and given his physique, he is a horse who has likely benefited from another summer break. The five-year-old looks a future chaser, but can win races over hurdles beforehand, and will set a good standard in early season novice hurdles over an intermediate trip.

Philip Hobbs

PILEON

FOLLOWING his encouraging fourth in a slowly-run race behind Chantry House on debut (same race as Pipesmoker), Pileon won two small novice events at Catterick and Ffos Las, before putting up a career-best in the Martin Pipe, back at Cheltenham. Off a mark of 138, he came within a short-head of landing the concluding race at this year's festival, after which the handicapper put him up another 5lbs. Never too far away, he travelled really well at Cheltenham, and despite suffering an agonising defeat, it was a run which promised much for the future. Runner-up on his second start in an Irish Point, he made huge progress last season and could now form part of what appears to be a very strong team of novice chasers in the Philip Hobbs stable. At home on deep ground, he should have little trouble in staying 3m this season.

POTTERS VENTURE

RACED keenly when third in a maiden hurdle at Uttoxeter last October (faded from two out), Potters Venture improved significantly a month later, when he won a Chepstow maiden in commanding fashion. Having taken over with a circuit to run, he kept up the gallop to fend off Stick With Bill (won twice subsequently), and although he didn't run again afterwards, he is expected back this autumn. Currently rated 125, he would certainly be of interest in handicap company, whilst chasing is another option. His exuberant way of going suggests to me that he might be best over a stiff 2m4f – 2m5f, as he also raced freely in his Irish Points, when not quite seeing out the trip.

SPORTING JOHN

HAVING impressed me when winning his maiden Point in Ireland, it was pleasing to see Sporting John rattle up a hat-trick over hurdles in impressive fashion last winter. A smooth defeat of Harry Senior (Grade 2 winner) set the tone, and after following up at Exeter, he ran out a decisive winner at Ascot. Given how he had travelled in his earlier races, it is hard to believe that he gave his true running in the Ballymore, where he looked to be struggling with a circuit to run. I thoroughly expect him to prove that run to be all wrong, and although he could scale greater heights as a hurdler, he looks a chaser-in-waiting and could develop into a very smart novice if sent straight over fences. He remains an exciting prospect.

ST BARTS

ALBEIT at a lower level, St Barts is another decent prospect for staying novice chases and could develop into a decent handicapper in time. A fortunate winner of a Point for Ed Walker (left in front at the last when the leader ran out), he showed signs of greenness that day, and improved throughout last season, winning twice from four starts over hurdles. A winner on heavy ground at Uttoxeter, it was similar conditions when he won a 2m7½f handicap at Ascot, where he stayed on strongly. He begins the new campaign on a mark of 125, from which he will be interesting in staying novice handicap chases in the mid-winter.

TRUCKERS PASS

A HORSE who first caught my attention when finishing runner-up in an Irish Point, having swerved badly late on, which surely cost him victory. Following 10 months off, he made his debut under Rules in a bumper at Warwick, where he ran a sound race to chase home *Leading Prospect* Soaring Glory. The pair pulled nicely clear and marked themselves down as nice prospects, but whilst the winner followed up under a penalty at Ascot, Truckers Pass again finished runner-up, at Exeter on New Year's Day. Visibility was extremely poor that day, but he appeared to be travelling strongly at the top of the home straight, and was, perhaps, outstayed on soft ground. Clearly talented, it could be that he is better suited when there is less emphasis on stamina, and he remains a horse of some potential. I would like to see him out nice and early, whilst the ground isn't too bad.

WILDFIRE WARRIOR
SHAPED with promise in a couple of Warwick bumpers earlier this year (contested the same two races as David Bridgwater's Comotion), Wildfire Warrior looks as though he will appreciate a stiffer test of stamina once sent hurdling. His dam is a half-sister to the high-class hurdler Lady Rebecca (winner of the Cleeve Hurdle in 1999, 2000 and 2001, when the race was run over 2m5f) and he showed enough to suggest that he can make an impact in novice hurdles. Rather surprisingly, Philip Hobbs was 0-24 in bumpers last term.

Anthony Honeyball

KID COMMANDO
A WIDE-MARGIN bumper winner, Kid Commando bolted up on his hurdling debut at Plumpton in January, then finished a sound third in the Dovecote at Kempton. The son of Robin des Champs jumped well and had the opposition strung out when he won his Irish Point, so chasing is an option, whilst after just the two starts over hurdles, handicaps (from an opening mark of 136) is the alternative. He could step up in trip this season.

KILCONNY BRIDGE
IMPRESSED when winning a bumper at Plumpton, Kilconny Bridge finished runner-up on her first start over hurdles (1m7½f) , but rattled up a hat-trick in testing ground, latterly winning twice in the space of six days. Rather like stable-mate Kid Commando, she likes to race prominently and get on with things, and given how she won at Ludlow last time, she could easily still have more to offer this season. Now rated 126, she is another Irish Point-to-Point winner, so has plenty of options open to her. She is at her best on soft ground over a staying trip, and she was ridden with more restraint when coming from behind to win her Point.

MONT SEGUR
A FIVE-YEAR-OLD half-brother to Terrefort and Vino Griego, Mont Segur was an eye-catcher on debut, when flashing home in third at Wincanton, just one place behind *Leading Prospect* Sizable Sam. Held-up, the penny dropped up the home straight, passing several horses, and he would have gone very close but for hanging to his left in the closing stages. Dropped slightly in trip (an extended 1m6f), he got off the mark at Ludlow on his second start. Ridden in mid-field on this occasion, he travelled strongly into the straight, and took control of the race soon after. Despite shifting to his left again (not as dramatically), he ran out a very taking winner, marking himself down as a nice prospect for novice hurdles. His sire French Fifteen wouldn't necessarily be the most common (at this early stage) from a jumps perspective, but the pedigree is certainly there on the dam's side, and he is a very interesting horse going forward. He looks to have plenty of speed.

WINDSWEPT GIRL
OWNERS Geegeez.co.uk have a couple of promising mares to look forward to over hurdles this season, with **Coquelicot** the obvious one. She completed the hat-trick in the re-routed Listed event at Kempton in mid-March, but arguably more intriguing – in the long-term – is the year older Windswept Girl, who won easily on her sole start, at Taunton. Ridden patiently by Rex Dingle, she was nudged along on the outside around the home bend, and drew right away inside the final couple of furlongs. There is plenty of stamina in her pedigree, so she won't mind a longer trip once sent hurdling.

Ruth Jefferson

BUSTER VALENTINE
HAVING shaped with promise on chase debut (at a time when the stable's runners were improving for their reappearance), Buster Valentine appreciated the longer trip when winning a novices' handicap at Market Rasen in November. He jumped soundly in the main and showed a fine attitude to fend off the runner-up, but unfortunately picked up an injury that day which forced him to miss the remainder of the season. Expected to be back in action this winter, he will find life tougher off his revised mark (135) but he remains completely unexposed as a chaser, and could improve further once stepping up to 3m.

CLONDAW CAITLIN

HIGHLY progressive in her first season with Ruth Jefferson, Clondaw Caitlin now rates an exciting prospect for the novice chase division. Only seventh on her debut for the stable at Aintree, she stripped fitter when winning a bumper at Wetherby, and returned to the Yorkshire track to make a winning hurdling debut – a race which Jefferson had won 12 months earlier with Mega Yeats – on Boxing Day. Only third into the home straight, the daughter of Court Cave stayed on really strongly, drawing right away from the back of the last. That form worked out well, with the runner-up going on to finish third in the Dawn Run at Cheltenham, whilst the third won her two subsequent starts for Amy Murphy, and Clondaw Caitlin easily carried a penalty to success at Newcastle, teeing up a crack at Kelso's Premier Novices' Hurdle. The heavy ground probably negated the slightly shorter trip and she travelled best to lead two out. Yet again, strong at the finish, the five-year-old will relish stepping up in distance this season (both on running style and breeding) and boasts experience from Irish Points, having run three times in that sphere.

Alan King

COLOURS OF MY LIFE

MADE a hugely encouraging debut in a bumper at Newbury – won by *Leading Prospect* Gran Luna – when beaten less than five lengths into fifth. The biggest priced of the three Alan King-trained mares in the field (the other pair also finished in the first six), this daughter of Arcadio made eye-catching progress around the home bend and then up the straight. Having hit the front two furlongs out, she faded late on, but it was a very promising run, and she should have little trouble in finding a winning opportunity in a bumper if starting off down that route. The first foal of a Stowaway mare, who is a full-sister to Grade 1 winner Outlander, Grade 2 winner Western Leader, and several other multiple winners, she has a good jumping pedigree. I will be disappointed if she doesn't develop into a nice mare and win plenty of races in time.

EDWARDSTONE

THIRD in a trio of bumpers the season before last, Edwardstone made the perfect start to his hurdling career, when beating subsequent Tolworth winner Fiddlerontheroof at Wincanton. Despite refusing to settle, he moved up well to lead early in the straight, and showed the superior speed after the last. He then beat another subsequent Graded winner, when conceding 6lbs to Harry Senior at Aintree, where he again looked to win the race with a fine turn of foot on the run-in. The heavy ground appeared against him in the Grade 2 Rossington Main at Haydock, although he ran a fine race in defeat, doing little to dent the favourable impression he had made earlier in the season. Once again keen (despite wearing a first-time hood), he was delivered to win the race when jumping on at the last, only to be collared on the line (something we saw more than once on that card). The hood was left off when he ran a sound race to finish sixth in the Supreme, and from a mark of 142, is an obvious contender for the better 2m handicaps. If he settles slightly better in the early part of his races, he has the potential to rate higher, and will be at his best when the emphasis is on speed rather than stamina.

ES PERFECTO
AN expensive purchase on the back of a runaway Irish Points success, Es Perfecto debuted in what looked a competitive bumper at Kempton, and wasn't helped by the lack of pace. The race developed into a sprint and having been held-up (and also having stumbled slightly on the home bend) he couldn't match the turn of foot of the winner, but still ran with plenty of credit. More than capable of winning a bumper if ridden more positively, I suspect that he will be sent straight over hurdles, when an extra half-mile will probably prove ideal. A five-year-old chestnut by Shirocco, his dam is a full-sister to Corskeagh Royale (runner-up in the 2008 Champion Bumper) and multiple winners Shadow Eile and As You Like, so he has a good pedigree, and seems versatile ground wise. He looks to have a really bright future.

HARAMBE
WINNER of last year's Greatwood Hurdle, he wasn't too far away when brought down at the last in the Betfair Hurdle on his only subsequent run. Still relatively lightly-raced, it would seem sensible to try him over fences now, and it is worth remembering that he finished placed in a Grade 2 as a bumper horse. Versatile in terms of ground, he often shapes like he will stay 2m4f (although he has yet to win beyond 2m2½f around Market Rasen) so there should be plenty of opportunities for him if he does indeed head down the novice chase route.

JAY BEE WHY
IMPRESSED with the way he travelled when winning a maiden Point for Colin Bowe and Barry O'Neill (placed horses both won next time to advertise the form), he was sent off second-favourite for a Newbury bumper, but refused to settle early and never really got into the contest. Having won on a sounder surface in Ireland, it could be that he found the heavy ground against him, and he is certainly worth another chance when he returns.

THE GLANCING QUEEN
FIFTH in the 2019 Champion Bumper, she of course went on to win the Grade 2 mares' bumper at Aintree, and returned to action in this year's Champion Bumper, finishing eighth behind Ferny Hollow. She travelled well once again, and given the lay-off,

it was understandable that she tired in the straight. Hopefully she enjoys a clear run this season, as she could easily develop into a very smart novice hurdler against her own sex, with the Dawn Run the obvious end-of-season target. She has been in action on the Flat during the summer.

TRUESHAN
A SMART three-year-old on the Flat last year, Trueshan was a horse who I hoped would be sent juvenile hurdling, although it became clear in the autumn that it would not be happening. He twice beat subsequent Northumberland Plate winner Caravan Of Hope early last year, with Alignak (won his next two) back in third on the second of those occasions, when the winner shouldered a penalty. Following a second at Haydock, in another competitive event over 1m6f, the son of Planteur ran out an impressive winner of the valuable Old Rowley Cup, beating First In Line (won next time), and his season ended by beating another smart prospect, Hamish, in a conditions event at Newbury.

He returned to action in June, when shaping well behind subsequent Group 3 winner Dashing Willoughby, after which he won a Listed event at Haydock, again beating Alignak.

At the time of writing, it still unknown if he we will be sent hurdling this season, but I genuinely hope that he is. His form is solid, he has the size to take to it, and he relishes an easy surface. He should have no problem in staying the trip over hurdles, and he is trained by one of the best dual-purpose trainers in the country, so he has plenty going for him. If he does get the go-ahead, Trueshan could easily develop into a high-class novice, with the Supreme at Cheltenham and Aintree's Top Novices' Hurdle probable spring targets; his Flat speed would be a potent weapon around a track like Aintree.

Tom Lacey

ADRIMEL

WAS a couple of lengths in front when Make Me A Believer (Chepstow bumper winner for David Pipe) fell three out in a maiden Point at Ballyarthur, leaving him clear to score comfortably, and he made the perfect start under Rules, winning a bumper at Uttoxeter by 26 lengths. He faced stiffer opposition when defying a penalty at Doncaster, beating The Edgar Wallace (won at Hereford next time), with the pair a mile clear of the remainder. Prominent for a long way in the Champion Bumper, he dropped away inside the final half-mile, but can be expected to bounce back once upped in trip over hurdles.

TEA CLIPPER

WINNER of his first three starts over hurdles last season, Tea Clipper couldn't get to the front-running Cervaro Mix on his final start, when proving his stamina over an extra half-mile. Up a further 4lbs to 134, the five-year-old is now set to go chasing, and the prospect of fences over that sort trip should bring about further improvement. A Point-to-Point winner, his hurdling lacked fluency at times, but he appeals as the type who will improve for seeing a fence. All of his form to date has come on a relatively sound surface.

Emma Lavelle

KILLER CLOWN

THE first of a trio of second-season novice hurdlers to keep tabs on for the Emma Lavelle stable, Killer Clown made steady progress in three starts over hurdles, whilst leaving the impression that he would benefit greatly for a bit more time. Lavelle and husband Barry Fenton are well adept at bringing horses along patiently and hopefully they will be rewarded again this season, with this Getaway six-year-old, who won his sole start in Irish Points. Runner-up in a Warwick bumper the season before last, he begins this season on a mark of 124, and ended the last campaign with a decent third at Ascot, staying on well over 2m5½f.

NAMIB DANCER

UNLUCKY not to have won at the first attempt over hurdles last season, he was still travelling well in front when making a complete mess of the final flight at Wincanton, and he might well have won at Kempton had he been a little more fluent at the last, when he shifted to his right a little. Following a short lay-off, he again travelled reasonably well when sixth behind Chantry House at Newbury, and is surely capable of winning races from a mark of 119. He is one to note in novice handicap company, and given that all of his form is on good ground, might be one for the early weeks of the season.

RED ROOKIE

FINISHED third in an Irish Point, Red Rookie is a well-built son of Black Sam Bellamy who won both starts in bumpers last season, starting off at Exeter. Wearing a hood for his Rules debut, he was given plenty of daylight on the wide outside, and he joined issue going well inside the final quarter-mile. Drawing 12 lengths clear on the run-in, he readily saw off Big Bresil, who advertised the form by winning over hurdles a month later. Red Rookie made it two-from-two in bumpers when justifying short odds at Uttoxeter on Midlands Grand National day, when making all to beat just two rivals comfortably. Along with *Leading Prospect* Hoi Polloi, he looks to form part of a nice team of novice hurdlers at Bonita Stables.

RUNSWICK BAY

A BUMPER winner at Wincanton on debut, where he settled nicely just in behind the pace, and ran on strongly inside the final quarter-mile, despite showing signs of greenness. He failed to back that up at Warwick some five weeks later, perhaps the debut win taking more out of him than Emma Lavelle first thought. On the evidence of that Wincanton victory, he has more to offer once switched to hurdles, and it was nice to hear jockey Ben Jones provide a positive update in this year's *A View From The Saddle* section.

SAM BARTON

EMMA Lavelle boasted a fine record in bumpers last season, and although Sam Barton couldn't add his name to the list of winners, he made a promising start to his career when third at Exeter. The fact they went no sort of gallop will not have helped this five-year-old, whose pedigree screams stamina. He will need a longer trip once sent hurdling.

SHANG TANG

CAUGHT the eye on a couple of occasions in novice hurdle company last winter – notably when travelling very well at Taunton in January – Shang Tang has shown enough to suggest he can win races over hurdles, and in time, over fences. He should be capable of shedding his maiden tag over an intermediate trip and handles soft ground well.

Charlie Longsdon

GLENCASSLEY

WON what was the final race in England before racing was stopped due to Coronavirus, having earlier finished fifth in a good bumper at Exeter and filled the same position in a Listed event at Newbury. Allowed to stride on at Wetherby, he dictated matters under Aidan Coleman, and kept on well to score comfortably. A five-year-old by Yeats, he looks a nice type for novice hurdles, as he looks to possess plenty of size and scope for jumping.

ILLEGAL MODEL

FADED from two out in his only start in an Irish Point, Illegal Model made a winning debut for Charlie Longsdon in a 2m7½f novices' hurdle at Lingfield, where he stayed on well, having travelled best to lead two out. The runner-up franked the form by winning twice over fences subsequently, whilst the third home had looked a nice prospect when winning at Uttoxeter earlier in the season. It was, therefore, slightly disappointing that we didn't get to see the six-year-old again, but it looks as though the Charlie Longsdon Racing Club have found a useful staying prospect, who clearly handles testing ground.

Donald McCain

CHUVELO

RUNNER-UP to Uhtred (Listed bumper winner for Joseph O'Brien and Gigginstown) in a valuable sales bumper at Fairyhouse, Chuvelo won bumpers at Carlisle and Bangor on his first two starts for Donald McCain and owner Tim Leslie. He travelled really well at Carlisle and won with a fair bit in hand, before he made all to beat an ordinary field at Bangor. He then attempted to concede 10lbs to Good Time Jonny at Musselburgh, and whilst he had no chance with the impressive winner, he ran well again and was clear of the remainder. The winner went on to run respectably when ninth in the Champion Bumper, and Chuvelo should be more than capable of adding to his tally in novice hurdles this season. Versatile in terms of ground conditions, he is a full-brother to Double Seven, who finished third in the 2014 Grand National, so should certainly stay much further in time.

GAELIK COAST

A FORMER Irish Points winner, Gaelik Coast had been sick after his bumper runs and following his reappearance at Carlisle, won novice hurdles at both Doncaster and Bangor. A convincing winner on Town Moor, he showed a fine attitude to win a deeper race under a penalty, and he begins the new season on a mark of 130. Having jumped well and shown good pace when winning his Point for Donnchadh Doyle, he has the option of going chasing and should stay an extra half-mile if required this season. He looks quite progressive.

TEASING GEORGIA

WINNER of a three-year-old fillies' bumper (1m4½f) at Wetherby for Stuart Crawford, the daughter of New Approach was purchased in January by Donald McCain. Having travelled sweetly into the straight, she drew clear to score with plenty in hand, and although the form doesn't amount to much, it was a pleasing enough debut. She looks capable of making an impact against her own sex over hurdles.

THE CON MAN

RETURNED from a year off last December, and progressed to win handicaps in soft ground at Kelso and Ayr. Now rated 138, he jumped well when easily justifying favouritism in a Monksgrange maiden when trained by Colin Bowe, and now rates a decent prospect for novice chases in the North this winter. He saw the trip out well when stepping up to 2m5f last season and has raced exclusively on testing ground. Haydock's Grade 2 Altcar Novices' Chase could be a good option for him in the New Year, when he would likely get his ideal conditions.

Graeme McPherson

ASK BEN

ALTHOUGH he failed to get his head in front, Ask Ben ran a couple of sound races in defeat last term, and now rates a good prospect for the staying novice chase division. Fourth to Stoney Mountain in the Betfair Stayers' Handicap Hurdle on reappearance, he was still upsides at the last, and still a clear second with half-a-furlong to run. He ran a similar race at Cheltenham in December, where he was short of room on a couple of occasions, but still ran on really well to beat all bar the well-handicapped Goodbye Dancer, who might well have defied a 10lbs rise but for falling at the last on New Year's Day. The seven-year-old picked up an injury when pulling-up at Sandown in February, but has recovered well and is expected to return in the autumn, when he will head straight over fences. A strong stayer who is now rated 138, he clearly copes well with big-field handicaps, something which could stand him in good stead later in the campaign.

Rebecca Menzies

ONWARD ROUTE

DESPITE not getting his head in front in two starts last term, Onward Route shaped with considerable promise in a couple of bumpers for Ruth Jefferson, and should do well in northern novice hurdles for his new yard. Unable to cope with *Leading Prospect* Easy As That on debut, he kept on well despite leaving the impression that he wasn't exactly in love with the testing ground. He showed the benefit of that initial experience when travelling with ease at Newcastle, where he looked the most likely winner for most of the straight. Possibly just beaten by a stronger stayer, he is a half-brother to Policy Breach (finished runner-up to Petit Mouchoir in a Punchestown Festival bumper back in 2015) who was a good-ground winner for Kim Bailey. Being six, he is likely to head straight over hurdles on his return, and he will now sport the silks of John Wade.

RETURN TICKET

LIKE Onward Route, Return Ticket finds himself in training with Rebecca Menzies, having been sold by Richard Collins to John Wade. The Getaway seven-year-old is another who shaped well in defeat last term, especially the last twice, when runner-up at Catterick and Kempton. He bumped into a progressive novice on each occasion, but should be more than capable of shedding his maiden tag on his return. At his best on a sound surface, he is one to note in the early part of the season, and he also appeals as the type who will be well-suited by a strongly-run handicap over the minimum trip.

Kelly Morgan

RED INDIAN

LIGHTLY-RACED as a chaser, Red Indian has still only had the six starts over fences, and ran a hugely encouraging race on his reappearance at Haydock in January. The eight-year-old has an enthusiastic way of going, so dropping back to just shy of 3m might prove fruitful in time. He is now set to embark on a hunter chase campaign, and given that he is still officially rated 139, is a high-class recruit to that discipline. We also know that trainer Kelly Morgan does well in this sphere, having saddled Top Wood to place in the 2018 and 2019 Foxhunter at Cheltenham, before providing her with her biggest victory to date at Aintree. If the ground came up soft at the Grand National meeting, that race could be the ideal spring target for Red Indian.

UBETYA

HAVING shown promise in a bumper at Market Rasen and when runner-up behind St Barts at Uttoxeter, he returned to the Midlands venue to win a maiden hurdle over the minimum trip. A strong-traveller, he then headed north to contest the Grade 2 novice hurdle at Kelso, where he moved smoothly to the top of the home straight. A good jumper of hurdles, he is one to note in novice handicap chase company from a mark of 129. He will need to learn to settle if he is to stay further, but he is clearly talented, and is a nice prospect for young trainer Kelly Morgan.

Hughie Morrison

MISS AUSTEN

MORE renowned for his exploits as a Flat trainer, Hughie Morrison boasts an enviable record under National Hunt rules in recent seasons. Last season alone he saddled eight winners from just 19 runners (42% strike rate), with Not So Sleepy (winner of two Ascot handicaps) and Third Wind (winner of a Pertemps Qualifier before finishing fourth in the final at Cheltenham) his winners over hurdles, whilst his record in bumpers stood at five winners from seven runners (71%). Miss Austen was one of three mares who won in the division for Morrison, and she created a really good impression when winning at Ludlow in January, after which her trainer pinpointed Aintree's Grade 2 as the long-term aim. Expected to return in the autumn, she could bid to provide the trainer with back-to-back wins in the Listed event at Cheltenham in November (won the race last year with Urban Artist), after which she would have the option of going hurdling.

Neil Mulholland

MILKWOOD

A GOOD-GROUND bumper winner the season before last, Milkwood made a winning start over hurdles on similar ground at Hereford, where he travelled really well to come from off the pace to score with plenty in hand. Third on soft ground at Wetherby, he again travelled notably well when runner-up on his handicap debut at Wincanton in early-December. Up another 5lbs for that solid effort, this unexposed son of Dylan Thomas appeals as the type to land a nice handicap when getting his favoured conditions. Given that he is at his best when the emphasis is on speed, he could be out fairly early in the season.

ROOKIE TRAINER

BEAT the promising Truckers Pass (Philip Hobbs) by a head in an Irish Point, and made a pleasing debut for Neil Mulholland, when runner-up at Fontwell in January. Having failed to shine in a couple of runs for Kayley Woollacott, the six-year-old underwent wind surgery on arriving with Mulholland, and he looks more than capable of winning races over hurdles (for Noel Fehily Racing), on the evidence shown at Fontwell.

SOLWARA ONE

A SIX-YEAR-OLD by Gold Well, who represents the Neil Mulholland Racing Club, Solwara One made an encouraging start to his career, when runner-up to Ask A Honey Bee in a bumper at Wetherby in February. The winner was much more experienced, having won a couple of bumpers and run four times in Irish Points, and he went on to finish mid-field in the Champion Bumper. Solwara One was never too far from the pace and travelled up well, being just about last off the bridle, before his inexperience probably told. Given his age, he is likely to head straight over hurdles.

Olly Murphy

ALLAVINA

SHAPED with promise when third behind a subsequent Listed winner in a Huntingdon bumper, Allavina travelled well that day, and duly stepped forward to win at Market Rasen on her second start. She again moved nicely and picked up well inside the final quarter-mile. Bred to appreciate going up in distance, the daughter of Getaway looks more than capable of winning races in the mares' novice hurdle division this season. Given her pedigree, she might also appreciate a more galloping track.

BREWIN'UPASTORM

A REGULAR fixture in Jumpers To Follow, Brewin'upastorm has featured as a *Leading Prospect* in each of the past two seasons, and he remains a high-class prospect for chases up to 2m4f. A winner at Carlisle on his first start over fences last October, he came from last to first to win what was a strongly-run and strongly-contested beginners' chase, beating Good Boy Bobby by a head. He then went to Taunton, where he beat course specialist Southfield Stone easily, giving Paul Nicholls' runner 6lbs in the process. Sadly, he picked up an injury there, which forced him to miss the Henry VIII, and he ended up heading straight to the Arkle without a prep-run. Having missed the break, he was on the backfoot from the off, but was working his way into the race when unseating Richard Johnson at the top of the hill.

Exeter's Haldon Gold Cup is a race that makes plenty of appeal as a starting point for this season, whilst the Colin Parker back at Carlisle is another option, and it is worth noting that he has won first-time-out in each of his three seasons to date. Huntingdon's Peterborough Chase could be the ideal race for him before Christmas, whilst Kempton's Silviniaco Conti Chase is another Grade 2 to consider. 2m4f around an easy track might well end up being his optimum, so we could see him contesting the Melling Chase at Aintree, if things go to plan earlier in the campaign.

CHAMPAGNESUPEROVER

A WIDE-MARGIN winner at Ayr on debut, he travelled comfortably and drew right away to win by 16 lengths, and although it didn't appear to be the strongest of races, it was hard not to be impressed by the manner of victory. He didn't come off the bridle to win in a canter, which set up a crack at Newbury's Listed bumper a month later, for which he was sent off the 2-1 favourite. The least-experienced of those to finish in the first four, he came home in third, in what was a falsely-run race. Anchored at the back to begin with, he soon found himself much closer on the wide outside, and he was probably just about last off the bridle up the home straight. The race developed into a sprint inside the final half-mile, and he was unable to quicken on this much quicker ground. A big son of Jeremy, he will appreciate a stiffer test of stamina once sent hurdling in the autumn, and clearly handles soft ground well. He looks a really nice long-term prospect, who should enjoy a good season.

COLLOONEY

ONLY seen twice last season, when he didn't appear to appreciate the deep ground on either occasion. Runner-up in an Irish Point (had Fiddlerontheroof back in fourth), he jumped up well two out before his effort levelled out, again on soft ground. A six-year-old by Yeats, Collooney appeals as though he will appreciate going up in trip on decent ground and could, therefore, be one for staying handicaps. Lightly-raced, he also has the option of going chasing and there should be more races to be won with him in time.

DOCTOR KEN

OLLY Murphy continues his rapid ascent as a trainer, enjoying Grade 1 success for the first time last season with Itchy Feet, and he looks to have a lot of exciting un-raced youngsters in his stable at present, several of which I have included in this section. The first of those is this attractive four-year-old by Doctor Dino, sire of Grade 1 winners Sharjah, Sceau Royal, Master Dino and La Bague Au Roi. Out of Kendoretta, Doctor Ken is a half-brother to unbeaten chaser Salsaretta, and on breeding and looks, is very much one to look forward to at this stage. He is owned by Diana Whateley.

EWOOD PARK

A GOOD-LOOKING five-year-old by Shirocco, who Adrian Heskin speaks highly of in this year's *A View From The Saddle* section, he is another of the bunch of potentially nice youngsters in training with Olly Murphy. With his owner, Max McNeill, being a big Blackburn Rovers fan, Ewood Park has an eye-catching name, and is one to look forward to in a bumper to begin with, after which he could go hurdling.

FLETCH

ANOTHER really good-looking five-year-old, Fletch was purchased at the 2018 Derby Sale (€250,000) and he filled the eye the first time I saw him, in the pre-training yard of Francesca Nimmo and Charlie Poste. By Kayf Tara, his dam is a Robin des Champs mare who is a half-sister to Un Atout, who once promised plenty for Willie Mullins and Gigginstown (Grade 1 winning novice hurdler), so he has a lovely jumping pedigree. With that in mind, he might be one who will be seen to better effect as a hurdler, but is likely to have a run in the bumper beforehand.

GO DANTE

FLETCH will carry the silks of owner Barbara Hester, who has plenty to look forward to, as she has several un-raced horses to unleash this autumn. Another of those is Go Dante, who is another Kayf Tara, this time a four-year-old out of Nicky Henderson's Listed winner Whoops A Daisy. He cost €170,000 at last year's Derby Sale and is another who is likely to start off in a bumper in the coming months.

GUNSIGHT RIDGE

LOOKED to be one of the more exciting recruits from the Irish Points sphere this time last year (featured in Jumpers To Follow) but finished only fourth in a bumper at Southwell last October, after which we didn't get to see him again. Keen in a fairly slowly-run race, he perhaps found the ground softer than ideal, and the race did work out quite well. Ridden really positively when winning his Point, it could be that he needs a stiffer test, and I wouldn't be surprised to see him leave the Southwell form behind once sent hurdling.

HERE COMES McCOY

A FIVE-YEAR-OLD by Dylan Thomas, he won a newcomers' bumper at Warwick in January, where he showed a fine turn of foot to put the race to bed, and he was very strong through the line. Saving ground throughout, he cut every corner and might well have been best positioned in a race which looked a shade rough on the home bend. At this point, Aidan Coleman and Here Comes McCoy slipped up the inner, and once he got organised with a couple of furlongs to run, he picked up stylishly. Those directly in behind went on to shape well enough again (without winning) in bumpers, so there is reason to believe the form is above average, and he looks a smart prospect for novice hurdles.

I K BRUNEL

A SECOND-SEASON novice over hurdles last term, I K Brunel won twice from four starts. A winner at Fontwell on his reappearance, he stayed the trip well when upped to 3m for his final start at Musselburgh, where he travelled really well. Like several from the stable, he was being readied for Aintree when racing was suspended, and could now head straight over fences on his return. Seemingly at his best on soft ground, Haydock's valuable Betfair Stayers' Handicap Hurdle would be another option, should his connections opt to have one more start over the smaller obstacles. He would appear to have the right kind of profile for that race.

The same connections (McNeill Family and Prodec Networks Ltd) also have **The Wolf** for similar events, and their trainer will, no doubt, want to keep the pair apart for as long as possible. They are two nice horses for 3m novice chases this winter.

ITCHY FEET

AS stated on the previous page, provided his trainer (and owner) with a first win at the top-level, when winning the Scilly Isles Novices' Chase, and he begins the new season on a mark of 154. 2m4f seems to be his trip, so the Old Roan at Aintree would be one option in the early part of the season, after which he is another (like Brewin'upastorm) who could be considered for the likes of the Peterborough Chase and Kempton's Silviniaco Conti. There was still a full circuit to run when he unseated Gavin Sheehan in the Marsh at Cheltenham, and he remains completely unexposed after just the three chase starts. Although it was once thought that he was at his best on good ground, the pick of his form has come on soft.

LINELEE KING

ANOTHER who really impressed me when winning his Point-to-Point, he finished runner-up in a Chepstow bumper (Olly Murphy subsequently bought the winner) before winning on soft ground at Sedgefield. Ridden patiently, the grey stayed on well in the closing stages, readily justifying his short odds. Unable to make an impact in the Champion Bumper, he is another who will win races over hurdles before he goes chasing. Aidan Coleman was particularly complimentary about his jumping when I interviewed him for the *A View From The Saddle* section.

NO RISK DES FLOS

A HORSE who I gave a brief mention to in last year's publication, No Risk des Flos is a half-brother to both Vision des Flos and Umndeni, by an improving young sire (No Risk At All) who I am a big fan of. Epatante, Allaho and Esprit du Large flew the flag for him last year, and this grey is another who is likely to start off in a bumper in the coming weeks/months. The five-year-old is an athletic-looking individual and is another promising youngster who will carry the silks Diana Whateley.

The same owner has another five-year-old with a nice pedigree at Warren Chase, in the shape of **Lord Of Kerak**, who is a Martaline half-brother to Hell's Kitchen.

NOTRE PARI

A SMOOTH winner at Aintree in December (at a time when the stable was going through a quiet spell) he was then sent off favourite for the Lanzarote Hurdle, and he wasn't completely done with when falling at the final flight. Dropped back into novice company to win comfortably at Fontwell the following month, he begins the new season on a mark of 135. Although he could go straight over fences, he remains lightly-raced over hurdles so might make his return in a handicap, and something like the Silver Trophy at Chepstow would be an option, as he seems well-suited to intermediate trips.

ROCK THE HOUSE

FINISHED sixth behind *Leading Prospect* Sizable Sam, in a race which I expect to work out well. Indeed his stable-mate Dubai Guest (8th) franked the form by winning at Musselburgh, and having travelled well for a long way, Rock The House looked like he would take a hand in the finish before he tired late on, perhaps being inconvenienced by racing up the inside of the track. A half-brother to Nicky Henderson's Pistol Whipped, he looks more than capable of winning a bumper in the autumn, before he is sent hurdling.

TIGERBYTHETAIL

ANOTHER un-raced horse with a very nice pedigree, he is a four-year-old by Yeats out of Talktothetail, making him a half-brother to both Roksana (rated 152) and Robin Roe. Like the last-named, Tigerbythetail is owned by Barbara Hester, and he was a *Leading Prospect* in this publication four years ago, following an impressive display in a Warwick bumper. Sadly, we never got to learn how good Robin Roe could have been, but there is no denying that his dam has produced two very smart horses to date, and it is hoped that this youngster joins the list of her winners on the track. He will start in a bumper, and on pedigree alone, is one who I am particularly looking forward to seeing.

Dr Richard Newland

TASTE THE FEAR

DR NEWLAND has a fine record with horses that he receives from other trainers, and Taste The Fear made a winning debut for his stable in a bumper at Uttoxeter in December. The five-year-old had shaped with promise on his second start in Ireland, when fourth at Navan, and he looks to have a future over obstacles. Having travelled with purpose throughout, he had the opposition beaten early in the home straight, and was probably value for more than the official winning margin. He handled heavy ground well that day, having earlier ran twice on good ground for trainer Roger Joseph McGrath.

Paul Nicholls

ASK FOR GLORY

DESPITE only running twice last term, Ask For Glory again showed plenty of promise, finishing fourth at Newbury before relishing the longer trip to win a small novice hurdle at Wincanton in a canter. Given that he only shed his maiden tag in February, he will remain a novice until the end of November (under the amended rule for this season), so he could have one more run over hurdles, before going chasing. Already a winner of an Irish Point and a bumper, he has bags of scope for chasing and jumped well when winning between the flags for Donal Coffey. He could take a big step forward over fences.

GLENLIVET

MADE his debut in a bumper at Chepstow last October, Glenlivet travelled notably well that day before fading late on. In fact, he was still on the bridle when hitting the front around two furlongs from home, suggesting a less-demanding test would be more suitable. A full-brother to Knockgraffon, he was given plenty of time to mature, and would likely have run again in the spring on better ground. It will be interesting to see if Paul Nicholls opts to run in another bumper on his return, or sends him straight over hurdles.

FIDELIO VALLIS

FAR too keen when beaten on his British debut at Uttoxeter (as he was when runner-up over 2m1½f at Auteuil) and also when a faller at Chepstow in January. Allowed to stride on next time, Fidelio Vallis appreciated the change of tactics and made all to win easily at Wincanton. He continued his progression by scoring under a penalty at Kempton under similar tactics (took over with more than a circuit to run), when he hurdled really fluently. Despite not racing as freely, he was still very enthusiastic, which means he is likely to remain over the minimum trip for now, although Harry Cobden suggested after his Wincanton win that he rides like a horse who will need further in time. Now rated 138, he looks another smart prospect for novice chases (should he go down that route), especially if he can relax a little, opening up more opportunities over a shade further. Paul Nicholls did state after his Kempton win that he had also been suffering with ulcers earlier in the campaign, so he is a horse who could take another big step in the right direction this winter. He is another who is eligible for novice hurdles until the end of November, so Cheltenham's Grade 2 Sharp Novices' Hurdle might be one early-season option, should he not go chasing right away.

GREANATEEN

RATTLED up a hat-trick of wins in impressive fashion once sent chasing last season, he then shaped well in defeat when fourth in the Grand Annual, from a mark of 150. A little short of room when making a mistake two out, his effort on this occasion can be marked up, and the lightly-raced son of Great Pretender has the potential to improve further as a chaser. Some of the better 2m handicaps in the early part of the season can be quite uncompetitive at times, and he could easily land a nice pot before taking his chance in a better grade.

HITMAN

AN interesting recruit from France, where he won on the last of his three starts over hurdles at Pau. Runner-up on debut, he was ridden with exaggerated waiting tactics, but made eye-catching progress into the home straight, and it might well have been a different result had he not made a mess of the last. Either way, it was a most encouraging start and he was ridden more prominently when running out next time. He held a clear lead when appearing to jump one of the hedge markers, but he made amends just eight days later, when running out a convincing winner. Again ridden patiently, Hitman showed a fine turn of foot after the last to score by eight lengths, and it will be interesting to see what mark he is given in the UK. The four-year-old handicap hurdle at Chepstow in October – sponsored by this publication for the past three years – would be one option, as would the Masterson Holdings Limited Hurdle at Cheltenham. It is likely that he will have a light campaign this season, with chasing in mind for next year.

PIC D'ORHY

RATED 151 following his win in the Betfair Hurdle, Pic d'Orhy will be one of the highest rated hurdlers going chasing this season. Despite the bunched finish casting a slight doubt over the strength of this year's Betfair form, he kept on well to fend off the runner-up, to whom he was conceding 11lbs. An early casualty (unseated at the second) on his sole start over fences in France, he took a

McFABULOUS

A *LEADING PROSPECT* in last year's publication, McFabulous improved steadily as the season went on, and ran out a facile winner of the rescheduled EBF Final at Kempton in March. The six-year-old, who was a Grade 2 bumper winner the previous spring, travelled like a dream at Kempton and thoroughly deserved the 13lbs hike in the handicap. Now rated 145, Paul Nicholls had suggested that the West Yorkshire Hurdle at Wetherby could be an early-season target, with the prospect of him then being campaigned in the 3m hurdle division. However, given that he is another who remains a novice until the end of November, he could return in the Persian War, a race that Nicholls has won seven times since 2000 (and six times in the past 13 years). He would likely set a very good standard in that event, so it would appeal as the perfect starting point.

similar fall when returning to Auteuil to contest the Grade 1 Prix Renaud du Vivier, on his second start for the Nicholls stable, last November. He will, therefore, need to jump more fluently now that he goes chasing, but he is sure to be well-schooled coming from this stable. Despite his form in France, better ground was believed to have helped him at Newbury, and he can make his presence felt at a decent level this season.

SAINT SONNET

ONLY ran twice for Paul Nicholls last season, winning comfortably at Catterick (next two home won their only subsequent starts in handicap company) before running better than his finishing position would suggest in the Marsh at Cheltenham. Having travelled well to two out, his effort levelled out, but he is still only five and very much unexposed over fences. Rated 147, he is likely to be aimed at the BetVictor Gold Cup, and could land a nice pot at some stage this season. The Caspian Caviar Gold Cup is another likely option at Cheltenham in December, and having had more time to acclimatise to his new surroundings over the summer, there is every reason to believe that he can improve again this season.

SOLO

A WIDE-MARGIN winner at Auteuil last November (where he was inclined to shift to his right at times), Solo made a blistering British debut in the Adonis Juvenile Hurdle, earning himself a huge official rating (157) which was subsequently the topic of much debate. He travelled sweetly, jumped slickly, and drew right away to record a very taking success. Only eighth in the Triumph, he moved well until coming down the hill for the final time, and it could just be that he is more of a long-term prospect than an out-and-out juvenile hurdler. He has the build of a chaser, and it is worth remembering that Clan des Obeaux and Frodon finished in a similar position in the Triumph before making up into high-class chasers (something also worth bearing in mind with Pic d'Orhy). It is likely that he will remain over hurdles for this season, and from a mark of 152 might not be the easiest to place (again, the Masterson Holdings at Cheltenham would seem a logical starting point against his own age group, whilst he could head back to France for the Prix Renaud du Vivier), but he remains an exciting prospect for when he does go chasing.

STRATAGEM

ANOTHER four-year-old, he actually beat Solo at Auteuil on his only start in France, and won once from two starts in England last season. Beaten at short odds at Bangor, he wore a tongue-tie when winning a small race at Kelso, after which owner/rider David Maxwell suggested that he is likely to head straight over fences this season. The grey – who cost is owner €260,000 last November – is a half-brother to Ziga Boy (dual winner of the Sky Bet Chase for Alan King) and races as though he will be suited by a stiffer test of stamina, so expect to see him go up in distance.

WHISKEY LULLABY

RUNNER-UP in an Irish Point for Colin Bowe, Whiskey Lullaby filled the same position in what appeared to be a well-contested Newbury bumper. The lack of pace wouldn't have played to her strengths, but she stayed on really well to finish runner-up behind one of this year's *Leading Prospects*, Gran Luna. A mare by Stowaway with plenty of size and scope, she could be one for the mares' novice hurdle at Chepstow in October (2m3½f), a race that Paul Nicholls has won for the past three years, with If You Say Run, Posh Trish and Silver Forever. Like the first-named pairing, this five-year-old carries the silks of Highclere, and she will appreciate stepping up in distance over hurdles. She looks a nice prospect for jumping.

Peter Niven

MALYSTIC

A WINNER of two bumpers, Malystic won just once from four starts over hurdles last season, but looks open to plenty of improvement. Having got no further than the second at Market Rasen, he bolted up in a maiden hurdle at Musselburgh, winning by 17 lengths. Outstayed by Pileon (runner-up in the Martin Pipe) when trying to concede 6lbs to the winner over 2m3½f at Catterick, he dropped back to the minimum trip to contest the Scottish Supreme Novices' Hurdle back at Musselburgh, where he was narrowly denied by Nicky Henderson's Fred. He probably would have prevailed had he jumped the final flight more cleanly, and whilst a mark of 140 looks stiff enough on the face of it, he does appeal as the type who will relish a strongly-run handicap over the minimum trip. From the family of the same stable's classy dual-purpose performer Clever Cookie, he seems at his best on a decent surface.

Fergal O'Brien

ASK A HONEY BEE

TOOK four attempts to win his Irish Point, but quickly rattled up a hat-trick for Fergal O'Brien, before finishing mid-division in the Champion Bumper at Cheltenham. He beat a subsequent winner at Southwell and had Tupelo Mississippi (won his next two) back in fourth when completing the hat-trick in what looked a good race at Wetherby, so his form is strong, and his running style would suggest that he will need a trip over hurdles. A resolute galloper, he couldn't go with the principals when coming down the hill at Cheltenham, but should be more than capable of returning to winning ways over hurdles.

BRIEF AMBITION

BEATEN much further in the Champion Bumper, Brief Ambition doesn't have too dissimilar a profile to Ask A Honey Bee, in that he boasts plenty of experience from Irish Points and bumpers. Runner-up to Glynn (impressive winner for Nicky Henderson at Doncaster), he won at the third time of asking between the flags, and beat the ill-fated Supamouse (wide-margin winner on Boxing Day) at Southwell, on his debut for the O'Brien stable. He probably wasn't best positioned when only fourth at Cheltenham (held-up in a slowly-run race) and he travelled well when runner-up in another Listed event at Newbury. He actually shaped much better than his finishing position at Cheltenham and is a bright prospect for novice hurdles, with the Persian War a possible early-season target.

BUTTE MONTANA

RUNNER-UP at Cheltenham on his racecourse debut, he travelled well in the heavy ground, and ran a race full of promise. Interestingly, the stable had won the corresponding race the previous two seasons, and he didn't run to anywhere near the same level in a Listed event at Ascot next time. By Presenting, he has a nice pedigree being from the family of In Compliance, and whilst he could well win a bumper on his reappearance, he will form part of what looks to be a strong team of novice hurdlers at Ravenswell Farm. It wouldn't actually be a huge surprise if he headed back to Cheltenham in October for that same bumper.

GLOBAL FAME

RAN well without winning in three starts in Irish Points (fourth behind Silver Hallmark and runner-up to Silver Sheen, who completed a hat-trick over hurdles in a Pertemps Qualifier at Warwick), Global Fame is another who won a Southwell bumper on his debut under Rules. Ridden with confidence, he won well despite looking a shade green, and he made a pleasing start over hurdles when runner-up to Harry Senior (won a Grade 2 next time) at Chepstow. He probably didn't need to improve on that to win at Wetherby, where he came right away in the closing stages, suggesting he will get further in time. He remains a novice until the end of November, so again the Persian War would be an option, although he looks to have been handed a lenient opening mark (129) should his connections consider the handicap route. He will jump a fence in time, and looks a really nice prospect.

LIOSDUIN BHEARNA

ENDED the previous campaign with a couple of handicap hurdle wins, Liosduin Bhearna then ended last season with a smart performance in a handicap at Doncaster, on what was his first start over 3m. He saw the trip out well (although they didn't go any sort of pace) and being a full-brother to Cloth Cap (won twice as a novice before finishing third in the Scottish Grand National), he should get even further in time. He handled the heavy ground really well at Doncaster (slightly surprising as his brother prefers good ground) and he is now set to embark on a novice chase campaign. He begins this season on a mark of 139 and is the type to do well in handicaps.

SILVER HALLMARK

A *LEADING PROSPECT* in last year's publication, he made the best possible start over hurdles, winning in stylish fashion at Chepstow, reversing bumper form from the previous season with McFabulous. He jumped much better than the runner-up and stretched right away in the closing stages, staying on strongly over the minimum trip. He then finished tailed-off in the Tolworth Novices' Hurdle on his only subsequent start, although he was set to return to action at Newbury the weekend after racing was suspended. A good-looking grey with plenty of stamina in his pedigree (half-brother to mud-loving stayer Gayebury), he jumped well when winning a well-contested Irish Point, and is set to head straight over fences on his return. With plenty of scope for improvement as he goes up in distance, he remains a bright prospect for novice chases over 2m4f and beyond.

MINELLA TARA

A FINAL fence faller (held every chance) on his sole start in an Irish Point, Minella Tara justified strong market support when making a winning start for his current connections in an all-weather bumper at Lingfield. Ridden patiently, he showed a fine turn of foot to quicken to the front off the home bend, and readily saw off a previous course-and-distance winner. He failed to back that up in a better race at Kempton, but he wasn't right afterwards and can prove this running all wrong in time. Given the pace he showed when winning at Lingfield, he would appear quick enough to start off over the minimum trip once sent hurdling.

THE BEES KNEES

AN Irish Points winner who was purchased on trials day at Cheltenham, he hadn't been with Fergal O'Brien for long when making a promising Rules debut in a bumper at Huntingdon. He travelled well to lead, and although he couldn't go with the impressive winner, it was an encouraging start and he might well have got to the front sooner than ideal. Prior to winning his maiden over in Ireland, he had matched strides with the highly-touted Sir Gerhard for a long way, and was a tired third when falling at the final fence. He finished third on his recent reappearance at Market Rasen, where he again lacked the pace of the front two, but there could be significant improvement forthcoming once he is sent hurdling over an extra half-mile.

Jonjo O'Neill

ADICCI

GOT the better of Neff (wide-margin winner next time) at Plumpton on his first start over hurdles, and would have justified very short odds at Sedgefield but for falling at the last. Finished only mid-field in the EBF Final, he shifted to his left at times that day and possibly didn't fully see out the trip, having seen plenty of daylight on the wide outside. He had earlier given the impression that he wanted stepping up in distance, so is certainly worth another chance off what looks a fair mark (124).

DARSI IN THE PARK

HAVING failed to complete on his first two starts, he won an Irish Point at Lingstown for Donnchadh Doyle, beating stable-mate Captain Drake (now with Harry Fry, for whom he finished runner-up in the Midlands Grand National and is now rated 142) by three lengths. Having shaped with promise before unseating his rider at Perth, Darsi In The Park defied market weakness to win a heavy-ground maiden hurdle at Uttoxter, before going on to finish third in a handicap at Wincanton. He didn't travel particularly fluently on either occasion, so perhaps slightly better ground might help, and he remains on a potentially lenient mark (120). He will be interesting in novice handicap chases over 2m4f or thereabouts.

MAYPOLE CLASS

ANOTHER who will be of interest in novice handicaps over fences is Maypole Class, who jumped well when runner-up in an Irish Point before joining Jonjo O'Neill. He was an easy winner of an ordinary race at Lingfield (2m3½f, heavy) before running really well in a much stronger contest at Wincanton. He travelled very well that day, and a cleaner jump at the last might well have made the difference between winning and losing. He struggled in heavy ground when upped in distance at Ascot when last seen (perhaps he just got away with the ground in weaker company at Lingfield) and will be suited by intermediate trips over fences. He begins the new season on a mark of 123.

PALMERS HILL

PROVIDED Jonjo Jnr with a first Cheltenham winner, when winning in November 2018, and made a hugely encouraging return from 15 months off the track, when runner-up at Kempton in February. He travelled strongly and looked to have been delivered to perfection, hitting the front after the last, only to be collared by the rallying Downtown Getaway. The winner failed to frank the form in the Silver Plate, but the third home actually won that festival consolation race, so the form looks strong, and it is hoped that he remains sound now, and can be seen on a more frequent basis. Up to a mark of 137, he could be another who now goes chasing (won a Point-to-Point by 20 lengths as a four-year-old) and could be one who ends up in the novices' handicap at the festival, if rated similarly come the spring.

PAPA TANGO CHARLY

GIVEN the impression he made when winning his Irish Point, it was slightly disappointing that Papa Tango Charly couldn't win a race under Rules last season, but he certainly shaped with promise when second at both Ascot and Newbury. Again, he will probably come into his own as a chaser in time, but he can surely be placed to win over hurdles beforehand, and looked like a horse who needed time to fill out last year. His best efforts to date have come on soft ground and the five-year-old might well have benefited (physically) for his summer at grass.

TEDHAM

LIKE Papa Tango Charly, he is in the ownership of yard sponsor Martin Tedham. He ran well when a fast-finishing third in the valuable Betfair Stayers' Handicap Hurdle at Haydock, and was then hampered when a beaten favourite in a Pertemps Qualifier at Warwick. I have long been of the opinion that Tedham is capable of winning a nice prize or two, and perhaps, he is another who will flourish for going chasing. A good-looking six-year-old by Shirocco, his sole win to date came on good ground, and he travels like a horse who could be much better than his current mark (131). If he were mine, he would be going chasing, hopefully winning a couple of novice events to build up his confidence, before pitching him into handicap company. There could be a big race in him come the spring.

Ben Pauling

ONE TOUCH

TWO from four since joining Ben Pauling from Michael Scudamore, One Touch won a Doncaster novices' hurdle on his second start last season, making all to score with something to spare. A former winning Pointer (trained by Francesca Nimmo), he jumped big and bold, so is likely to come into his own as a chaser. He was pulled-up quickly on his final start and reportedly bled, which is of obvious concern, but he clearly possesses a good deal of ability, and he has a current rating of 131.

SHAKEM UP'ARRY

FAILED to win in four starts over hurdles last season, he was still in front when over-jumping at the fourth last at Leicester on debut. He then chased home Mister Coffey and Shishkin in a couple of decent events at Newbury, before finishing down the field in the Ballymore. Still a novice for this season, he is rated 127 over hurdles, so should have little trouble in finding a winning opportunity before heading into handicap company. A sizable six-year-old with a stout pedigree (full-brother to Imperial Bay) he should appreciate going up in distance.

THE MACON LUGNATIC

A BUMPER winner at Newbury the season before last, he wasn't too far away when blundering away his chance at Leicester on his hurdles debut (pulled-up straight away), then won twice at Doncaster before the season came to an end. Having made all to win an EBF qualifier on soft ground, he returned to the same track to win in similar fashion on better ground, under a penalty. Now rated 129, he is likely to be running in handicap hurdles this season, although he hurdled particularly fluently at times, so should have no problem when the time comes to go chasing. The six-year-old son of Shirocco looks to have plenty of scope and remains lightly-raced.

YOUR DARLING

LOOKED an exciting prospect when beating Flinteur Sacre (won easily next time) in a bumper at Newbury on his racecourse debut, Your Darling then disappointed at Warwick when pulled-up, having been sent off at odds-on. Both his trainer and Henrietta Knight, who had done the pre-training with the horse, were extremely complimentary about him after his Newbury success, where he really did look like a horse with a very bright future. Not short of speed, he will start off over the minimum trip once sent hurdling. Following that impressive victory at Newbury, there was talk of both the Champion Bumper or (more likely) a trip to Aintree, so he is clearly a horse who is held in high regard by his trainer, and it is very much hoped that he proves his Warwick running to be all wrong upon his return.

Richard Phillips

PICANHA

AN Irish Point-to-Point winner in November 2018, he made a winning start for Richard Phillips and Liz Prowting in a bumper at Exeter some 13 months later. Ridden patiently, he was pushed up into contention on the turn for home, and he really began on to stay on strongly down the centre of the course. Appearing to relish every inch of the 2m1f trip, he was too strong for the placed horses in the closing stages, and although the runner-up was beaten next time (surely didn't run to the same level), the race worked out particularly well, with the third, fourth and fifth all winning bumpers before the season was out. An injury prevented Picanha from running again last season, but he is reportedly ready to return in the autumn, when he will need a trip once sent hurdling, as stamina seemed a strong point in both starts to date. The six-year-old is Phillips' only bumper winner during the past five seasons and the son of Malinas looks capable of making up into a really nice novice hurdler, over 2m4f and beyond.

Ella Pickard

GETAROUND

STAYED on well to take second on his debut in the Point-to-Point sphere, he was ridden more positively when winning at the second attempt, over 2m4f at Upcott Cross. He jumped well on that occasion and drew clear in the closing stages, again suggesting that staying will be his forte. Third in a bumper at Ffos Las, he travelled well for a long way and probably would have appreciated a stronger gallop. More use was made of him on his second start at Chepstow, when he made all and ran out a taking winner, with the race in safe-keeping halfway up the home straight. Unsuited by the slowly-run race in Listed company at Newbury next time, the grey made a winning debut over hurdles in March, staying on strongly on soft ground over 2m7f at Exeter. Again making all, he jumped well and ran out a very taking winner, marking himself down as a smart long-term prospect.

Last year, Ella Pickard had just eight horses in training and it could be that this well-bred son of Getaway puts her on the map. A half-brother to strong-stayer Dandy Dan (Kim Bailey) and Gordon Elliott's smart mare Bigbadandbeautiful, Getaround remains a novice over hurdles until the end of November, and is likely to remain over the smaller obstacles until losing that novice status, after which he will be sent chasing.

David Pipe

EXTRA MAG

MISSED the whole of last season, but is expected to return this year, and remains a lightly-raced six-year-old with more to offer. A faller with the race at his mercy on his first start in England, he then won at Exeter, before chasing home Precious Cargo (conceding 7lbs) at Kempton. He had several subsequent winners in behind that day, including Not So Sleepy, and he will be of interest in handicap hurdles, which should be run to suit as he has been keen in the past. He doesn't have a rating at the time of writing, but he was rated 132 when a non-runner in last year's Imperial Cup, and he is an athletic sort who will also take well to fences. If over his injury, he could easily make up for lost time.

ISRAEL CHAMP

A TWO-TIME Listed bumper winner last season, Israel Champ relished the testing ground at Cheltenham and Ascot, where he gave *Leading Prospect* Soaring Glory 4lbs and a beating. Dictating matters from the front, that was strong form, and it was disappointing that he was unable to make an impact in the Champion Bumper, back at Cheltenham, where he faded from half-a-mile out. An impressive 12-length winner of his maiden Point, he might appreciate going up in distance over hurdles, and there are sure to be more races to be won with him. It could be that he will be at his best when able to dictate in small fields in deep ground, so pay particular attention to him when he might get an uncontested lead.

MAKE ME A BELIEVER

SHOWED a fine attitude to fend off the challengers when winning a Chepstow bumper last October, after which we didn't get to see him again. The runner-up was placed in a Listed event (behind Israel Champ) next time, whilst there were a couple of subsequent winners further down the field, and the five-year-old held every chance when falling in his sole Irish Point (race won by Adrimel, twice a bumper winner for Tom Lacey last season). A half-brother to King Roland, he looks capable of making an impact as a novice hurdler this season, when he shouldn't have a problem in stepping up in trip.

> ## MARTINHAL
>
> A FALLER when still in contention four out in his Irish Point, Martinhal was well-backed and justified the support when making a winning start for David Pipe and owner Lynne MacLennan, in a bumper at Huntingdon. Ridden prominently, he tracked the pace until the home bend, when he quickened clear in taking fashion. Pushed out, he won with plenty in hand, and the Westerner five-year-old looks an interesting prospect for novice hurdles. David Pipe looks to have a good team for that division this season and Martinhal could end up being the pick of the bunch.

PANIC ATTACK

HUGELY impressive when winning a Listed bumper at Market Rasen on her racecourse debut (when trained by Willie Mullins) she was bought privately and made her first start for her current connections in the Weatherbys Champion Bumper. She began to back-pedal around the same time as Israel Champ, eventually coming home in 18th. Back against her own sex, she can win more races, and although not overly big, she clearly has a big engine. Her pedigree doesn't scream that of a jumper, but Cliffs Of Dover (who is also by Canford Cliffs, and out of a Galileo mare) was a prolific hurdles winner for Paul

Nicholls, and offers up hope in that regard. She looks all about pace and will be best suited when the emphasis is on speed.

SIRUH DU LAC

THE winner of the Plate at last year's Cheltenham Festival, he took a horrid-looking fall in the same race this year (off a 9lbs higher mark), when still in front at the second last. The seven-year-old has since been switched from Nick Williams to David Pipe, and he remains lightly-raced after just the 10 chase starts. He is actually still a novice over hurdles so always has that as an option, but it is likely that he will be aimed at the BetVictor and Caspian Caviar Gold Cups, back at Cheltenham.

UMBRIGADO

ENDURED a rather frustrating campaign last season, starting at Haydock, where he didn't appear to see out the trip in the Betfair Stayers' Handicap Hurdle. Dropped right back to the minimum trip at Ascot, I then expected him to go well in the Martin Pipe at Cheltenham, but he never really made an impact under Jack Tudor. Still only six, he has time on his side and will, hopefully, now go chasing. He jumped well when runner-up in an Irish Point (showed pace and was probably outstayed) he can make his mark at intermediate distances as a novice chaser this term. It is worth remembering that his first defeat under Rules came in a Grade 1 at Aintree, and he remains fairly lightly-raced.

Alastair Ralph

BILLINGSLEY

HUGELY progressive when switched to handicap company over fences, winning his last three starts last season, latterly at Haydock and Newbury. The eight-year-old clearly handles testing ground really well, and given that he only ever seems to just do enough, the handicapper still might not have caught up with him. He will return on a mark of 136, so he will need to progress once again, but he is lightly-raced as a chaser and was improving all the time when last seen. He did shift to his right on occasions last season, so might be worth trying on a right-handed track at some point.

DRENAGH

TRAINER Alastair Ralph doesn't boast the strongest of records in bumpers (just three winners from 36 runners overall) so it is notable when one of his string catches the eye in that sphere. Drenagh actually shaped with plenty of promise in a couple of bumpers last season, and appeals as the type to appreciate going up in distance over hurdles. Third behind Faivoir (won again next time) at Bangor, he then chased home Wetlands at Newcastle, with the pair a long way clear. A gutsy effort on that occasion, he boasts plenty of experience from Irish Points, and could prove to be well bought for just £12,000 in January.

GIOVANNI ROYALE

ANOTHER who shaped with a degree of promise in a bumper last season was Giovanni Royale, a four-year-old by Schiaparelli, who comes from a nice family. Despite being beaten 43 lengths in the end, he made eye-catching progress from the back of the field at the halfway point, before keeping on well to finish fourth behind *Leading Prospect* Bear Ghylls. There is plenty of stamina in his pedigree, so he ought to have no problem in stepping up in distance when he goes hurdling, and he is another to monitor in the novice division.

Nicky Richards

CASTLE RUSHEN

A HALF-BROTHER to *Leading Prospect* Marown, Castle Rushen made a pleasing start to his career when winning a heavy-ground bumper at Ayr. Held-up off the pace, he travelled really smoothly down the far side, and was still going well when hitting the front halfway up the home straight. Despite looking a shade green, he knuckled down well, and was well on top in the closing stages. He was then sent off odds-on to follow up over the same course-and-distance, when he was beaten in what turned into a sprint up the home straight, but remains very much a nice young prospect. Once sent hurdling, he is sure to be suited by some better ground and an extra half-mile, and it will be disappointing if the son of Fame And Glory can't emulate his year-older half-brother in making a decent impact in the novice division.

GLENDUFF

BEATEN favourite in a couple of bumpers the season before last, Glenduff made a winning debut over hurdles at Carlisle on Colin Parker day, lowering the colours of Faustinovick. Clearly appreciating the extra half-mile, he made steady progress in the final mile of the race, and was delivered with a well-timed challenge between the final two flights. After disappointing at Newcastle, he bounced back (following a 103-day break) on better ground at Doncaster in March. He travelled much more kindly on that occasion, running a sound race to finish third. A half-brother to Champion Bumper winner Relegate, he will come into his own once sent chasing, and looks on a very fair mark at present (125). With that in mind, he could start off in a handicap hurdle, alternatively he would make plenty of appeal in a novices' handicap chase.

RIBBLE VALLEY

A *LEADING PROSPECT* in last year's book, Ribble Valley made the perfect start over hurdles, winning easily at Hexham and again at Wetherby. He really did look full of potential at that stage, but then raced too keenly when runner-up to Master Debonair in the Kennel Gate at Ascot just before Christmas. He would have returned in the spring – when I personally thought that the Scottish Champion Hurdle would have been a suitable target – and he will be of interest in decent quality handicaps over the minimum trip. He remains very lightly-raced and has won four of his six career starts. Currently rated 141, I wonder if his trainer will consider another trip south for the Greatwood in the autumn.

WETLANDS

LIKE Castle Rushen, he won a bumper for leading owner Trevor Hemmings last season, and is another who can do well over hurdles this year. Fourth on heavy ground at Newcastle on his first start, the Westerner gelding showed the benefit of that experience when returning to the same track to win at the second attempt. Despite still looking green, he finished strongly to win a shade comfortably, with the front two a long way clear. He is another who should have little trouble in stepping up in distance, as and when required.

Lucinda Russell

BOLLINGERANDKRUG

A FIVE-YEAR-OLD by Getaway, he shaped with a degree of promise in a bumper at Musselburgh, when finishing third behind one of this year's *Leading Prospect*s Easy As That. Held-up for the first half of the race, he made some progress leaving the back straight, and having initially looked to be outpaced, stayed on inside the final three furlongs. He actually looked as though he would finish a clear second until tiring in the closing stages, shaping like a horse who would benefit for the experience, and also for a stiffer test of stamina.

MAX APPEAL

A BUMPER winner at Ayr in March, Max Appeal won what turned into a dash inside the final half-mile, lowering the colours of Castle Rushen, who had won at the same track on debut. He raced keenly in the early part of the race, but given the sedate pace, that is understandable, and he was still racing enthusiastically when joining issue halfway up the straight. He was in receipt of plenty of weight from the runner-up, but he picked up really well to make a winning debut. A five-year-old by Kayf Tara, he is another to note for the Lucinda Russell yard, once sent hurdling.

Jeremy Scott

DASHEL DRASHER

ANOTHER of last year's *Leading Prospect*s, Dashel Drasher ran a blinder on chase debut against Champ at Newbury, before unseating Matt Griffiths at the first, when re-opposing the subsequent RSA winner. He came out just five days later and won for the first time over fences at Haydock, where he jumped well and won with plenty in hand. Forced to miss the remainder of the season, he should be back in the autumn, and from a mark of 145, will be of interest in handicap company, if he can sharpen up his jumping.

It is also worth noting that Jeremy Scott has a four-year-old full-sister to Dashel Drasher in his yard (un-named and currently in the ownership of his wife, Caroline).

Michael Scudamore

DO YOUR JOB

AN expensive purchase (£150,000) after he won an Irish Point-to-Point for Colin Bowe, he joined Claire Dyson, for whom he ran just once, at Uttoxeter in December. Quite keen-going out in front, he jumped well in the main, and only gave best approaching the final flight. The front two went on to advertise that piece of form, and after switching to the yard of Michael Scudamore, Do Your Job ran another sound race when runner-up at Newbury in late-February, where he chased home one of this year's *Leading Prospect*s Brinkley. Tracking the pace, he eased into contention early in the home straight, and was the only horse to challenge the winner from the last. Well-beaten in the end, the omission of the final flight probably didn't help. A chasing type, he jumped boldly when winning his Point, and although he probably won't reach his full potential until sent over fences, he remains an interesting and lightly-raced six-year-old.

Oliver Sherwood

BALLAQUANE

AN eye-catching second on his racecourse debut, in a Wetherby bumper in March, he came from off the pace to chase home the more-experienced Glencassley. Pushed along turning in, the son of Scorpion really found his stride inside the final quarter-mile, and was doing his best work in the final couple of hundred yards. A five-year-old with plenty of stamina on the dam's side, Ballaquane would be of interest if reappearing in another bumper, but given his connections, I would expect him to go straight over hurdles on the back of such an encouraging introduction.

NORLEY

LIKE Ballaquane, Norley carries the silks of Trevor Hemmings, and he also shaped with promise on debut in a bumper at Warwick. A Yeats five-year-old who is closely-related to the same owners' Fionn Mac Cul (winner of two novice hurdles for Venetia Williams), he is another who came from off the pace, and was still last of the main group down the side of the track. Having looked as though he would finish mid-division, he is another who really found his stride late-on, staying on nicely to take fifth place in what looked a competitive race. The front four all had the benefit of having had a previous run, and he is another who will appreciate an extra half-mile once sent hurdling.

Dan Skelton

CADZAND

PLACED in two bumpers last season, the highlight of each performance was the way he travelled, and he also travelled with purpose when winning his Point-to-Point for Sophie Lacey. Keen in the early exchanges at Newbury, he was held together for most of the home straight, and only asked to pick up inside the final quarter-mile. He came home in

third, closing on the second at the line, and he built on that when chasing home *Leading Prospect* Sizable Sam at Warwick. This is a race that has already been covered on numerous occasions in this year's publication (I expect it to work out well) and, once again, he travelled with real purpose into the home straight. Having settled slightly better, he swept into the lead around the home bend, perhaps hitting the front a shade sooner than ideal. He did little wrong and should have little trouble in winning races once sent hurdling.

FAIVOIR

BEAT Favori de Champdou (bumper winner for Gordon Elliott and Gigginstown) in his sole Point-to-Point, when neither horse was foot-perfect in the closing stages. Faivoir refused to settle early on at Huntingdon, which probably cost him in the closing stages, when he was unable to get to Presence Of Mind, who franked the form by winning on his hurdling debut on New Year's Day. Bridget Andrews was aboard the five-year-old for his final two starts, firstly at Bangor, when he again raced freely. He had enough left in reserve to finish strongly inside the final furlong, and he followed up in more straightforward fashion back at Huntingdon. Anchored right out the back, he picked off rivals one-by-one, and is another nice prospect for novice hurdles. The better ground probably helped last time, and if he learns to relax, he could have a very bright future.

MIDNIGHT RIVER

ANOTHER for the novice hurdle division, Midnight River failed to win a bumper last season, but he twice finished third, and has a nice jumping pedigree. From the family of Royal Guardsman and Iris Royal, the five-year-old debuted in what turned out to be a really good bumper at Worcester, coming from well off the pace to finish in front of impressive Chepstow winner Cadmar. Israel Champ, Benson and Papa Tango Charly were further down the field, and following a 101-day break, Midnight River filled the same spot at Wetherby. Again ridden with restraint, he moved really well into contention, and he kept on well without ever looking like getting to the front two. The five-year-old is described by Harry Skelton (see *A View From The Saddle*) as a chaser of the future, but he looks more than capable of winning races over hurdles this season.

WEST CORK

WON twice from five starts over hurdles last season, West Cork had earlier impressed with the speed he showed to reach the leaders en route to winning an Irish Point for Timmy Hyde. He jumped well late on that day, and it wasn't surprising to see him appreciate coming back in distance over hurdles last year. A strong-traveller, he is well-bred being a full-brother to the likes of William H Bonney, Tiqris and Midnight Maestro, and he is now likely to go chasing. He appeals as the type to win more races over fences this year, and will be at his best up to 2m4f.

WILDE ABOUT OSCAR

ANOTHER who forms part of what looks a strong team of novice hurdlers for Dan Skelton, Wilde About Oscar also carries the black-and-white silks of Mike and Eileen Newbould (owners of *Leading Prospect* Third Time Lucki). The five-year-old travelled well on debut at Southwell, before winning with ease at Warwick. Fourth in Newbury's Listed bumper, a stronger gallop would have suited that day (as it would for most of the field), and he will certainly appreciate a stiffer test of stamina once sent hurdling. A full-brother to Whiskey In The Jar, soft ground holds no fears to him, and he is yet another nice prospect for novice hurdles.

Sue Smith

JAYAAAH

AN imposing son of Yeats (filled the eye in the paddock ahead of his debut second at Carlisle), Jayaaah went on to again finish runner-up at Market Rasen (beaten by Champion Bumper fourth Third Time Lucki) and, perhaps, felt the effects of those two relatively quick races when only fourth at Haydock. Given his physique, it could also be that he found the track a bit sharp, and he ought to appreciate a stiffer test once sent jumping. Although he is unlikely to reach his potential until he goes chasing, his progress should be monitored in northern novice hurdles.

RARE CLOUDS

A HORSE who featured in this section last year, Rare Clouds didn't win a race, but ran well on a couple of occasions and from his current mark (109) can surely be placed to shed his maiden tag. It could be that he goes chasing before too long – being a full brother to stable-mate Vintage Clouds – and he remains a young horse of potential. He also remains at the right end of the handicap.

The same owner (Trevor Hemmings) has a nicely bred un-raced five-year-old at Sue Smith's, **Yeats Venture**. He is a half-brother to Trevelyn's Corn (a Point-to-Point winner for Colin Bowe and a maiden hurdle winner for Paul Nicholls).

Suzy Smith

ANIMAL

AN Arcadio four-year-old, he made a winning debut at Market Rasen in February, winning a nine-runner bumper by eight lengths. Never far from the pace, he travelled comfortably under Aidan Coleman, and quickened up nicely with a couple of furlongs to run. Well-positioned throughout, it was a likeable performance, and he was his trainer's sole bumper winner (from just seven runners) last season.

Jamie Snowden

ANYTHINGFORLOVE

WON both starts in bumpers last season, Anythingforlove is a mare by Black Sam Bellamy, who would probably have gone on to Aintree and taken her chance in the Grade 2, had the season not ended prematurely. A half-sister to 2017 Gold Cup winner Sizing John, she clearly boasts a very good pedigree to go jumping, and she also demonstrated a fine attitude on both starts. Both breeding and running style suggest she will improve when going up in distance, and she has raced exclusively on testing ground to date.

CHARLIE GEORGE

SOMETIMES the naming of a horse really catches the eye and this is another case-in-point. Owned by Sir Chips Keswick, who was chairman of Arsenal F.C. until May of this year, Charlie George is a four-year-old by Presenting and has been named after their former striker. He scored the winning goal in the 1971 FA Cup Final (completing the double for his side), and Jamie Snowden was particularly positive about his namesake when I spoke to him during the summer. Described as a good-looking individual, he is a half-brother to Cobbler's Queen (a winner over hurdles and fences for Henry Daly) and is bred to appreciate a decent surface.

KILTEALY BRIGGS

TWICE a winner over hurdles when heading north last season, he was pulled-up in the Albert Bartlett when last seen. He was reportedly sick immediately after the festival, but is expected to return in the autumn, when he will be sent novice chasing. Runner-up in his sole Irish Point, he finished one place ahead of Shishkin on that occasion, and there should be more races to be won with him as a staying chaser. Both of his wins last season came on heavy ground.

MUSTANG ALPHA

IMPRESSED me with the good turn of foot he showed when winning an Irish Point for Mick Goff, Mustang Alpha probably found the ground too soft when making his debut under Rules in a bumper at Cheltenham, and he shaped much better over hurdles at Huntingdon next time. Off the track since (last November), the Stowaway five-year-old is expected to return in the autumn, and given his liking for decent ground, I would expect him to be out fairly early.

THEBANNERKINGREBEL

A LISTED novice hurdle winner last season, he then returned to Haydock and ran with huge credit in the Grade 2 Rossington Main, where he looked the likely winner jumping two out. He faded late on in the Betfair Hurdle on his final outing of the season, and although he has the option of going chasing, it seems more likely that he will be campaigned in the better handicap hurdles this season. He remains on a mark of 141, and should be placed to win again from that rating.

THOMAS MACDONAGH

ANOTHER who relished testing ground last winter, Thomas Macdonagh won a maiden at Hexham, a handicap at Wetherby, and a novice at Ffos Las. A strapping son of Black Sam Bellamy, he has always appealed as the type who would come into his own once sent chasing, and he will head down that route this year. He jumped soundly when placed in a couple of Irish Points for Denis Hogan, and he could develop into a really nice staying handicapper in time. Despite the fact that he has yet to win beyond 2m4f, he often gives the impression that he will improve once going even further, and he gets on particularly well with Page Fuller, who was aboard for two of last season's three victories.

Sandy Thomson

SIRWILLIAMWALLACE

SHAPED with promise when runner-up to Nickolson in a bumper at Ayr the season before last, he improved steadily on his first three starts over hurdles, chasing home another *Leading Prospect* (Marown) on his second run, before staying on strongly to win over 2m5f at Kelso. He slightly disappointed on his handicap debut and was already beaten when quite badly hampered two out (eased down afterwards), but he remains on a fair mark (121) and would be of interest if sent chasing. Clearly at home on soft ground, he has a very

stout pedigree, so will have no trouble in going up to 3m over fences.

Colin Tizzard

BUCKHORN GEORGE

CAUGHT the eye in both a bumper and a maiden hurdle at Chepstow, before chasing home Sporting John at Exeter. He then pulled-up at the same track, before winning a Wincanton maiden hurdle on his final start, when upped to 2m4f for the first time. A good traveller in his races, the grey stayed on strongly, suggesting that he will get even further in the future, and after idling when clear, rallied well to win on the line. Left on a mark of 124, he is one to note in either handicap hurdles or novice handicap chases.

ELDORADO ALLEN

ONE of last year's *Leading Prospects*, Eldorado Allen returned from 13 months off with a solid second at Sandown (looked the likely winner when getting to the lead at the final flight) off a mark of 145. Unable to recapture that form, he remains a really bright prospect for fences, given the impression he made earlier in his career. I was taken with the manner in which he jumped en route to victory in a Sandown maiden hurdle in November 2018, and he had jumped equally as well at Auteuil on his final start in France. He looks to have bags of scope for fences, and he could easily make up into a Graded class novice, between 2m and 2m4f. To date, he has raced exclusively on soft ground or worse.

FIDDLERONTHEROOF

COLIN Tizzard went into the Cheltenham Festival with a strong-looking team, particularly in the novice hurdle division, but things didn't exactly go to plan, and I think it is safe to assume that – for one reason or another – the majority of the stable's runners failed to run to their earlier form. That started in the very first race, as Fiddlerontheroof backed out of it approaching three out. The imposing six-year-old had earlier developed into a very smart novice, culminating in Grade 1 success in the Tolworth at Sandown. An Irish Point-to-Point graduate, he has the build of a chaser, and is likely to head straight over fences upon his return. Runner-up in the Persian War on his reappearance last season, I would expect him to be campaigned over intermediate trips this year and he could, once again, start off at Chepstow's two-day meeting in October. Tizzard likes to use the 2m3½f Listed novices' chase as a starting point, with Cue Card

(2011) and Finian's Oscar (2017) successful for the stable in recent years. The Rising Stars at Wincanton would be another possible early-season target, although I suspect both races will also be considered for *Leading Prospect* The Big Breakaway.

HARRY SENIOR

ANOTHER who was progressive in novice hurdles prior to the festival, Harry Senior got off the mark over Christmas when stepped up in trip at Chepstow, and followed up in the Grade 2 Classic Novices' Hurdle at Cheltenham on trials day. He travelled well on the soft ground that day, and powered home down the centre of the course, staying on strongly from the back of the last. Pulled-up in the Albert Bartlett, he made a fairly serious error on the first circuit, after which he failed to regain his position. Rated 143, there is a chance that he could be aimed at something like the Betfair Stayers' Handicap Hurdle at Haydock, but it is more likely that he will head straight over fences, to form part of what looks a really strong novice chase squad. He moved well when finishing third (not fluent two out and pecked at the last) in an Irish Point.

LIEUTENANT ROCCO

ANOTHER who failed to complete in the Albert Bartlett (also pulled-up), Lieutenant Rocco had earlier won heavy-ground novice hurdles at Chepstow and Warwick, where he looked another useful prospect for fences in time. On both occasions he finished really strongly over an extended 2m3f, and he only gave best after two out at the festival. Currently rated 139, he wouldn't be too far behind the likes of Harry Senior at this stage, and is also likely to form part of the Tizzard novice chase team. Clearly at his best in deep ground, he might be one who flourishes during the middle part of the season. Only third on his second start in the Point-to-Point sphere, it could be that he was big and weak at the time (given his physique), and his dam is a full-sister to First Lieutenant.

SEYMOUR PROMISE

COLIN Tizzard saddled just one bumper winner last season (that being *Leading Prospect* Rose Of Arcadia) but another who shaped well – in what I thought was a good race at Kempton – was Seymour Promise. A Flemensfirth four-year-old, who is a half-brother to Mahler's Promise (won a bumper and a maiden hurdle for Seamus Mullins) he is another who would have been inconvenienced by the lack of pace, especially as he was held-up. Still last turning for home, he picked up well down the inside and looked green when getting upsides. He should, therefore, come on plenty for that initial experience, and given his physique, is likely to improve once sent hurdling.

Nigel Twiston-Davies

GOOD BOY BOBBY

A HORSE who I have always had plenty of time for (a *Leading Prospect* two years ago), Good Boy Bobby won once from four starts over fences last season, and appeals as one who could land a nice handicap from an opening mark of 146. Sold as part of the Rooney 'National Hunt' dispersal, he will return to action sporting the silks of Simon Munir and Isaac Souede, and having proven his stamina over an intermediate trip at the December meeting last year, the BetVictor Gold Cup looks an obvious starting point. The Colin Parker would be another option at Carlisle, where he ran so well on debut against Brewin'upastorm. Still only seven, he could well have a big day in him this season.

LET IT LOOSE

AN un-raced four-year-old owned by Carl Hinchy and Mark Scott, Let It Loose is a full-brother to First Approach, who won a Point for Donnchadh Doyle, and three times for Noel Meade (one bumper and twice over hurdles). This son of Robin des Champs is one to look forward to in the autumn, when he could start off in a bumper, although he will probably want an extra half-mile (on breeding) once going hurdling.

ONE TRUE KING

UNABLE to win in five starts in Irish Points, Cormac Doyle sent him over to Barbury, where he won impressively over 2m4f, perhaps finding the longer distance against him on home soil. He certainly showed that he possesses plenty of pace when winning a 1m6f Ludlow bumper on his first start for Nigel Twiston-Davies, where he made all (as he had done at Barbury) to win unchallenged. Despite that victory coming on soft ground, the easy ground in stronger company probably didn't help him in the Champion Bumper, and he will be of interest once sent hurdling under less-demanding conditions. The five-year-old finished a respectable tenth at the festival, having moved well for a long way, and given the trainer's record, he could be one who we see quite early, possibly heading up to Perth at the end of September for a meeting the yard does well at.

THE MICK PESTON

THE winner of a three-year-old bumper at Hereford last December, a victory that didn't look likely

MOSSY FEN

ANOTHER who carries the colours of Messrs Hinchy and Scott, Mossy Fen stayed on strongly when winning an Irish Point, and he made a winning Rules debut over 2m7f at Worcester last October. Prominent throughout, he jumped really well, and ran out a taking winner in the end. He followed up at Aintree – initiating a double for connections, who also won with Riders Onthe Storm at their local track – before finishing fourth on his first start over 3m at Cheltenham. Still only four at the time, it was a big ask for a young horse, and he bounced back to win the Grade 2 Leamington Novices' Hurdle at Warwick, where he again jumped well, and stayed on strongly over 2m5f. That was a gutsy performance, and his season ended with a respectable fifth in the Ballymore, where he moved really well to the top of the hill. Everything about last season suggested that he will improve for going chasing, when he should have little trouble in getting the 3m trip. I have touched upon the possibility of him being aimed at Haydock's Betfair Stayers' Handicap Hurdle (see *Big-Race Trends*) but it would seem more likely that he now heads straight over fences.

for a long way. Green and nudged along, The Mick Peston picked up well leaving the back straight, and stayed on strongly to win what was no more than an ordinary event. He finished really well, however, and not being asked to race again will probably have benefited the son of Shirocco, who looked a big individual for his age. From the family of Ipsos du Berlais (looked promising early in his career for Noel Meade and Gigginstown), it will be interesting to see how he has developed, physically, since that debut win.

TORN AND FRAYED

SHAPED better than the finishing position might suggest in a bumper the season before last, Torn And Frayed again performed with credit (in defeat) on occasions last term. Just touched off in maiden hurdles over 2m5f at both Warwick (form worked out well) and Ascot, he looks a stayer in the making, and from a mark of 125, has the option of heading into handicap company, too. There should be races to be won with him this season.

Tim Vaughan

AERONISI

A FOUR-YEAR-OLD by Kalanisi with quite an eye-catching pedigree, he is un-raced at present, but is a half-brother to Carrigeen Lotus, who won a bumper at Cork before finishing third in the Grade 2 event for mares at the Dublin Racing Festival. She is a mare with plenty of size about her and their dam (Carrigeen Lonicera) is a half-sister to Minella Indo. Given his breeding, I hope we get to see Aeronisi in a bumper in the autumn.

BOHEMIAN MAESTRO

A FIVE-YEAR-OLD by Mahler, who made his racecourse debut behind festival runner-up Pileon, in a novice hurdle at Ffos Las in January. Well-beaten in the end, he shaped better than the bare result, making ground down the far side before fading, and also giving the impression that better ground might help (his pedigree also suggests this). I was hoping to see him step forward later in the season, but we obviously didn't get to see him again, so hopefully that improvement will be evident when he returns.

CLEMENCIA

MADE his debut for the Tim Vaughan yard in the Fred Winter at the festival, where he ran a sound race to finish fifth behind Aramax. He had earlier won by a wide-margin at Cork (when trained by Brendan Duke) and subsequently contested Graded juvenile events in Ireland. He was never too far from the pace at Cheltenham, and after briefly looking like he might lose his position coming down the hill, he battled on really well and was only a length or two down at the last. Upped 1lb (to 135), he is likely to reappear in the four-year-old handicap at Chepstow in October (sponsored by this publication in recent years) and he looks more than capable of making his presence felt in handicap company from his current mark. He will get further in time, and is also a maiden on the Flat, so that could be an option at some stage, too.

Lucy Wadham

MARTELLO SKY

A WELL-BRED filly who hails from a family Lucy Wadham (and owner/breeder Tim Wood) knows well, Martello Sky made a winning debut, in a Fakenham bumper. By Martaline, she enjoyed the soft ground, and stayed on strongly, sweeping around the outer off the home bend to win going away. She ran another sound race when runner-up to Allavina at Market Rasen, again showing a willing attitude, and can win again over hurdles.

TRINCOMALEE

A WARWICK bumper winner last April, Trincomalee won a novice hurdle at the same course last season, when he travelled notably well. Likely that the better ground helped him on that occasion, he had earlier shaped well in good company at Sandown and Newbury. Dropping back in distance probably didn't suit when returning to Warwick, and from a mark of 128, he will be interesting in handicaps over an intermediate trip, back on a sounder surface.

There is also the option of going chasing and he certainly appears to have the size and scope to take to fences. Given that he is already seven, that could well be the way to go, although he is another who remains a novice over hurdles until 1st December, having only won for the first time in February.

Paul Webber

GUMBO FLYER

TRAINER Paul Webber enjoyed a first Cheltenham Festival success in March (saddled the runner-up in two successive renewals of the Champion Bumper back in 2005 and 2006), when Indefatigable won the Martin Pipe, and 12 days earlier, he introduced a nice sort in the shape of Gumbo Flyer, who finished runner-up in a Huntingdon bumper. A Rail Link four-year-old, he came from behind to chase home Martinhal, with Fortunate Fred (shaped well at the same track previously) back in third. Green up the home straight, he finished clear of the third, showing plenty of promise, and given the stamina on his dam's side, he should improve when going up in distance over hurdles.

Alistair Whillans

CORRIEBEN REIVER

USEFUL in bumpers the previous season, Corrieben Reiver made a winning start over hurdles last October, despite not jumping particularly fluently. He stayed on really well, suggesting that he could get further in time, and it was a shame that he was forced to miss the remainder of the season. A couple of horses in behind advertised that form later in the season, and the six-year-old chestnut is expected to return this side of Christmas.

K C BAILEY

ALISTAIR Whillans has Corrieben Reiver's four-year-old half-sister (by Norse Dancer) in his Borders stable. She is named K C Bailey (presumably named after the trainer) and is expected to run in a mares' bumper in the coming months, when she will sport the same multicoloured silks of John and Liz Elliot. As a sire, Norse Dancer boasts a decent strike-rate in bumpers, with Yanworth (twice a winner in that sphere) his most notable jumper to date.

Harry Whittington

STICK WITH BILL

HARRY Whittington was another trainer to gain a first festival success in March, with Simply The Betts landing the 'Plate' just two races after Saint Calvados ran a stormer to finish runner-up in the Ryanair Chase. He also saw his Rouge Vif hit the frame in the Arkle, so it was a hugely creditable week for the Lambourn trainer. All three of those runners carry the silks of Kate and Andrew Brooks (who are the main owners in his stable) and Stick With Bill is one the owners can look forward to in staying novice chases this season. Twice a winner in heavy ground over 2m4f, he saw the race out really well under top-weight at Sandown, before bumping into the potentially smart Lieutenant Rocco at Warwick. He has the size to take to fences, and the scope to progress from his current mark of 132.

YOUNG BULL

ANOTHER six-year-old for staying novice chases, Young Bull is a similar type to Stick With Bill (rated 1lb higher on 133), and he won three times over hurdles last winter. He completed the hat-trick on his first start in a handicap (off 127) and possibly needed the run – following a short break – when keeping on for second, on his first start over 3m+ (3m2f). Once switched to fences, he should be capable of dropping back to 2m4-2m5f to begin with, as he appeared to appreciate being ridden positively over that sort of distance, and is another who handles deep ground.

Christian Williams

DEFUTURE IS BRIGHT

Runner-up in two of his three Irish Points when trained by Mary Doyle, he finished runner-up to Exeter bumper winner Picanha on debut, and bounced back to put forward a similar effort on his third outing, having been hampered on his second start. He jumped well in the main, and probably found the trip too sharp on his first few starts over hurdles, before finishing third at Ascot once upped to an extended 2m7f. He disappointed on his final start, but back over an intermediate trip and switched to fences, he could be interesting off his current mark of 101. I would certainly expect him to improve once sent chasing.

FIVE STAR GETAWAY

SIMILAR comments apply to Five Star Getaway, who is another from the Christian Williams stable that could be capable of significant improvement once upped in trip over fences. This six-year-old actually got his head in front in the Irish Points sphere (later disqualified for a banned substance) and was fairly highly-tried last season. Pulled-up at Aintree on debut, he showed glimpses of promise behind The Big Breakaway at Chepstow, before finding the shorter trip against him when finishing behind Sporting John at Exeter. On his final start

of the season, he ran better than the bare result (hampered on the home bend) and is another to note in novice handicap chases, whilst there is also the option of running in another handicap hurdle beforehand. He is currently rated just 94.

LIMITED RESERVE

REPRESENTS the same connections (All Stars Sports Racing) as Welsh Grand National winner Potters Corner (a *Leading Prospect* in Jumpers To Follow some five years ago), and he has been another flag-bearer for the Christian Williams stable. The winner of handicap hurdles at Haydock in November and December 2017, Williams brought the eight-year-old back to win handicaps at Taunton and Sandown (valuable Grade 3) last season. Not overly big, he is a nimble jumper, however, and is well worth a try over fences.

WIN MY WINGS

TWICE a winner over hurdles, she ran well for a long way in the Persian War, and although she disappointed when last seen at Ludlow, that was her first start for four months, and it is likely that her trainer had one eye on the spring. Win My Wings likes decent ground and is a winning Irish Pointer, so is yet another who can win races over fences, especially when kept to her own sex.

Evan Williams

BOLD PLAN

A *LEADING PROSPECT* in last year's book, Bold Plan improved for his reappearance in the Silver Trophy when winning smartly at Haydock on Betfair Chase day. Things didn't go to plan in two subsequent starts, but I expect that he will now be sent chasing, and he jumped brilliantly when beating New Age Dawning (won twice from three starts for David Pipe) in his maiden Point. I was slightly concerned that the ground would be too lively for him the day he won at Haydock, but he proved he is versatile in that respect, and I expect him to make up into a really nice chaser. Currently rated 138, I expect him to be campaigned over intermediate distances to begin with.

FADO DES BROSSES

FEATURED in Jumpers To Follow last year (*Point-to-Point Graduates*) and got off the mark at the third time of asking over hurdles, staying on well to win in heavy ground at Chepstow. He jumped well up the straight, and it took him every yard of the 2m3½f trip to get there, but he now appeals as the type who could land a handicap once going even further. He certainly has scope to improve from his current mark (128) and there is also the option to go chasing, although after just the three runs, I suspect that he will return in a handicap hurdle.

MACK THE MAN

ONE who will likely be sent chasing this season, Mack The Man made giant strides in handicap hurdles last season, and was still in contention when being brought down at the final flight in the Betfair Hurdle. Ironically, he was brought down by Lightly Squeeze, who he had beaten at Warwick at the beginning of the season (off 115). He defied a 7lbs rise when beating Protektorat (won a Listed race next time) and Song For Someone (won the Grade 2 Kingwell later in the season) at Sandown on Tingle Creek day, where he coped well with the heavy ground. He travelled very well that day, capping a memorable afternoon for all concerned, with Esprit du Large having won the Henry VIII just 35 minutes earlier. Versatile in terms of ground, he should stay further over fences, and should certainly win more races.

QUOI DE NEUF

ANOTHER who is likely to be contesting novice chases between 2m and 2m4f, he failed to add to his sole success to date (a maiden hurdle at Aintree in November 2018) last season, but did run well on his first couple of starts, notably when fourth in the Greatwood. Going back up in distance will probably help him this season, and he was impressive when winning his Point-to-Point in Ireland as a four-year-old. He showed plenty of speed that day, so might prove best up to intermediate trips.

Ian Williams

DRAGON BONES

WE only saw Dragon Bones once last season – when winning a competitive bumper at Worcester – but given how that form worked out, she will be very much of interest when returning this season. A Passing Glance half-sister to Flawless Escape (bumper and hurdles winner for Gordon Elliott), she belied her odds of 50-1 at Worcester, where she raced prominently throughout. Having looked briefly outpaced early in the home straight, she battled on really well to regain the lead close home, and she is yet another who we might well have seen in the Grade 2 at Aintree. She is expected to go hurdling in the autumn.

Jane Williams

MONSIEUR LECOQ

RATED 149 over hurdles, Monsieur Lecoq has the size and scope for fences, so it is hoped that he now goes novice chasing. The winner of the Welsh Champion Hurdle on his reappearance, he ran a huge race (off 7lbs higher) to finish a close third in the Greatwood, after which he finished runner-up in the Betfair Exchange Trophy at Ascot. Although he was unable to bridge the gap into Graded company over hurdles, he could easily be of that level as a novice chaser, especially during the middle of the season on his favoured soft ground.

I was always of the opinion that stepping up to 2m4f might open up further opportunities, but he looked a non-stayer when tried in the National Spirit Hurdle at Fontwell in February. I would, therefore, expect him to revert to the minimum trip for the start of this campaign.

Nick Williams

LE CAMELEON

TWICE a winner over hurdles last season – a maiden at Chepstow and a handicap at Stratford – Le Cameleon is now set to go chasing, and certainly has the build to take to it. He was strong at the finish when winning at Stratford on the eve of the Cheltenham Festival, suggesting that he can go back up in distance in time, and he clearly handles soft/heavy ground. Still only five, he is currently rated 125 and has plenty of scope for improvement.

YGGDRASIL

A THREE-YEAR-OLD by Kapgarde, he is out of the mare Margerie, making him a half-brother to Nick Williams' former stable-star Siruh du Lac. Yggdrasil is also owned by John White and Anne Underhill, and he will be campaigned in juvenile hurdles this season. His pedigree suggests that he could be more than just a juvenile hurdler, so it will be fascinating to monitor his progression, as youngsters from this stable invariably improve considerably for each run, certainly in the early days. Interestingly, Siruh du Lac switched yards over the summer and is now in training with David Pipe, as is Le Grand Rocher, another in the same ownership. At the time of writing, there was no indication that Yggdrasil has also moved to Pipe, although the owners also have the likes of Ramses de Teillee, Israel Champ and Umbrigado among their horses in training in the Pipe stable.

ONE FOR THE TEAM

PLACED three times earlier in the season, including in the Pertemps Qualifier at Warwick, One For The Team won for the first time over hurdles at Newbury in February, landing a good-ground handicap over 3m by 14 lengths. Never far from the pace, he took over halfway up the home straight, and drew right away to record a taking success. Now rated 140, he is expected to go chasing, and being a tall, rangy individual, he could step forward again over fences. By Shirocco, he is out of the good race-mare One Gulp (a smart performer, trained by Paul Webber) and clearly appreciated the sound surface when last seen. After just seven career starts, he remains open to plenty of improvement, and he could develop into a smart staying novice, under the right conditions.

Venetia Williams

ESPOIR DE GUYE

FINISHED runner-up to subsequent festival winner Simply The Betts on his debut over fences, Espoir de Guye then won impressively in handicaps at Exeter and Ascot, appearing to relish the mid-winter ground. Up a stone for the Ascot success, he had almost three months off before Cheltenham, where he was pulled-up in the novices' handicap chase. He faded coming down the hill, but still looks capable of making his presence felt in handicaps during the winter, on his favoured testing ground. Having been ridden prominently when winning at Exeter and Ascot, he was held right up at Cheltenham, perhaps missing the break slightly. Caught wide throughout, it could be that the change of tactics had an impact on his performance, and he certainly isn't one to write off based on that one performance. I would expect him to be considered for the BetVictor and Caspian Caviar Gold Cups, with the ground likely to be more suitable in December.

FANION D'ESTRUVAL

HAVING impressed with how he jumped when winning over fences in France, Fanion d'Estruval made a really smart British debut, when turning a competitive-looking novices' handicap at Newbury into a bit of a procession. That victory came off 137, and he never really travelled with the same verve when held-up in the Wayward Lad over Christmas. To his credit, he kept on well up the home straight, and might have benefited from more positive tactics around the tighter track. Now rated 150, he shouldn't have any problem in stepping up in trip in time, although the Haldon Gold Cup – over a stiff 2m1f at Exeter – might be the ideal starting point in the autumn. He is another who clearly enjoys deep ground, and being only five, remains open to plenty of improvement.

★★★★★ ★★

COMMODORE MILLER
TICKS ALL THE BOXES
FOR CHAMPION TRAINER
NICKY HENDERSON

COMMODORE MILLER

Bay Three Year Old **By Blue Bresil - Milliegait (Tobougg)**

10% interest £5,000 including all costs October 2020

A LEGENDARY LUNCH AND STABLE VISIT WITH THE CHAMPION TRAINER AWAITS (*see Back Cover*)

CONTACT **HENRY PONSONBY** 01488 638718 Mobile 07836 242007
EMAIL: henry@henryponsonby.com   WEBSITE: www.henryponsonby.com

Steven Keating
Equestrian Art

View the complete Steven Keating collection
available from Rowles Fine Art
53 Mill Street, Ludlow, SY8 1BB

HACKED UP
Oil on Canvas | Signed
Framed: 52.5" x 64.5"

£4,950

CLOSE FINISH!
Oil on Canvas | Signed
Framed: 44" x 56"

£4,500

JONATHAN BURKE

JAMIE CODD

AIDAN COLEMAN

ADRIAN HESKIN

BRIAN HUGHES

BEN JONES

JEREMIAH McGRATH

JONJO O'NEILL Jnr

NICK SCHOLFIELD

HARRY SKELTON

A View
FROM THE SADDLE

JONATHAN BURKE

BIG BRESIL *(Tom George)*

A WINNER over hurdles in Exeter in February, hurdles were only ever an inconvenience to him – given his size – and he has already schooled over fences. He didn't really jump well in Exeter, he was very careless over his hurdles, but his raw ability got him through, and he showed a good attitude to win, sticking his head down from the back of the last.

When I schooled him over fences, he paid them a lot more respect, and I am looking forward to riding him in novice chases, as I am hopeful that he will improve a fair bit. An exciting horse for Mr Brookhouse, his lack of experience doesn't worry me, and he could develop into a very nice staying chaser.

BILLINGSLEY *(Alastair Ralph)*

LIKE last year, I thought I would include one horse who impressed me when riding against them last season, and I have gone for Billingsley. He won his last three races and I was very taken by his performance in Newbury, when I finished second to him. He went a proper gallop, making all, after which I thought he might be an ideal type for the Red Rum in Aintree. I came from off the pace and was getting to him, as he never seems to do an awful lot in front, but was never getting by him. Given the gallop he set that day, I think there is more to come, and from a rating of 136, he can win a big 2m handicap at some point. Watching him, he reminds me a little of Bun Doran, who I was lucky enough to win the Desert Orchid Chase on last Christmas.

BOOTHILL *(Harry Fry)*

SEAN Bowen's misfortune meant that I got to ride him in a bumper in Kempton. He was very keen in what was a strongly-run race, but he took me to the front, and really quickened up. Given how hard he pulled for the first mile, it was a very taking performance, as he really did pick up well and finished strongly through the line. He probably would have gone on to take his chance in a festival bumper – whether that would have been Aintree or Punchestown was still to be decided – and I would say that he will now go straight over hurdles. He did plenty wrong at Kempton, so must have a massive engine, and I certainly wouldn't mind getting my leg over him again at some stage.

COOLBANE BOY *(Liam Burke)*

A HORSE who will, hopefully, fly the flag for my Dad this season. He ran well in a maiden hurdle last October, after which we tried to put him through the sales ring, which was always the plan. Unfortunately, he's not an overly-big horse, so didn't stand out, but it could be a blessing, as he ended up winning a bumper in Thurles, beating a well-touted horse trained by Willie Mullins. He had again shaped well over hurdles before falling in Limerick over Christmas, and was given a good ride when winning his bumper. A nice compact sort, he made a pleasing return in Gowran during July, and again finished in the frame in Kilbeggan. There are races to be won with him over hurdles and I am hopeful that he can win a nice handicap for us this season, perhaps once meeting some easier ground in the autumn.

HOOLIGAN *(Tom George)*

A FINE, big horse who won in Warwick in March, and will, therefore, benefit from the amended ruling which means he will remain a novice until the end of November. He is a chaser in the making, but will benefit from some more experience over hurdles, so it will be a help that he is able to run in one or two more novice events at the start of the campaign. He finished very strongly in Warwick so won't mind going up in distance, and I had dropped him right out, as he was quite keen, but he relaxed through the race and jumped well considering it was his first run over hurdles. He will have learnt plenty, having come through horses, and he beat a good horse. A horse with a big engine, he enjoys soft ground – so will be a good horse to follow through the winter months – and if things go right, he should have a big future.

JAVA POINT *(Kim Bailey)*

A HORSE I rode twice last season, and I was very taken with him in Ludlow, on a track which wouldn't have suited him at all. A big imposing horse, who jumped very well and finished second behind a nice horse of Nicky's (Henderson). He handles soft ground well, has a nice way of going through his races, has a good attitude, and he backed that run up by running well behind Chantry House in Newbury. Despite not having won over hurdles, I think he could go straight over fences, and is a nice prospect for staying novice handicap chases, around big galloping tracks. He should be very competitive off a mark of 119.

LIEUTENANT ROCCO *(Colin Tizzard)*
ANOTHER who I didn't ride, but a horse who really caught my eye last year. I was actually heading to the car in Chepstow when I saw him in the stable yard, so I put my bag in the car and went back in to the course to watch him. He was very impressive that day, and also when following up in Warwick. He disappointed in Cheltenham, but I know that Robbie (Power) thinks a lot of him, and I would imagine that he will go over fences now. As a model, he stands out, being a good-looking chestnut with a white face, and I look forward to seeing him progress over fences.

OSCAR ROBERTSON *(Tom George)*
RAN well in a bumper in Chepstow, when he was very babyish (he was quite stressed in the parade ring beforehand) and it took him most of the race to realise what was happening, but he then went straight over hurdles and won well in Wetherby. He didn't back it up – back in Wetherby shortly after – but, I think he is a horse who will leave that form behind and excel over fences. He will start off in a novices' handicap chase, and he will benefit from going up to 3m. He handles soft ground well, and begins the season at the right end of the handicap (rated 120). He has done well, physically, for his break, and I can see him developing into a really nice staying chaser in time.

SPRINGFIELD FOX *(Tom George)*
GIVEN that he won twice over fences last season, I am hoping that we haven't missed the boat with him, but I think that he could win a big one at some point this season. He had a couple of nice runs over hurdles, then came alive when switched to fences. He jumped brilliantly in Chepstow and galloped the opposition into the ground, and it was the same in Exeter. He was actually a little sketchy at the first couple, as I had to rush him to get him away from the start, but once he got into a rhythm, he was very assured. From being a couple of lengths clear on the home bend, he ended up winning 17 lengths that day, and is a thorough stayer, who loves soft ground. Now rated 142, I think there is a big race in him when getting his conditions, and the likes of the Welsh National and Eider are likely targets.

TEA CLIPPER *(Tom Lacey)*
I RODE him in Huntingdon, in what was a funny race, with the eventual winner Cervaro Mix going off a long way clear, and it was probably a winner that

got away. We had planned to ride him in the middle of the pack, as he was going up in distance, and he should really have an unbeaten record, having won his earlier three races. Going over fences should help him, as although he jumped hurdles well, he was a bit careless, and he will have more respect for fences. A lovely big horse, who probably had a bit of filling out to do over the summer, I look forward to seeing what he can do over fences.

I also won aboard **Sebastopol** for Tom last season, and he is another who should do well over fences. I won on him in Musselburgh, despite him not handling the track. He jumped well and found plenty for pressure that day, and he is a horse who will appreciate a step up in trip. A lovely horse, he showed a good attitude to win.

THERE'S a few more I wanted to give a mention to, starting with my flagship horses, **Black Op** and Summerville Boy. Black Op was actually being saved for the Mildmay Novices' Chase in Aintree, so it was a shame for him that racing was stopped, but he should come back in a fresh horse. We did a lot of work with him at the start of last season and it was paying off, as he was very neat in Kempton, having earlier been a horse who needed forcing a little. Now rated 150, we will think about the Hennessy (Ladbrokes Trophy) for him, and he ran very well at the track last year, when second to Champ.

I'm looking forward to **Summerville Boy** this year, as I think I rode him a little too handy in the Stayers' and if I had dropped him out further, he might have gone closer. I would have liked the opportunity to have gone to Punchestown with him in the spring, and he was earlier very impressive in the Relkeel.

Another of Mr Brookhouse's who I am looking forward to is **Lets Go Champ** who had a setback, but will be back in training this year. He's been on the walker at Roger's twice a day since February, and is a gorgeous model of a horse, who showed us plenty of nice things before meeting with his setback. A big, tall horse with plenty of filling out to do, the time off might not have done him any harm.

Kakamora was another Point-to-Point winner who featured in this book last year, and he was just starting to do things right and impress us at home when racing was suspended, so probably would have run in a bumper in the spring.

Finally, **Coupdebol** finished sixth in a strong maiden hurdle in Newbury, then also met with a small setback. He was only four when running and was a huge horse, so again should have benefited for his break. He was a bit keen in Newbury, but gave me a great feel, and I'm looking forward to seeing him back.

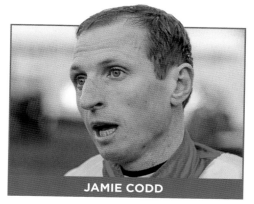

JAMIE CODD

BALLYADAM (*Gordon Elliott*)

THIS is a very, very smart horse. He won his Point-to-Point for Wilson Dennison in Portrush last October, before Gordon bought him for Cheveley Park. Prior to running in a bumper in Navan, his work had been very good, but things just didn't work out on the day.

The ground was very heavy, he pulled a bit hard, Patrick (Mullins) was exceptional from the front on the winner, and the race just didn't pan out as we hoped, so I wasn't overly hard on him in the finish, and he came out the next day in Downpatrick to win without coming off the bridle. We saw a glimpse of what he could do that day, but he is going to be a better horse again this year. A horse I love to bits, I think he could be a very smart two-miler for the novice hurdle division this season, and he could be a Supreme Novices' horse.

BOB OLINGER (*Henry de Bromhead*)

THIS isn't a horse I have ridden or had anything to do with, but he was hugely impressive when winning his Point-to-Point in Turtulla by 15 lengths, then was sold to Robcour. He won the Point-to-Point bumper in Gowran, beating a nice horse of Gordon's, again looking a very smart, and I think that he is a serious horse.

A five-year-old by Sholokhov, he is a half-brother to Myska (Listed winner for Willie Mullins) so has the pedigree as well, and I think he could be the real deal. I don't think that he will have any problem over the minimum trip for the time being, before going up in distance.

Coqolino chased him home in Gowran and he had won his maiden very easily in Ballindenisk prior to Christmas, before being purchased by JP (McManus). A five-year-old by French Fifteen, he is a nice horse, who could himself end up being Graded class, which suggests that Bob Olinger could be very smart indeed.

FISTON DES ISSARDS (*Gordon Elliott*)

A LOVELY horse who had beaten Boothill (bumper winner for Harry Fry) when winning in Loughanmore for Colin Bowe, he came back to Gordon's and got going through the winter, but was taken home quite early by his owners, Noel and Valerie Moran, to give him a bit more time. A lovely big son of Buck's Boum, they felt that being patient with him would be the best thing to do, and I know Colin really liked him last year. He should have little problem in winning his bumper, and he can progress from there. I think the time that his owners have given him will benefit him, and he is a lovely long-term prospect.

GALLYHILL (*Nicky Henderson*)

HAILS from the same nursery as the likes of Simonsig and Slate House, Gallyhill is the most gorgeous horse to look at, so it is understandable that Henrietta Knight was keen to buy him (on behalf of Mike Grech). A beautiful five-year-old by Getaway, if he can back up his looks with ability going forward, he could be very nice indeed. Not short of pace, he won around a tight track in Kirkistown – something which wouldn't have suited him – so it was even more creditable that a big horse like him could go around those sharp bends and win first time up. He's obviously going to a good home in Seven Barrows, and although the form of his win might not have worked out particularly well, I expect him to improve massively when hitting those bigger, galloping tracks, like Newbury, this winter.

GARS DE SCEAUX (*Gordon Elliott*)

A FOUR-YEAR-OLD by Saddler Maker, who won a maiden in Borris for Denis (Murphy). His work at home beforehand had been very good, but he is a big horse, who is going to furnish into a very nice horse with the more time he gets. He made a little mistake at the second last in Borris – which probably looked worse than it actually was – and recovered well to win nicely. Given his size and pedigree, he is likely to need a trip in time, but he is a horse with a huge engine, and is going to be very exciting in the long-term. He is going to Gordon, JP (McManus) bought him, and I would expect to see him run in a bumper in the winter.

The runner-up **Magic Tricks** has also been bought by JP and also joined Gordon, and he is a full-brother to Abacadabras. He is a completely different type to Gars de Sceaux, and I would expect him to be a lot sharper for this season, as his brother was a good bumper horse and, of course, finished second in last season's Supreme Novices' Hurdle. A four-year-old by Davidoff, I think he will also develop into a really nice horse, and the form of their Point-to-Point is working out, with the third having won a maiden hurdle over in America.

GERRI COLOMBE *(Gordon Elliott)*

ANOTHER Saddler Maker four-year-old, he is a horse who Colin Bowe has always liked, and he won in Lingstown in March, beating myself and **Lakota Warrior** (trained by Denis Murphy) by a head, and I think the two of them will reach Graded level in time. The pair of them quickened up nicely from the back of the last, there wasn't much between them, and the two of them look like nice staying horses for the future. Gerri Colombe was subsequently bought by Mags O'Toole, for Robcour, and Lakota Warrior – who is a half-brother to Run Wild Fred – is now with Dan Skelton. His sire, Valirann, is a bit of an unknown at this stage, whereas Saddler Maker needs no introduction. Both horses should be capable of winning soft ground bumpers, before stepping up in trip over hurdles.

GUARDINO *(Ben Pauling)*

AN Authorized four-year-old, who I rode to finish second for Denis (Murphy); he's a lovely horse, who has since joined Ben Pauling. A slick horse, the race got away from us that day, with the winner jumping out and gaining a bit of an easy lead, but I wouldn't be surprised if the second ended up being the better of the pair. I'd imagine that he would have no problem in winning a bumper, he's a horse who wouldn't really want heavy ground in the depths of the winter, and he should appreciate some nice ground come the spring.

PETIBONOME *(Henry de Bromhead)*

FIRST past the post in Lismore, he was disqualified for going the wrong side of a bale. Pat Doyle had been very positive about him before he ran, and he must have a very good constitution, as he took an absolute mother-and-father of a fall in Bellharbour – in what was the first four-year-old maiden of the season – on his debut. For him to come out and (essentially) win just five weeks later suggests that he is a hardy horse; an ordinary horse wouldn't be able to back that up so quickly. He was going to win in a common canter and he isn't short of gears, so dropping back in distance won't be a problem at all.

QUEENS BROOK *(Gordon Elliott)*

A MARE who was exceptional when winning her bumper in Gowran, decimating a good field of mares in heavy ground, and she ran a very good race in Cheltenham, to finish behind two horses of Willie's (Mullins) who are likely to become proper Graded horses over jumps. Had the season not ended when it did, she could have easily gone on to the mares' bumper in Aintree, or the Champion Bumper in Punchestown, but she had a hard enough race in Cheltenham, so it might have been a blessing-in-disguise that she couldn't run again. Her future is all about jumping, and although she has won on deep ground, I don't think it is a necessity to her. I had ridden her before she joined Gordon, when she was with Aidan Fitzgerald, and I'm confident that she will handle nice ground, as well. She has plenty of stamina in her pedigree, so I think we will see the best of her as she goes up in trip, and she is very straightforward, so looks to be a really exciting mare for Noel and Valerie Moran.

QUEENS BROOK

SIR GERHARD *(Gordon Elliott)*

A MAIDEN winner in Boulta for Ellmarie Holden, he was bought by Gordon on behalf of Cheveley Park Stud, and I rode him when he did a couple of really nice pieces of work last season. He would have run in a bumper in the spring, had the pandemic not caused the suspension of racing, but the break certainly won't have done him in any harm. His work was on par with that of Ballyadam at the time, so I would be very hopeful that he can win his bumper. A five-year-old by Jeremy, he should be versatile in terms of ground, without wanting extremes.

I COULDN'T leave out **Envoi Allen** (who I have included in each of the past two years) after what he achieved again last season, despite obviously not riding him on the track. He was exceptional throughout the whole of last season, rounding it off with a great performance in Cheltenham in the Ballymore, where he certainly wasn't stopping, suggesting that he will have no problem in stepping up in trip. A graduate from Colin Bowe's yard, he has always schooled very well at home, and we are all looking forward to him getting going over fences. The hope is that he continues to progress

GARS DE SCEAUX

and ends up a Gold Cup horse of the future.

Moving on to a few bumper horses who I rode last season and were worthy of a mention, starting with **Easywork**, who I won on in Down Royal at the beginning of the season, and he progressed considerably after that, ending up with him finishing second to Envoi Allen in the Ballymore. Riding him handier has certainly been a help to him, and if he takes to fences, he could also become a live contender for the RSA. He's not a massive horse, but he's got a serious engine, and he ran a massive race in Cheltenham.

Farouk d'Alene is another who I won on for Gigginstown, winning bumpers in Down Royal and Naas. He was very impressive at Christmas, but this horse is crying out for a jump, so the fact that he was able to win two bumpers speaks volumes. He was still green the last day in Naas, but he showed a very good attitude, and will be a lovely horse going forward. A good galloper, he will improve considerably for a hurdle and a trip.

The third is a horse called **Ajero**, who is a half-brother to Charbel and is now with the same connections (Kim Bailey). He pulled my arms out when finishing third in Thurles, in what was a good bumper. He won't want stepping up in distance, and in fact, Kim could probably run him on the Flat if he wanted to at some stage. If he achieves half as much as Charbel did, I think his owners will be pleased, and if he learns to settle, he could develop into a nice horse for them. His sire, Red Jazz, is of slight concern, but Charbel is also by a sprinter, so the dam is obviously a strong influence.

Reverting back to the Point-to-Point horses; even though the season was cut short, and we lost around eight weeks (there will be plenty of high-class youngsters to run in the autumn, when the maidens are sure to be very competitive), the quality was still very good.

Glenglass is a gorgeous, big four-year-old by Ocovango who won in Tallow for Colin Bowe, and he has a nice pedigree. He went through the sale in Cheltenham back in February, and is another who is now with Gordon (Elliott).

Another who has gone to Gordon is **Hollow Games**, a four-year-old by Beat Hollow, who won by a wide-margin for James Doyle in Turtulla, the same track that Bob Olinger won at. He was left clear two out, to win by a distance in the end, and winning in the manner of a horse who could end up being pretty smart. He is obviously going to a good home, and I think that he will make up into a very nice stayer in time.

Brandy Love was another very impressive winner for Colin (Bowe), when winning an early four-year-old maiden over 2m4f in Cragmore, and Willie (Mullins) has subsequently bought her. She is a nice filly by Jet Away.

Finally, another who won impressively for Colin (Bowe) is **Velvet Elvis**, who won in Nenagh, and has since joined John McConnell. He looks a hardy individual and is a half-brother to Black Benny, who won plenty of races for Shane Broderick and Barry Connell. A four-year-old by Shirocco, he could give John and his new owner(s) plenty of fun.

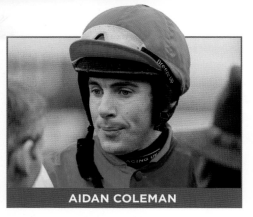

AIDAN COLEMAN

ALLAVINA *(Olly Murphy)*

A LOVELY mare by Getaway, who benefited from her debut run at Huntingdon to win at Market Rasen. The form of her debut third is strong, and she quickened up well to win nicely, giving weight to a nicely-bred filly trained by Lucy Wadham. She has the size to go on over jumps and is bred to get a trip, so there should be plenty to look forward to, given the programme for mares nowadays. She could be very nice; I like her a lot.

GEORDIE B *(Venetia Williams)*

ENDURED a slightly frustrating campaign last season, when he was due to go chasing after his first run, but picked up a knock, and by the time he came back it was too late to go over fences. He actually ran really well at Newbury on what was his first start in handicap company, but didn't fire at Doncaster when he returned. Hopefully, he can leave that behind now and enjoy a better season, as he is more mature now and will go chasing. As I said last year, he is a horse with a lot of ability. His novice hurdle form reads well and given that he is a fine big horse who looks made for fences, he is one to look forward to in soft ground this winter.

GLENCASSLEY *(Charlie Longsdon)*

A HORSE who Charlie has always liked at home, hence why he was quite highly tried on his first two starts in bumpers, before winning at Wetherby. Fifth at Exeter on debut, in a race which rode like a good contest, he then filled the same spot in a Listed bumper at Newbury, when he raced keenly for Sam (Twiston-Davies). He was a lot more professional at Wetherby and he's a very nice horse to look forward to over hurdles. I would imagine that he will start off over 2m, then step up in trip.

HERE COMES McCOY *(Olly Murphy)*

THE winner of a newcomers' bumper at Warwick,

he was ultra-impressive and I couldn't pull him up after the line, which is always a good sign. I didn't have a lot to do with him at home before he ran, so it was a pleasant surprise to win in the manner that he did, having travelled really well throughout. He showed a good bit of speed once in front and he galloped right through the line, so there is a chance that he could just be very, very good.

JETAWAY JOEY *(Olly Murphy)*

ANOTHER horse who benefited from his debut, when running really well at Market Rasen, then he went to Fontwell and won nicely. We have always liked him, he has always done everything well at home, and he was much sharper and more professional at Fontwell, where he travelled much more kindly for me. The form of the Market Rasen race worked out well and the extra furlong probably helped him when winning, as his pedigree suggests that he will develop into a stayer. A fine big horse, he will be well suited by soft ground, and he is one I am particularly looking forward to.

KID COMMANDO *(Anthony Honeyball)*

HE was very impressive when winning a Fontwell bumper by 18 lengths and, perhaps, he was feeling the effects of two fairly quick runs when only fifth in a Listed bumper at Ascot just before Christmas. He then switched to hurdles and won hard-held at Plumpton before finishing a good third in the Dovecote Novices' Hurdle. Once he learns to settle, I think he will improve for going an extra half-mile this season and from a mark of 136, he is one to note in handicaps. A Point-to-Point winner in Ireland, he is a brilliant jumper and will make a chaser in time, although after just two runs, he is likely to remain over hurdles for now.

Another from Anthony's who is worth noting in handicaps is **Kilconny Bridge**, who is very straightforward. I won twice on her last season and she rounded off the campaign by completing a hat-trick over hurdles. She wants a trip and is a very good jumper, and there will be plenty of opportunities for her going forward.

LINELEE KING *(Olly Murphy)*

I WON a bumper on him at Sedgefield and although he disappointed in the Champion Bumper, I am still hopeful that he will develop into a nice horse. He will make up into a proper chaser down the line, as he stays well and he is as good a jumper as you could wish to school at home; he is very athletic. A nice kind horse, who has a nice way of going, jumps amazingly well and has won a Point-to-Point, so has all the attributes you need as a

LINELEE KING

staying chaser. Before that, I expect him to do well in novice hurdles when he will appreciate a more galloping track.

NAMIB DANCER *(Emma Lavelle)*
A HORSE who I only rode once when runner-up in a Kempton novice hurdle, when a slight error at the last didn't help. He should have won on debut at Wincanton, when he made a much more serious mistake, and he then ran well behind Chantry House at Newbury on his final start. Given how he travels, it will be disappointing if he can't win races, especially as he enters handicaps, which should really suit him as they will go that little bit quicker, and he can be delivered late. He wants good ground and looks on a fair mark (119).

SAM BROWN *(Anthony Honeyball)*
VERY lightly-raced, he returned from a long lay-off to win impressively at Lingfield, and followed up just 11 days later in a Grade 2 at Haydock, where his stamina came into play over 2m4f. In hindsight, I probably rode him all wrong in the Reynoldstown, as he likes to be closer to the pace and, perhaps, with a bit more space. It could also be that the race came quickly enough for him after his two wins, but being as ground dependant as he his, he needed to get out and take his chance. Rated 152, there are plenty of options with him, but something like the Charlie Hall might suit him as a starting point. Soft ground is essential and given his conditions, I think he is a very good horse.

SONG FOR SOMEONE *(Tom Symonds)*
A HORSE with a fantastic attitude and that is what won him the re-routed Kingwell, as 2m around Kempton would be too sharp for him, but he wouldn't lie down and pulled it out of the fire. He's a great jumper so he does have the option of going chasing, but he is still only five turning six, so he could continue to run with credit in the Graded hurdle races. Ideally, he probably wants an extra half-mile, but he does handle heavy ground which brings his stamina into play over the minimum trip. A very straightforward and uncomplicated horse, he will hopefully pick up another nice race or two this season.

TO conclude, I thought I would touch upon both **Paisley Park** and Put The Kettle On. Obviously it was disappointing not to win a second Stayers' Hurdle on 'Paisley', but he actually did well to finish where he did, as most horses who have that kind of problem would pull-up. Without wanting to make excuses, he pulled off two shoes and wasn't really happy from an early stage, but it was Lisnagar Oscar's day so take nothing away from him and his connections. The heart issue obviously came to light afterwards and it wasn't as if he had a bad season before that, having won a Long Distance Hurdle and a Cleeve, where he showed plenty of pace to run down Summerville Boy after giving him head-start off an easy lead. I retain every faith in him and I'm really looking forward to getting him out again.

Put The Kettle On obviously provided me with a festival winner in the Arkle, having earlier won on her in the trial at the November meeting. I had ridden Plan Of Attack to win at Aintree for Henry (de Bromhead) a couple of weeks earlier, which is how the ride came about, and she was a very good jumper for a novice. She won going away in the Arkle and could go back up to 2m4f, with the new mares' chase a possible target. It was a fantastic training performance to produce her to win an Arkle on the back of almost four months off, and she is a fine mare to be associated with.

PUT THE KETTLE ON

ADRIAN HESKIN

AUTONOMOUS CLOUD *(Colin Tizzard)*

THE first of the un-raced horses which I will put forward, he is a lovely four-year-old by Flemens-firth, out of August Hill, who was a winner over hurdles and fences for Philip Hobbs. I rode him over in Ireland when he was with Sean Doyle (Monbeg Stables) – who we buy a lot of horses from – and he gave me a very nice feel. He might not be one you see an awful lot of this year, but he is a name to remember, and the McNeill Family own him in partnership with Terry Warner. I believe he will carry his yellow silks this season, and I can see a galloping track like Chepstow suiting when he debuts in a bumper.

CHAMPAGNESUPEROVER *(Olly Murphy)*

HE was the standout amongst our bumper horses from last season, winning impressively at Ayr, which was only what we all hoped he would do, in truth. He had shown us plenty at home before-hand, and being by Jeremy, soft ground was probably a help to him, whereas he probably found Newbury a little on the quick side. In fairness, that race worked out well and we rode him with his future in mind (held up), which wasn't ideal in a steadily-run race. I'm very much looking forward to him going over hurdles, and although he might start off over 2m, we will probably step him up before too long.

EWOOD PARK *(Olly Murphy)*

A FIVE-YEAR-OLD by Shirocco, who impressed with everything he did at home last season and was ready to run in a bumper in the spring. We were all very excited by him before racing was suspended, so it was a little disappointing that he didn't get to run, but he will probably run in a bumper in the autumn, before he goes hurdling. Max (McNeill) is a big Blackburn Rovers fan and this horse is obviously named after their stadium.

I K BRUNEL *(Olly Murphy)*

AN uncomplicated horse, who is versatile in terms of ground, and did little wrong last season, winning at Fontwell and Musselburgh, where he stayed well on his first start over 3m. It was unfortunate that we lost the Grand National meeting, as the Sefton Novices' Hurdle – a race which we won in 2017 with The Worlds End – had been his long-term target, but he remains a very exciting prospect for fences. Having graduated from the school of Charlie Poste and Francesca Nimmo, he is a very good jumper, and is one who I am particularly looking forward to riding in staying novice chases.

RAYAPOUR *(Willie Mullins)*

RATED 97 on the Flat in Ireland, he looks a very smart recruit and although we were unbale to get him out as a juvenile last season, he has strengthened up well for the break, and judged on his Flat rating, should make up into a smart novice hurdler. The form of his last run in France has worked out very well, and he is a horse who would be more than capable of running well in a decent handicap on the level, either before he goes hurdling or next summer.

RESTANDBETHANKFUL *(Olly Murphy)*

ANOTHER recruit from Sean Doyle at Monbeg Stables, he is a four-year-old by Califet who does everything very well. He was bought to run in a bumper towards the end of last season, but again didn't get to run. He looks to possess plenty of speed and will make his debut in a bumper in the autumn. As with Champagnesuperover, he is part owned by the Bryceland Brothers (Patrick and Scott) and I will wear their silks aboard him this season.

Another of Olly's to note would be **Tamar Bridge**, a big five-year-old by Jeremy, who has taken a lot of time to come to hand, and it might be a while before we get to see him, as he will need heavy ground. He is yet another potentially nice youngster, however, and – along with I K Brunel – is co-owned with Prodec Networks Ltd.

THE WOLF *(Olly Murphy)*

ANOTHER from Olly's who we are looking forward to over fences, he wasn't the best jumper of a hurdle, but we expect him to improve for going chasing. He was still learning throughout the whole of last season and it took him a while to fully find his feet, but going forward he is another to look forward to as he matures. I actually opted to ride **Kiltealy Briggs** (Jamie Snowden) – who also forms part of what looks to be a strong staying novice chase squad for us – at Cheltenham, thinking the occasion might have been a bit too big for The Wolf

CHAMPAGNESUPEROVER

I K BRUNEL

at that stage, but he handled himself very well and ran a lovely race. Going to the festival might actually have made a man of him.

Whilst touching upon our staying novice chase team, I must also give a mention to **Escaria Ten** (Gordon Elliott), who is the type who could win a nice novice handicap at some point. He definitely wants a trip, and the softer the ground the better for him.

THREEUNDERTHRUFIVE *(Paul Nicholls)*

I ALWAYS think it takes a good horse to win a bumper around Chepstow, where he was workmanlike but still very green. He has schooled very well and like Champagnesuperover, is one of our brighter prospects for the novice hurdle division. Again, having won on heavy ground, he is another who will need a trip in time, but is another lovely youngster to look forward to.

Also trained by Paul, **Shearer** (another Blackburn Rovers link) is another name to note. A four-year-old by Flemensfirth, I have yet to sit on him, but they seem to like him down in Ditcheat.

WHERE IT ALL BEGAN *(Gordon Elliott)*

A FOUR-YEAR-OLD by Yeats, he has a good page being a half-brother to Rathvinden (winner of the National Hunt Chase for Willie Mullins) and Chapel Stile (multiple winner for Nicky Richards), and was ready to run in his Point-to-Point in the spring, before racing was suspended. He has a nice staying pedigree, but can still be expected to show up well in a bumper before he goes over hurdles, and he will be ready to run in the autumn. He is another who is part-owned with the Bryceland Brothers.

YOUMDOR *(Willie Mullins)*

A new recruit to the team, he was purchased during the summer following a win over 1m2f at Deauville in late-May and will be going juvenile hurdling. A lovely three-year-old by Youmzain, I schooled him a couple of times when he arrived in England (prior to him having a break, before he moved to Ireland) and he gave me a really nice feel. He gives the impression that he is a horse who is blessed with both speed and stamina, so staying the trip over hurdles shouldn't be an issue, and he will be trained by Willie Mullins.

THE WOLF

BRIAN HUGHES

BIG BAD BEAR *(Nicky Richards)*

THE first of a lovely bunch of youngsters that Nicky has in his yard, he is a horse who would have benefited from some nicer ground in the spring had the season not been cut short. He ran really well first time out at Aintree, then won at Wetherby and Carlisle, before pulling-up back at Wetherby. He made a nasty mistake early on and struggled to get into the race on the bad ground. He probably got away with soft ground over 2m, but he certainly didn't want it, and will improve for better ground this season. An athletic horse, he is a very neat jumper.

CASTLE RUSHEN *(Nicky Richards)*

A FAME And Glory half-brother to Marown, who you will read about shortly, he is one of four lovely young horses who Trevor Hemmings has in training with Nicky. He won a bumper first time out, then got outsprinted up the straight in a muddling race, but I'm sure that he would have had no problem in winning another bumper under a penalty. He jumps well at home and is one to look forward to over hurdles, when he might need an extra half-mile.

CHUVELO *(Donald McCain)*

A HORSE I loved last year, winning his first two starts in bumpers for Donald and Tim Leslie. He won well at Carlisle, when I dropped him in and he travelled very well, and then in a weak race at Bangor, before he attempted to concede a double-penalty to a horse of Tony Martin's who went on to finish ninth at Cheltenham. His form is strong and he has done nothing wrong to date. I'm looking forward to him going over hurdles, and despite his pedigree, he is not completely devoid of pace, so could start off over 2m. He will stay further in time and seems versatile in terms of ground.

CLONDAW CAITLIN *(Ruth Jefferson)*

A LOVELY mare, who did nothing but improve throughout last season. Well bought and well trained, she ran well despite finishing only seventh in a bumper at Aintree, then she won a bumper and a novice hurdle at Wetherby, when Henry (Brooke) rode her. I rode her to win a second mares' novice hurdle, under a penalty at Newcastle, before she beat the boys in the Grade 2 Premier Novices' Hurdle at Kelso. She handles a dig in the ground and probably outstayed the opposition on what was very tacky ground. There would be plenty of options for her going forward, but she finished runner-up in the third of her Irish Points and would have no problem jumping fences.

I also won aboard **Bally Conor** for the same owners, Mr and Mrs Russell, and he would be another who could jump a fence. A nice strong sort, he stayed well at Haydock. And, whilst touching on Ruth's horses, I can't not mention **Waiting Patiently**. He ran a massive race in the Tingle Creek, before which he had been to Pontefract for a canter, so I was very hopeful. It was obviously disappointing that he picked up his injury, as he would have had his ground all year and the Ascot Chase would have set up perfectly for him, but thankfully it wasn't a career-threatening injury, and hopefully he will be back this year for all the big races. Despite his age, he has still only had the 13 runs in his life.

GAELIK COAST *(Donald McCain)*

SECOND in a bumper on his first start the season before last, he was quite sick after his second start at Haydock, so probably needed the run on his reappearance at Carlisle. He was well recommended before being purchased, so it wasn't a surprise to see him come good and win his two novice hurdles, and the form of his Bangor win was franked when the third horse won easily at Kelso for Paul Nicholls. I'm not sure if he will go chasing this season or next, but in time he should make up into a really nice 2m chaser.

GLENDUFF *(Nicky Richards)*

A WINNER at Carlisle on his debut over hurdles, after which I'm not so sure the ground was totally in his favour at Newcastle in The French Furze, as he ran much better, back on better ground at Doncaster. That race probably wasn't run to suit, as we just hacked and then it turned into a sprint, and he is more of a staying type. Another grand horse, he's unexposed, so could have another run over hurdles, but the main aim with him will be jumping fences. A half-brother to Champion Bumper winner Relegate, I actually won a bumper and a novice hurdle on his mother (Last Of The Bunch) for the late Alan

GLENDUFF

Swinbank. A light-framed horse, I'm fairly sure that he got stuck in the mud at Newcastle, so better ground is preferable.

MAROWN *(Nicky Richards)*

A FINE big scopey horse, who would have had another run but for the season being cut short. I included him last year, having won a bumper the season before, and he won both of his novice hurdles at Ayr in good style. It would have been nice to get that little more experience into him, but it wasn't to be. He has done nothing wrong to date and given his physique, you would like to think that he could be a very nice chaser. He clearly handles soft ground, but being by Milan and being a good-mover, better ground shouldn't be a problem to him. He will also have little trouble in stepping up in distance.

RIBBLE VALLEY *(Nicky Richards)*

ANOTHER who I included last year, he won his first two starts impressively, then things just didn't quite work out at Ascot. It was the first time that he had been away overnight, so perhaps it was the trip down, but he just didn't show up on the day. He got very worked up on the way to post and I couldn't do anything to drop his head, so he over-raced with me. He had no ill effects from that and was spot on ahead of the spring, when he would probably have run at Aintree or Ayr, and given how he moves, some better ground might have helped him. I certainly haven't lost any faith in him.

THE CON MAN *(Donald McCain)*

A HORSE who loves soft ground, he ran just the once the season before last when winning easily at Carlisle, and he returned with a solid second at Haydock, beaten by Marie's Rock, who won a Listed event next time. He probably should have won himself next time, but the race didn't go to plan with a horse breaking down in front of me, then he recorded two wins in the second half of the season, at Kelso and Ayr, and also ran well at Ascot. Now rated 138 over hurdles, I would expect him to go chasing and he should make up into a nice staying novice this winter. He is very ground dependant.

WETLANDS *(Nicky Richards)*

ANOTHER bumper winner owned by Trevor Hemmings and another who might not have wanted the ground as soft as it was last season. He won at Newcastle on his second start, beating an experienced sort. He is another who jumps well at home and another who, in time, will be a nice stayer. Like all four of Mr Hemmings' horses with Nicky, they are big, good-looking horses who are future chasers, and it is just about getting there, but I have no doubt that they will win their share of races on the way. It could be that he starts off over 2m, but an extra half-mile certainly won't be an inconvenience.

TO wrap things up, I wanted to give a positive mention to a couple of horses trained by Brian Ellison and owned by Phil Martin.

Firstly, **Windsor Avenue** who won his first two starts over fences in impressive fashion, before disappointing at Doncaster. He wasn't right that day, but I retain the faith in him and am hopeful he will bounce back.

And, **The King Of May** is one who might be capable of winning a nice 2m handicap chase.

He beat a subsequent Grade 1 winner on his chase debut at Carlisle, then ended his campaign with a win off a 6lbs higher mark at Sedgefield. He wouldn't want the ground too deep and it is worth remembering that he wasn't beaten too far by We Have A Dream in a Listed juvenile hurdle on his first start in Britain. He's only six and still unexposed as a chaser.

RIBBLE VALLEY

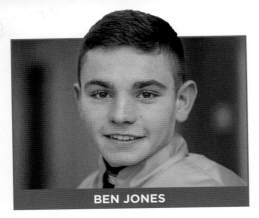
BEN JONES

DE RASHER COUNTER *(Emma Lavelle)*
ALTHOUGH it hasn't been discussed at this stage, I would have thought that he would go back to Newbury for the Ladbrokes Trophy, a race which we won 12 months ago. I couldn't really leave him out here, as he provided me with my biggest win to date. I had ridden him in his prep-run over hurdles at Uttoxeter and luckily for me, Adam (Wedge) was up at Newcastle to ride Silver Streak, so I kept the ride. He loves Newbury and is only 6lbs higher than last year, plus the form worked out really well with The Conditional winning at Cheltenham, so I would say the Ladbrokes Trophy will be his race again. The ground was too tacky for him when we pulled-up in the Midlands Grand National at the end of last season.

DON ALVARO *(Philip Hobbs)*
THE only un-raced horse in my list, he is a four-year-old by Muhtathir (sire of Envoi Allen) and is a half-brother to Oliver Sherwood's smart mare, Papagana. I gave him a spin around Exeter when we took a few of the youngsters for a canter, and he is a horse I like a lot, who does everything profession-ally, and is a lovely prospect. He's a big horse, who needed another summer to fill into his frame, but all being well we will see him this season in a bumper.

Wildfire Warrior would be another of our youngsters to note. He ran twice in bumpers last season without winning, but both races were decent events, and he wants stepping up in trip on soft ground, so it bodes well that he was so competitive. He will be one to follow in the middle of the winter, and he jumps very well.

EVERGLOW *(Philip Hobbs)*
I WAS lucky enough to give him his first piece of work and have liked him ever since. He is very professional in what he does at home, and ran well when placed in bumpers at Chepstow and Chelten-ham in the first half of last season. He was due to run at Newbury in the valuable sales bumper, but that obviously didn't take place, and he is another horse who will benefit for a trip and softer ground. He jumps like a buck, so is another to look forward to in novice hurdles. A big solid unit, he will be a 3m chaser in a couple of years' time.

JATILUWIH *(Philip Hobbs)*
HE won five times over hurdles last year and jumps fences well at home. A winner over fences in France, where he gained plenty of experience, he has a brilliant temperament, and I think he will give his owner Mr Maxwell a lot of fun when going chasing. A winner of a Cheltenham handicap last season, he is a very nice horse, and whatever route they take with him, he should win more races.

PEMBERLEY *(Emma Lavelle)*
A HORSE who I rode four times last season, winning once on soft ground at Hereford, he's a real old-fashioned chasing type, who should improve for fences. He does everything right in his races and ran well at Newbury on his final start, where he got done for a bit of speed, in what turned into a sprint. The final flight being omitted wasn't in his favour on that occasion and fences should just slow the opposition down a bit more. He wouldn't want the ground too soft and trips around 2m4f would be fine going forward.

PILEON *(Philip Hobbs)*
I WAS lucky enough to get the ride on him at the festival in the Martin Pipe, where he gave me a lovely spin. It was an incredible feeling to go so close and now I can look back at the run in appre-ciation, but it was hard to take on the day. As for the horse himself, he's still a bit babyish and back-wards at home, but he's learning all of the time, and he coped well with the big field at Chelten-ham, which was a slight concern beforehand. He's already had a pop over a fence, so I would expect him to go novice chasing, and he would definitely be one to look forward to in that division.

We look to have a nice bunch of novice chas-ers and another would be **Kalooki** who was sticky over his hurdles early on, but his jumping improved throughout the season. Still not foot-perfect, I think he will back off his fences and respect them more than hurdles.

POTTERS VENTURE *(Philip Hobbs)*
A WINNER at Chepstow last November on his second start over hurdles, he was then forced to miss the remainder of the season but will be back

this year. Placed in an Irish Point-to-Point, he has schooled over fences at home, and could go chasing, although after just two starts over hurdles does have options. He jumps well and he could be a forgotten horse, having had a bit of time off.

RUNSWICK BAY (Emma Lavelle)
IMPRESSIVE on debut when I won a Wincanton bumper on him, he was a weak horse and didn't really give me the same feel on his second start at Warwick. I would expect him to leave that behind when he returns and I have already schooled him over hurdles. He jumps well and is one I am still looking forward, given how nicely he won on debut. Emma looks to have a nice bunch of novice hurdlers for the upcoming season and he will, hopefully, win a nice race or two.

SPORTING JOHN (Philip Hobbs)
OBVIOUSLY I have never ridden him in a race, but I ride him out every day at home. He is a horse who I have always liked a lot, but we didn't really know how good he was when we sent him to Exeter the first day. He absolutely bolted up, beating Harry Senior, and did the same on his next two starts. He's a horse who travels very well and jumps well,

and I'm sure he wasn't himself at the festival. I'd be happy to write off that run, he's still only five and although I'm not sure what they will do with him, he remains very exciting. If he goes chasing, jumping certainly won't be an issue, but they might just give him another year over hurdles, in which case I could see him going up in distance at some stage.

ST BARTS (Philip Hobbs)
ANOTHER horse who means a lot to me, he provided me with a big Saturday winner at Ascot in February, when winning in heavy ground. He's got a Pointing background and jumps very well at home, so he will be another to go novice chasing with and he loves testing ground. A nice staying trip on bad ground will be ideal for him, and he had earlier won at Uttoxeter (also on heavy ground) over 2m4f when Richard (Johnson) rode him.

He beat **Ubetya** that day and I went on to win a maiden hurdle on him for Kelly Morgan on his next start, back at Uttoxeter. He is another who will do well in novice chases this season, as he travels and jumps, and barely came off the bridle the day he won. He's only five and another who boasts lots of Pointing experience, and like St Barts, he coped well with testing ground last winter.

PILEON

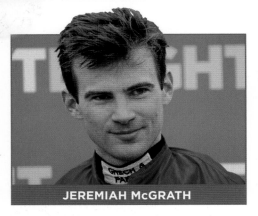

JEREMIAH McGRATH

ALLART *(Nicky Henderson)*
A VERY talented horse, who fell on debut, then won two small races, before running a very good race when fifth in the Supreme. A big horse, who will have no problem jumping a fence if they decide to go chasing, but from a mark of 143, he would be more than capable of winning a decent race over hurdles beforehand. A Shantou who enjoys some cut in the ground, he travels strongly, but should get 2m4f this season. I think not over-facing him after his fall at Ascot did him the world of good ahead of Cheltenham, and he is a horse with solid form, even going back to his bumper at Newbury, which was a strong race.

BOND'S LOVER *(Nicky Henderson)*
A MARE who ran only once last season, when winning in heavy ground at Newbury. She did nothing but improve at home throughout last year, and although she only ran the once, I would expect her to go chasing, as she is a very big mare. She enjoys a bit of soft ground, being by Flemensfirth, and like many of his progeny, she has a bit of attitude, but more importantly, she has the ability to go with it. The form of her Newbury win was franked by the fourth, who won a handicap next time and is now rated 135, and she should develop into a nice staying chaser in time.

CHAMP *(Nicky Henderson)*
ONE of the more obvious selections. We all saw what he did when staying on strongly to win the RSA last season, but I really do think that, with more intensive schooling behind him, he could be in for another big season. He is a horse who might appreciate spending a bit of time at Henrietta Knight's, but we all know that the engine and ability is there, and with a bit of luck, I would like to think that he will be lining up in the Gold Cup in March with a big chance. From the family of Best

Mate, I wasn't surprised that he stayed on as well as he did at the festival, and now he settles a lot better in his races, the longer trip is what he wants.

CHANTRY HOUSE *(Nicky Henderson)*
WE tend to school all of the horses in the autumn and then make the decision as to which will go chasing, but I would be very surprised if he didn't go straight over fences, and I think that he will improve again for it. Ran a belter when third in the Supreme, he will also improve for going up in distance, and I expect that he will end up a three-miler in time. An easy winner at Cheltenham and Newbury, he is a gorgeous big horse – by a sire that I am a big fan of, Yeats – he will make up into a very nice novice over 2m4f this season. He is a horse with a lot of natural ability.

I thought **Shishkin** was a little too obvious to include in my 'ten' but he, too, will go chasing, I would imagine. He put up an incredible performance in the Supreme, considering how much went wrong during the race, and I will be disappointed if he doesn't end up contesting the Arkle. He is a big horse, who will stay further, but I expect him to be campaigned over 2m this season.

FLINTEUR SACRE *(Nicky Henderson)*
RAN a good race on debut when second at Newbury, when he was a bit green, then he came out at Kempton, and barely came off the bridle to win. The better ground probably helped him that day, and he is clearly bred to be smart. Whilst I'm not going to say that he will be as good as his brother, he has done little wrong to date, his CV looks good, and he falls into the 'could be anything' category. A keen-going sort, he moves very well and is very sharp, so I would expect that better ground will always help him. I also expect that keenness to go as he matures.

GALLYHILL *(Nicky Henderson)*
AN expensive purchase (£450,000) at the Cheltenham sale last December, he is a lovely big horse by Getaway, and ticks all the boxes in terms of a horse of potential. He came into Seven Barrows for a short while, and did a small bit of work, then I actually schooled him over fences at Henrietta's (Knight) – as she buys for the owner and I ride out there, too – and he is a very talented young horse. An impressive Point-to-Point winner in Ireland, he is a big horse, so it wouldn't be a total surprise if he didn't run in a bumper, and instead rocked up in a novice hurdle first time out over 2m4f. He is a long-term project, and very much a staying chaser down the line.

GLYNN

GLYNN *(Nicky Henderson)*

WE only got to see him once last year, when I rode him to win impressively at Doncaster, after which we were considering both the Supreme and the Neptune for him. Nothing went wrong, but we worked him at Kempton a fortnight before the festival and he just didn't spark, so we decided to back off him. He would probably have gone to Aintree, under normal circumstances, and the lack of experience could just mean that he finds himself caught between a rock and a hard place this season, but he came from a good Point-to-Point school in the Crawford's, so he is very streetwise for a lightly-raced horse. A strong-traveller, it was 2m3½f the day he won at Doncaster, but I would have no issue in dropping back in trip. A chasing type for the future, he could be one for an introductory hurdle to begin with this season.

MARIE'S ROCK *(Nicky Henderson)*

A VERY talented mare, who remains unbeaten, winning both starts over hurdles last season, before meeting with a setback, which ruled her out of the Dawn Run at the festival. She won at Haydock on debut, before impressively winning a Listed race at Taunton over Christmas, and it wasn't a serious injury what kept her out, so she will be back in the autumn. Rated 144, the hope is that she could end up running in the Champion Hurdle, which gives you an indication of the regard in which we hold her at home. She wouldn't be the biggest mare, so might be better in the small-field mares' races to begin with, rather than lumping a big-weight in a handicap, but once she gains some more jumping experience, we believe that she could be a Grade 1 filly. She has lots of pace, and I have even mentioned to her owners (Middleham Park Racing) that she could be a good mare on the Flat at some stage. She will appreciate better ground.

PATROCLUS *(Nicky Henderson)*

PURCHASED at the festival sale, he finished second in an Irish Point-to-Point for Mick Goff, but did a couple of bits of work at home, and we really liked what we saw. A four-year-old by Shirocco, I rode him myself a few times in the spring, and is one that I would advise readers to keep an eye out for. Owned by Dai Walters, he will go down the bumper route this season.

TIME FLIES BY *(Nicky Henderson)*

A CHELTENHAM bumper winner last autumn, he then finished second in a Listed race back at Cheltenham, before running in a couple of Grade 2 novice hurdles. It could be that he had four relatively quick runs, and I think that he could be a nice second-season novice this year. He could be difficult to beat in an ordinary novice event first time out, then he will get his handicap mark, which could determine where he goes from there. I expect that he will improve for better ground, and there could be a nice race to be won with him at some point this season.

JONJO O'NEILL JNR

ANNIE MC *(Jonjo O'Neill)*

A GOOD mare last year, winning three times over fences, her mark (144) is probably at the top end of her limit, but there is a good programme for mares these days, so we are hopeful that she could pick one of those Listed events up at some stage. Last year, she still felt as though she had more filling out to do, so physically she may have improved, and I expect her to begin the campaign against her own sex. She relishes soft ground.

ARRIVEDERCI *(Jonjo O'Neill)*

WON a Wincanton maiden hurdle on his final start last season, I think there is plenty more to come from him this season and beyond. Still only five, he is lightly-raced and will probably remain over hurdles for now. His form was solid throughout last season, and from a mark of 128, I would like to think that he could win a decent handicap. He enjoys cut in the ground and will probably step up by half-a-mile this season. Further down the line, he has the size and scope to develop into a nice chaser.

ARRIVEDERCI

BUTTERWICK BROOK *(Colin Tizzard)*

A HORSE I rode three times last season, winning once at Taunton, where we beat a decent horse of Emma Lavelle's called Shang Tang. He then ran well under his penalty at Exeter, and I think he could be a horse who will improve significantly for going chasing. He will also be suited by going up in distance and has no problem in handling heavy ground.

COPPERHEAD *(Colin Tizzard)*

HE took a bad fall when well beaten at Cheltenham and he was quite sore afterwards, but if he comes back in time, the Hennessy (Ladbrokes Trophy) would appeal as the obvious race for him in the early part of the season. A course winner at Newbury, I then won the Grade 2 Reynoldstown on him at Ascot, and he is a big galloper, who might not have been suited by the Old course at Cheltenham. A bigger track would suit him better and he does handle soft ground very well.

ELDORADO ALLEN *(Colin Tizzard)*

I RODE him in the Contenders Hurdle, having run very well in a handicap, which was his first start in 13 months, so he might well have 'bounced' that day. He didn't quite pick up as I hoped he would, before disappointing at Cheltenham, although it has been well-documented that Colin's horses didn't appear to run to form at the festival. I would put a line through that, and he is a tall, rangy horse, so going chasing would suit him, and he remains quite exciting.

HARRY SENIOR *(Colin Tizzard)*

I RODE him at Chepstow on his first start over hurdles and I was mad about him. Another who failed to run his race at Cheltenham, he had improved with every run since the day I rode him, winning twice, including the Grade 2 on trials day. A horse I like a lot, chasing will bring about further improvement in him, and I think he could make up into a leading contender for the RSA this season.

It was lovely to be able to win on former Gold Cup winner **Native River** for the same owners last season, at a time when things were going really well for me, personally. Unfortunately for Richard (Johnson), he was out injured at the time, and thankfully, I got the ride. Aintree would be a possible starting point again, and time will tell if he is aimed at another Gold Cup, or trained with the Grand National in mind.

LIEUTENANT ROCCO *(Colin Tizzard)*

I'VE yet to ride him in a race, but he is a horse that Colin and his team have always liked at home, and before he disappointed at Cheltenham, he twice won on heavy ground, at Chepstow and Warwick, where he beat a solid yardstick in Stick With Bill. An Irish Point-to-Point graduate, I have ridden him a few times at home, and he could be another smart staying novice chaser if they send him down that route.

ROSE OF ARCADIA *(Colin Tizzard)*

A LOVELY big strong mare, who won an ordinary bumper at Taunton, but she couldn't have done it any easier. She galloped on strongly that day and would certainly have no problem in stepping up in distance, so should make a nice stayer over hurdles this year. An Irish Point-to-Point winner, she coped with the heavy ground and will have no problem jumping, although I have yet to school her.

Another filly who I rode to win a bumper and is worth noting would be **Maridadi** who won at Wetherby for trainer Hughie Morrison. A good strong daughter of Beat Hollow, I made plenty of use of her that day, and I think the plan might have been to head to Aintree had the Grand National meeting gone ahead.

SOARING GLORY *(Jonjo O'Neill)*

HE won his first two bumpers really well, then ran well against Israel Champ, on ground which would have been softer than ideal, in a Listed race back at Ascot. Having had a mid-season break, we were planning to run him at Aintree until the season came to an end, but he remains one who we are looking forward to. I schooled him before his summer break and he jumped well, and I think he will improve for better ground over hurdles. He has the speed to start off over the minimum trip.

THE BIG BREAKAWAY *(Colin Tizzard)*

ANOTHER who I haven't ridden in a race, but he is a horse that I have schooled plenty at home and I love him. I thought he ran well at Cheltenham, given that Colin's didn't appear to run up to their best during the week, and he was only a frame of a horse last year. I expect that he will have improved for another summer and being an Irish Points winner, jumping won't be a problem. Potentially top drawer, I think he could be quite special, and is certainly one to follow in the novice chase division.

COPPERHEAD

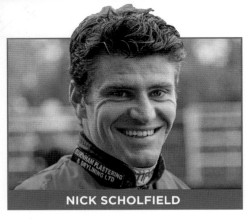

NICK SCHOLFIELD

CHAMPAGNE COURT *(Jeremy Scott)*
WON his first two starts over fences last season, then struggled in soft ground afterwards, and has since had a wind-operation, which should certainly help. We had been hoping that it would dry out for him at Cheltenham, but that didn't materialise, and I think the plan this season is to start off in the Betfair Stayers' Handicap Hurdle, as he is rated lower over hurdles and ran well in the Silver Trophy on his reappearance last year. He will then probably go down the handicap chase route, and as he wants 3m on good ground, something like the Sky Bet Chase could prove to be ideal.

FLYING SARA *(Jack Barber)*
A MALINAS filly who won a Taunton bumper on debut, beating Sabrina who won at Ascot next time. She picked up a little injury after that, which meant she missed the remainder of the season, so she might run in another bumper in the autumn, with the Listed race at Cheltenham one possible option. The time off might not have done her any harm, as she has grown a lot since, and she gave me a nice feel on debut, winning a shade comfortably.

GETAROUND *(Ella Pickard)*
I HAVEN'T ridden him in a race yet, but I have ridden him plenty at home and done lots of schooling on him, and he is a lovely big horse. A bumper winner at Chepstow, he won his novice hurdle in March, so remains a novice until the end of November. Ella might give him one more run over hurdles, but I think the plan is to go chasing and he jumps fences brilliantly. A proper stayer with a nice pedigree, he relishes testing conditions.

KISSESFORKATIE *(Jeremy Scott)*
A MARE who I included last year, she shaped well behind Silver Forever at Chepstow, and then behind the likes of Sporting John and Harry Senior over

2m1f at Exeter, before beating subsequent winners, Lunar Baby and Cill Anna (won her next three), at Wincanton. She still held every chance when falling on Boxing Day, after which she was given a break with the spring in mind. Her main target for the season was the Mares' Final at Newbury, which was obviously lost when the season was cut short, but there is talk of that race being re-staged early this season. I think she could be very well handicapped off a mark of 126, and when the time comes, she should jump a fence, too.

LIMITED RESERVE *(Christian Williams)*
I WON on him at Taunton, where he dug really deep in heavy ground, and he followed up by winning the valuable Grade 3 handicap at Sandown. He stayed on strongly that day on what was his first start over a staying trip, and he reminds me a little of the same connections' Potters Corner. An athletic horse, who jumps very well, he could take to fences and end up being a smart handicap chaser. He's a prolific hurdler who has won plenty of prize money, and he could easily add to his tally if sent chasing.

ONEUPMANSHIP *(Jack Barber)*
A LOVELY five-year-old of Jack's, who was still big and weak whilst running well in three bumpers last season, on ground that would have been softer than ideal. I schooled him just before he got turned away and he gave me a really good feel, so he could improve significantly when stepping up in trip over hurdles. He has had a wind-op over the summer and that should help, as his wind seemed to be catching him out at the end of his races on heavy ground. A horse that we have always liked, he is from the family of Thisthatandtother and Carlingford Lough, and he could just develop into a really nice staying hurdler.

ORRISDALE *(Jonjo O'Neill)*
A NICE horse owned by Trevor Hemmings, who I won on at Uttoxeter on his hurdles debut, and I think he would be of interest in handicap company off a mark of 122. A typical Trevor Hemmings horse, in that he will be a staying chaser in time, he is a big strong son of Oscar, and I think he will progress again this year.

PAPA TANGO CHARLY *(Jonjo O'Neill)*
GIVEN his reputation, he was slightly disappointing last season, but he still ran well when second behind both Igor at Ascot and The Big Breakaway at Newbury, then he boiled over at Doncaster, getting quite worked up beforehand. He's had a nice long break and was just a frame of a horse

PAPA TANGO CHARLY

that was the first time in his life that he had left Jeremy's farm. I loved the way he performed, as he had never even galloped on grass before that run, and he improved massively for the experience. He then won at Warwick, where he went through the race like a good horse, and was always doing enough. He was doing his best work late on and I didn't have to get too serious, so it was a pleasing performance, and he schooled well before he went on his summer break. A straightforward horse, who doesn't let anything bother him, I think he has a very bright future and he's a horse who I am very excited about. A good-mover, he wouldn't want deep ground and although he will stay further in time, he should be capable of starting off over the minimum trip.

last year. Having won his Point-to-Point, he was probably quite light afterwards, and he is still only five. He did an awful lot in a short space of time as a four-year-old and, therefore, should have appreciated the time off. He gives me a great feel and given his mark (128), I wouldn't be surprised if he turned up in a handicap at some stage. He will be a staying chaser in time and is a great jumper, but he is still a novice over hurdles, and should be capable of winning races this season.

SIZABLE SAM *(Jeremy Scott)*
A HORSE that I have always loved, having done everything right at home before he ran. A big chestnut with a fantastic attitude, he was very green on debut when runner-up at Wincanton, but

TEDHAM *(Jonjo O'Neill)*
ENDURED a frustrating season last year, missing out on qualifying for the Pertemps Final by one at Warwick, then he was meant to go to Aintree for the 3m handicap hurdle, and obviously that meeting didn't go-ahead. I schooled him over fences before he went out into the field, and he was electric, so I am hoping that he will go chasing when he returns. A horse that we still haven't seen the best of, there is a chance that he could be a bit better racing right-handed, but I retain the belief in him and, hopefully, this could be the season he delivers as he now looks to be the finished article. Better ground helps and granted a bit more luck, there is a big day in him.

TEDHAM

HARRY SKELTON

BEAKSTOWN *(Dan Skelton)*

AT his best on good ground, he didn't really get his conditions last season, but he ran encouragingly at Cheltenham in the novices' handicap, where he went through the race like a good horse. He travelled really well, but just couldn't pick up and see it out on the soft ground. A big horse with a big engine, we haven't over-raced him, and hopefully this season he can step forward to become the horse we hoped he would be.

We haven't yet made the decision as to where we will start, but expect to see him out nice and early before the winter ground comes. As he is still a novice, there should be plenty of options for him this season.

BEAKSTOWN

BOSS MAN FRED *(Dan Skelton)*

SURPRISED us a little when winning at Kempton first time up, he is a horse who is very laid back at home so can go under the radar a little, but he followed up at Southwell, then won a handicap at Doncaster. Put a line through his run in the River Don, when Bridget rode him, as he was never really

going and is much better than that. He will go chasing now, wants 3m, and is a really likeable horse. A big backward sort, to do what he was doing last year suggests that he is a horse with a good deal of ability.

Another for novice chases is **Northofthewall** who won three times over hurdles last season. We have given this horse plenty of time and he learnt as the season went on, including when running in the Lanzarote, which taught him plenty. I think you will see an improved horse again this year, and going chasing could be the making of him. A tough individual, he will develop into a good quality handicapper over fences.

CADZAND *(Dan Skelton)*

A HORSE with a lot of natural ability, he travelled really well when placed in two bumpers. A Point-to-Point winner, he has gone through his races very well and just got caught out with a bit of greenness at Warwick on his second start, when I probably got to the front a bit soon, and after looking at the crowd, was caught by a good horse of Jeremy Scott's. Quick enough to start off at 2m, he wouldn't want bad ground, so he will be out in October. He jumps well at home and has a touch of class about him, so hopefully he develop into a smart novice hurdler.

FAIVOIR *(Dan Skelton)*

I HAVEN'T actually ridden him in a race yet, but Bridget won bumpers on him at Bangor and Huntingdon, despite doing a lot wrong. Clearly another young horse with a lot of ability, we just need to channel him in the right direction, as he has been keen in his races and is a little babyish. He will need to learn to settle and being a bit raw, might take a run or two to find his stride, but he is a horse who obviously has a big engine. Only a frame, I expect him to be a lot stronger this year and will hopefully do well over hurdles, starting off over 2m.

MIDNIGHT RIVER *(Dan Skelton)*

FINISHED third in two bumpers last season, starting at Worcester in what turned out to be a very good race, then behind Ask A Honey Bee, who went on to run in the Champion Bumper. On both occasions I dropped him in and he was ridden for a proper education, in that I wanted him to settle, go through the race correctly and finished out to the line. He jumps well at home and I hope he will take fairly high rank as a novice hurdler, as I think he is pretty smart. A horse we have given plenty of time to, he's a great big strapping individual, who will want a trip, and although he is a chaser for the future, he should be winning races over hurdles this season.

PROSCHEMA *(Dan Skelton)*

A SMART horse on the Flat for Tom Dascombe, he missed the second half of last season, but is ready to return, and he will improve for good ground. He ran well first time for us at Chepstow, then he won at Wetherby, before picking up a little injury when returning to Wetherby in late-November. He will be out fairly early, and I think he could be well handicapped on a mark of 128, so I am hopeful that there is a good race in him.

PROTEKTORAT *(Dan Skelton)*

A HORSE who really improved throughout last season having had a wind-operation. He came from France and took a while to acclimatise, as can often be the case, and being a proper big horse who is beginning to come into his own, he is going to go chasing now. He won at Cheltenham on New Year's Day, then he ran well on trials day when he would have appreciated a stronger gallop, and it was similar in the Coral Cup when they went too slow for him. He will start off over 2m4f and we will see where we go from there and although he enjoys a bit of cut in the ground, the key to him is a strong pace, which helps him settle. We think he has a big future, and although I have to ride him patiently, he might grow out of that as he matures and gains more experience.

PROTEKTORAT

THIRD TIME LUCKI *(Dan Skelton)*

THE pick of our bumper horses last season. We were very pleased with his fourth in the Champion Bumper, where he stayed on up the hill really well, and he's a big horse, who has a lot of filling out to do. He can be keen and get lit up, which is why we have held him up in his races, but provided he settles, we will be able to ride him anywhere in time.

He has schooled well at home and will start off over 2m, and hopefully can make up into a top-class novice hurdler. A horse with a hell of a lot

of ability, his long-term future lies over fences and I suspect that we will be talking about him in next year's book, ahead of his novice chase campaign.

WEST CORK *(Dan Skelton)*

DID well last season, winning a couple of novice hurdles, before finishing second in the Grade 2 Dovecote at Kempton. Runner-up on his first two starts, we then dropped him back in trip, and although there is a chance that he will start off in a handicap hurdle (currently rated 139), he is a good jumper and will be going chasing before long. He will start off over 2m, but I'd have thought that he would want an extra half-mile as the season goes on.

WILDE ABOUT OSCAR *(Dan Skelton)*

ANOTHER of our bumper horses from last season, he got collared on the line at Southwell, when probably getting to the front a little too early, then won easily at Warwick. Bridget rode him in the Listed bumper at Newbury, a race that just didn't really suit, as they went very slow, which resulted in him being too keen. A horse with a very good attitude, he will go novice hurdling and, hopefully, he is another who will take pretty high rank. I would imagine that we will start over 2m, then build up as the season goes on, and he has a very bright future.

I ALSO wanted to mention a couple of un-raced four-year-olds. Firstly, one by Presenting called **Jersey**, who is out of Synthe Davis (won three times over hurdles and once over fences) and was going really nicely at home in the spring. He's enjoyed a good summer out at grass, and we feel that he's definitely a horse to look out for. Another in the same bracket is **Cousu Main**, who is by Buck's Boum, and we really liked what we saw from him in the spring, too. You won't see too much of them this season, but they are definitely two nice youngsters who should start off in a bumper at some point.

And, it is nice to be able to give a positive update on **Generation Text** and Interconnected, who both featured in this publication last year. Looking at his Irish Point-to-Point form (second to Sporting John), Generation Text is a very interesting horse, and we really liked what we saw at home last autumn. A real classy horse, he did everything easily, and jumps great, so will go straight over hurdles. **Interconnected** looks unbelievable, he has filled right out having had plenty of time to fill into his huge frame. Both only had small niggling injuries, but I doubt that we will see them before Christmas. Hopefully we can get both of them back, and all being well, they are two horses with exciting futures.

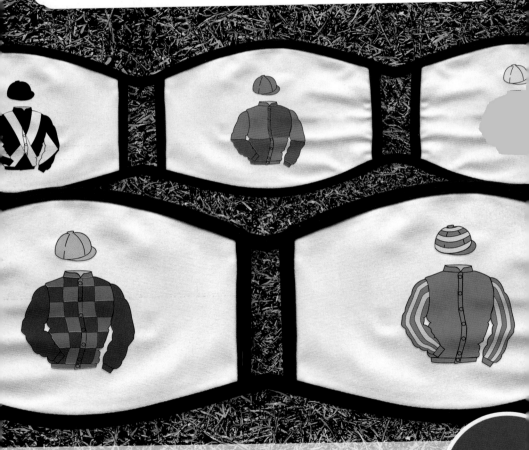

CREATE YOUR OWN
PERSONALISED SILKS
FACE MASKS

DESIGNED AND PRODUCED BY ⚜ WEATHERBYS

£9.9
(Plus P&

Call: 01933 304776 or visit:
wearyourcolours.squarespace.com

Cheveley Park Stud
RICHARD THOMPSON

The National Hunt string of Cheveley Park Stud continues to grow, and here Richard Thompson, son of the stud's owners David and Patricia, talks us through their plans for the upcoming season:

ALLAHO *(Willie Mullins)*
THERE is an argument to say that he could have run in the Marsh at Cheltenham, but Willie and his team were still comfortable after the RSA that he ran over the right trip and he's now hit the frame at the past two festivals. He did win over 3m as a five-year-old over hurdles, so he does stay, but would certainly have no trouble in dropping in distance, and there will be plenty of options for him this season. He remains lightly-raced and progressive.

A PLUS TARD *(Henry de Bromhead)*
WE were obviously slightly disappointed that he didn't win the Ryanair, but he still ran well despite not travelling as comfortably as he usually does in his races. He had earlier, of course, won the Grade 1 at Leopardstown over Christmas, beating Chacun Pour Soi. That was a wonderful performance and we have high hopes for him once again this season, when he will be aimed at the middle-distance chases.

BALLYADAM *(Gordon Elliott)*
A HIGH-CLASS prospect, he would have run in the Grade 1 bumper at Punchestown, had the festival gone ahead. A horse Gordon has always held in high-regard, he was a bit disappointing at Navan when he was too keen, but did it well at Downpatrick. We paid a lot of money for him, but have big hopes going forward, and he will probably start off over the minimum trip.

DEPLOY THE GETAWAY *(Willie Mullins)*
HE had a setback after we bought him, but Willie was pleased with his progress in the spring and he will start off in a bumper during the autumn, all being well. The vibes were positive about how he had recovered and we are hopeful that he can make up for lost time.

EL MERANO *(Willie Mullins)*
HE has had some issues and actually hasn't run for us yet, but probably would have run in the spring had the season not been cut short. Off the track since November 2017 (when he finished runner-up to Elixir d'Ainay in a three-year-old AQPS race) Willie certainly thinks he is worth persevering with, and hopefully he will finally make it to the track this season.

EN BETON *(Willie Mullins)*
RAN twice in bumpers last season and ran reasonably well at Thurles in March. He's a big horse and we are hopeful of improvement as he goes over hurdles this season. He will probably want a trip and I believe he has a future.

ENVOI ALLEN *(Gordon Elliott)*
WHAT more can I say about Envoi Allen? I'm sure we are going to head over fences with him and I would have thought that the RSA will be his end of season target. Going up in trip shouldn't be a problem, as he was running on well at the end of the Ballymore, and we will, hopefully, be looking at the Gold Cup with him at some stage, so I think the RSA makes sense. He has everything, however, so has all options open to him, and he enjoyed a good summer over in Gordon's.

FERNY HOLLOW *(Willie Mullins)*
WILLIE liked him from day one and although he is clearly a bit quirky and was beaten in his first couple of bumpers, he got the job done at Fairyhouse and then put up a smart performance under a beautiful ride at Cheltenham. Dropped right out, it was great to watch on what was a memorable day, providing us with a second successive win in the Champion Bumper, and completing a double following the earlier victory of Envoi Allen. We have big hopes for him now and if we can contain him mentally, he could be very good. The change of tactics appeared to help and given how keen he is, I would expect him to start off at 2m. If all goes

to plan, he will develop into a contender for the Supreme Novices' Hurdle at Cheltenham.

GLOIRE D'ATHON *(Henry de Bromhead)*
HE'S a four-year-old from France who hasn't run for us yet, but won on the Flat and has been with Henry since the end of last year. He might well have come out in the spring but for the season finishing prematurely, which means he retains his novice status for this season. He will start in a maiden hurdle.

JEWELLER *(Henry de Bromhead)*
WON his last two starts for Sir Michael Stoute when we stepped him up to 2m, he is a four-year-old who we thought could do a job for us as a hurdler, as Chief Justice did for us as a juvenile, winning a Grade 3 and a handicap at Aintree. He appreciated the step up in trip, so should stay well over hurdles, and the headgear was applied purely to help him concentrate.

LARQUEBUSE *(Gordon Elliott)*
NOT one of our stars, but she won three times for us last season and being a former Point-to-Point winner, you would hope that she can go on improving over fences and pay her way. She has won a bumper and twice over hurdles, so it would be nice to complete the set over fences this season.

MALONE ROAD *(Gordon Elliott)*
A HIGH-CLASS bumper horse, he has been sidelined since November 2018. Declared to run in a maiden hurdle in August, he was pulled out due to the ground, so we should see him soon. You can never be confident after such a lay-off, but we are certainly hopeful that the ability is still there.

QUILIXIOS *(Gordon Elliott)*
A THREE-YEAR-OLD who Tom Malone bought for us, after he won on his debut at Compiegne in France in March. It is early days with him, but at this stage the hope is that he develops into a Triumph Hurdle candidate, before which there are plenty of nice juvenile hurdles for him in Ireland.

ROSE OF ARCADIA *(Colin Tizzard)*
SHE is currently our only National Hunt horse in training in England, and she put up a really good performance to win a bumper at Taunton. She will want a trip in time, but has always shown Colin the right signs at home, and could have done no more than win as she did, so is another who we will look forward to this season. She will be campaigned in the mares' novice hurdle division.

SIR GERHARD *(Gordon Elliott)*
ANOTHER expensive purchase and another of our big hopes. Impressive when he won his Point-to-Point last November, he is another who was ready to run and might have been out in the spring. He is likely to be campaigned in bumpers this season.

NEWS FROM
France

You will have already read about a number of exciting prospects who have arrived in Britain from France, but there are several more who have moved to England or Ireland more recently, having shown promise on home soil. Several are mentioned in this section, along with a select number who remain in training in France.

LEADING PROPSECT Paros looks to be an exciting addition to Nicky Henderson's string and the horse who finished third behind him at Dieppe **Hacker des Places** has since been purchased by Owners Group and is now in training with Paul Nicholls. A scopey looking son of Great Pretender, he ran out a taking winner at Dax on his second start for Francois Nicolle, despite veering to his left at times (quite markedly at the first flight in the home straight). He appeared to be full of running as he crossed the line, and should make his mark in the juvenile hurdle division.

Nicholls also purchased the first and second from a three-year-old hurdle at Auteuil in March. The race was won by **Monmiral**, who travelled with purpose, and took up the running at the end of the back

straight. Ears pricked, he jumped well two out, and despite stepping at the last, ran out a taking winner (also trained by Francois Nicolle). A gelding by Saint des Saints, he is a half-brother to hurdle and chase winner Soulongy, and is in the ownership of John and Lisa Hales, Sir Alex Ferguson, and Ged Mason.

Monmiral had two-and-a-half lengths to spare over **Hell Red**, who is in the ownership of Sir Martin Broughton and Friends. A grey by Martaline, he is a full-brother to Hell Boy, a horse who has flourished since going chasing this year. He raced quite enthusiastically in the early part of the race and saw plenty of daylight out wide (probably not ideal). However, he still travelled up menacingly leaving the back straight and showed a good attitude to chase the winner all the way to the line. He covered a lot more ground than Monmiral, and they could be two nice recruits to Ditcheat.

Yet another three-year-old who won for trainer Francois Nicolle and has since changed yards is **Quilixios**, who was purchased by Cheveley Park Stud and is now in training with Gordon Elliott. The son of Maxios was still a couple of lengths down jumping the last, but picked up well inside the final furlong, scoring by 12 lengths in the end. I'm Walkin' (finished fourth from the same stable) went on to finish runner-up behind the exciting Heros d'Ainay in a Listed event at Auteuil (incidentally, the third horse from the Monmiral and Hell Red race finished back in sixth), and the ground was described as heavy when he made that successful debut at Compiegne back in March.

The McNeill Family have also purchased a three-year-old to go juvenile hurdling in Ireland, with **Youmdor** having moved to the yard of Willie Mullins. The Youmzain gelding showed a fine turn of foot when winning a handicap at Deauville in late-May (1m2f), where he came from off the pace under a confident Ludovic Boisseau. Ridden patiently, Youmdor travelled really well and picked up stylishly once seeing daylight in the home straight. It was a performance that suggests that he might be more about speed and it is also worth noting that he won over 7½f as a two-year-old. He could be one for a sharper track and better ground, but looks a bright prospect for hurdles.

Busselton is a Mastercraftsman three-year-old, who won on his hurdling debut for David Cottin, and has reportedly joined Joseph O'Brien. Sixth on his sole start as a two-year-old (at Angers in November 2019), he raced quite keenly in the early stages but settled better down the far side. He showed a good turn of foot to hit the front approaching two out, and having jumped the final two hurdles well (jumped well throughout, in fairness) he looked to score with a bit in hand. The runner-up **State Man** looks a sure-fire future winner, having come from off the pace, and is another three-year-old to monitor closely.

Gloire d'Athon is another who will sport the Cheveley Park silks, having won on the Flat at Cholet over an extended 1m6f for Alain Couetil. A four-year-old by Doctor Dino, he has been with Henry de Bromhead since the end of last year and would probably have made his debut for his new connections in the spring, had the season not been brought to a premature end. The positive is that he remains a novice for the full season, and although that form isn't the easiest to evaluate (certainly wouldn't appear to be particularly strong), he picked up well and won with plenty in hand, despite showing signs of greenness in the closing stages.

It will be interesting to see how he fares once sent hurdling this autumn.

Owner Mike Grech – who has bought expensive horses such as Gallyhill and Keskonrisk (both feature elsewhere in the book) – has acquired a well-bred un-raced four-year-old by the name of **I Am Maximus**. He's by Authorized and out of Polysheba (a Poliglote mare), making him a half-brother to Pointel, a winner over 1m6f for James Fanshawe. He also finished runner-up in a 2m handicap at Goodwood, suggesting there is plenty of stamina for jumping in his pedigree, and he is one to note in bumpers for Nicky Henderson.

I thought I would touch upon another couple of impressive winners who – at the time of writing – are set to remain in France, starting with the aforementioned **Heros d'Ainay** who won the Listed Prix Go Ahead on his racecourse debut for trainer Gabriel Leenders. A Sholokhov half-brother to Jonjo O'Neill's Arrivederci, he raced enthusiastically throughout and had the race sewn up when jumping two out. He dived at the last, but drew right away to record a striking success, in a race which was won by Kauto Star back in 2003. He heads the betting for the Triumph Hurdle with several firms, but I would expect to see him campaigned domestically.

And, secondly, **Happyday** looked a nice prospect when winning an AQPS race (a French bumper) over 1m4f at Vichy. Tracking the pace throughout, the grey looked as though he might be trapped on the rail with a couple of furlongs to run, but his rider was patient and the gap soon came. Having been nudged upsides, he quickly asserted in the closing stages, showing a good turn of foot, and putting the race to bed in a matter of strides, winning a shade cosily in the end. By Coastal Path and out of a Dom Alco mare, he boasts a lovely jumping pedigree and is a half-brother to Farnice, a five-time winner (won two Grade 3 chases) for Francois Nicolle. He could be a smart long-term prospect.

Finally, an update from France wouldn't be complete without touching upon **Easysland** who ran out a facile winner of the Cross Country Chase when last seen. Still only six, returning to Cheltenham to defend his crown next March will, no doubt, be the main aim for the season for him, and he might well follow a similar path back to the festival (via Pau, in February). The Grand National is another possibility in the spring, and although he will only be seven, he boasts considerably more experience than most horses of that age. Even at this stage, he is as short as 6-4 to win a second successive Glenfarclas Chase, making him the shortest priced horse (2-1 best) in any race at this season's Cheltenham Festival.

GRIZZMAN

Point-to-Point
GRADUATES

AMARILLO SKY *(Colin Tizzard)*

COLIN TIZZARD has added plenty of new blood to his squad for the upcoming season, with Amarillo Sky one of the more exciting recruits. A four-year-old by Westerner, he cost £280,000 at the Cheltenham Festival Sale, having won division one of a Borris House maiden (Gars de Sceaux won division two) just 11 days earlier, for Colin Bowe. Prominent throughout, he jumped very well for a debutant, and also displayed a good deal of pace, suggesting that he will be well-suited to shorter trip under Rules. His dam is an un-raced sister of Beg To Differ (won three times over hurdles and once over fences, for Jonjo O'Neill) so he is bred to stay further in time, but I suspect that he will be campaigned over the minimum trip to begin with, possibly starting in a bumper in the autumn.

Tizzard actually bought to the top three lots at the festival sale, all for the same owners (Romans, Taylor and O'Dwyer). The other pairing were **Killer Kane** (£300,000) and Shirocco's Dream. The former is an Oscar half-brother to three-time Grade 1 winner Go Native, so should possess the pace to drop in distance, having won with plenty in hand at Ballycahane for Donnchadh Doyle.

Runner-up to Leading Prospect (and now stable-mate) Rose Of Arcadia on debut, **Shirocco's Dream** (£260,000) won a mares' maiden at Borris House for the same handler, and is out of a sister to the high-class Captain Chris. She looks to possess plenty of size and scope for jumping, and stayed on strongly to score, suggesting that she might want 2m4f once going hurdling in the autumn.

BRANDY LOVE *(Willie Mullins)*

An impressive winner of a 2m4f maiden at Cragmore for Colin Bowe and Barry O'Neill, Brandy Love is a four-year-old by Jet Away, and looks to be an exciting recruit to the Willie Mullins stable. Taking on the boys, she got into a really good rhythm at the head of affairs, and had the opposition beaten a fair way out, suggesting that she won't have any trouble in dropping in distance under Rules. She crossed the line with eight lengths to spare in the end, but was value for a good deal more, and I would expect her to start off in a mares' bumper. Purchased for £200,000 at Cheltenham (February sale) just six days after winning, she is a half-sister to Topofthecotswolds, who won three times for Nigel Twiston-Davies. His winning form came on good ground, which bodes well for when Brandy Love encounters a sounder surface, and she could develop into a very smart mare.

CHOSEN PORT *(Olly Murphy)*

YET another winner for the Colin Bowe stable, Chosen Port won a four-year-old maiden in March, just five days before being purchased by Olly Murphy at the festival sale (£115,000). A well-bred filly, she tracked the pace at Ballycahane, and effortlessly moved into second place jumping two out. Asked to pick up, she quickly asserted, and was in control when jumping the final fence. A full-sister to Burtons Well (a useful soft-ground chaser for Venetia Williams and Trevor Hemmings) and a half-sister to Burton Port (also owned by Hemmings, and winner of the Mildmay Novices' Chase at Aintree), there are another couple of bumper winners in her family, so she should be up to making an impact in that sphere. Bred to appreciate a trip once sent jumping, she will carry the colours of Noel and Valerie Moran.

Gerry Hogan paid £85,000 at the same sale for the runner-up **Western Zara**, who is a grey by Westerner, out of a Flemensfirth mare. She made most of the running, and to her credit, rallied well once headed by the winner, beaten by two lengths at the line. She is now in training with Paul Nolan.

CLONDAW SECRET *(Gordon Elliott)*

A WINNER for Mick Goff at Boulta last December, Clondaw Secret is a full-brother to Clondaw Court, who also won a Point, before winning his first four races (a bumper and three hurdles) for Willie Mullins and Susannah Ricci. Travelling well just behind the pace, he jumped well under Shane Fitzgerald (particularly three out, when he was beginning to edge closer), and showed a good turn of foot to beat **Champagne Gold** (sold to Alex Elliott for £90,000 at the same sale and now in training with Henry de Bromhead) by a cosy two lengths. The form was advertised when the fourth **Minella Escape** (subsequently sold to Kevin Ross for £100,000, and also now in training with Henry de Bromhead) won comfortably at Bellharbour. A five-year-old by Court Cave, Clondaw Secret is just one of a clutch of exciting youngsters now in the care of Gordon Elliott, and he looks to possess the speed to win a bumper, before making an impact over hurdles.

FASHION NOVA *(Fergal O'Brien)*

FASHION NOVA showed much improved form to dead-heat at Bellharbour on her second start, having finished fourth on debut at Borris House a couple of months earlier. Ridden more prominently, the grey travelled with purpose on the front-end, and looked to have the race sewn up when kicking clear from two out. Collared on the line by Rose Milan, the form wouldn't be particularly strong, but the way she went through the race was eye-catching, and Fergal O'Brien – thanks to the buying prowess of partner Sally Randell – has done well with similar-priced purchases in recent seasons. Bought out of Donnchadh Doyle's yard for £42,000, the daughter of Flemensfirth is now in the ownership of Stewart Andrew, whose Ever Blessed won the 1999 Hennessy Cognac Gold Cup for Mark Pitman.

A five-year-old by Flemensfirth, Fashion Nova is bred to relish a trip – her dam is an un-raced half-sister to Bobs Worth – but I suspect that she will be capable of going well in a bumper against her own sex, before she goes hurdling. She should have no problem in coping with softer ground, also.

FISTON DES ISSARDS (*Gordon Elliott*)
A FIVE-YEAR-OLD by Buck's Boum, who won impressively at Loughanmore last October, Fiston des Issards was purchased by Gordon Elliott at Cheltenham the following month (£255,000), and has been given plenty of time by his new connections. Ridden positively by Barry O'Neill (for trainer Colin Bowe), he jumped well and was too strong for Boothill in the closing stages. The runner-up and the fourth, Smurphy Enki, both won bumpers in England in the New Year (and feature elsewhere in this year's publication), whilst the third Upandatit has since joined the Scottish yard of Nick Alexander, so is another for the notebook. As for Firston des Issards, there was a lot to like about the performance, and the patient approach might pay dividends in the long-run, with this good-looking chasing type. Out of a Robin des Champs mare, I don't envisage him hanging around in bumpers for too long. When we see him on the track, he will be sporting the silks of Noel and Valerie Moran, who have plenty to look forward to this season, with Queens Brook and The Bosses Oscar amongst their Irish string.

GARTER LANE (*Barry Connell*)
WELL-SUPPORTED on debut for Philip Fenton, Garter Lane justified favouritism when winning at Lisronagh last November. Having travelled smoothly into contention, she took up the running at the second last, and stayed on well to score, despite not being particularly quick over the final fence. A five-year-old by Getaway, she is a half-sister to a couple of bumper winners, and

she was purchased by Gerry Hogan at Cheltenham (£100,000) shortly after that debut success. She will represent leading owner, come trainer, Barry Connell.

Back in third was **Overnight Success**, who is a Jeremy half-sister to Samcro, and again caught the eye with how she travelled. She had run a sound race on debut the previous May, when again travelling with purpose before fading into fourth. That form reads well, with Grade 2 novice hurdle winner Clondaw Caitlin finishing runner-up, so appeared not to get home, so could be one to note over shorter under Rules.

She did run once more after that, when pulling-up at Borris House, in a race in which **Feuille de Lune** (since bought privately by trainer Kelly Morgan) finished second, and she, too, should appreciate dropping back in distance, having made most of the running. She was a beaten-favourite next time and her new trainer has bought well from the Pointing sphere previously – notably Timetochill and Ubetya – so it wouldn't be a huge shock if this daughter of Saddler Maker was another success story for her yard. Look out for her in a mares' bumper in the autumn.

GERICAULT ROQUE (*David Pipe*)
ONLY fourth in a maiden at Tallow in February, the bare result doesn't tell half the story here, as Gericault Roque was travelling with purpose when badly hampered three out, when he was all but brought to a standstill. Much to his credit, he got back into the race, and came into shot as the front three crossed the line, closing all the time, eventually beaten less than eight lengths. He must have lost more than that at the third last, so it really was an eye-catching debut, and he has since been bought privately by owner Bryan Drew, and is now in training with David Pipe. A four-year-old by Monmartre, his half-brother won over fences in France (2m1f) and he doesn't look short of pace, on the limited evidence we have available to us. He might well go under the radar, whereas the front three all subsequently sold for relatively big money at Cheltenham's February sale.

The winner **Glenglass** was given a positive mention by Jamie Codd (*A View From The Saddle*) and is now in training with Gordon Elliott, having been purchased for £155,000. A big-looking son of Ocovango, he struggled around the tight bends, so might be value for a bit more than the winning margin, and is likely to appreciate a galloping track under Rules. Incidentally, the runner-up was purchased for £100,000 by Ian Ferguson, and the third for £82,000 by Tim Vaughan.

GRIZZMAN *(Tom Lacey)*

A four-year-old by Al Namix, who possesses a speedy pedigree, Grizzman won an open maiden at Larkhill for Sophie Lacey and Tommie O'Brien. From three out, him and the runner-up (a fellow four-year-old debutant) began to forge clear of the opposition, and they became locked in a protracted duel for the remainder of the 2m4f contest. In tight at the penultimate fence, the grey picked up well on the run to the final fence, and was quicker over it, which probably sealed the victory. He looks to have plenty of scope for jumping when the time comes, but in the meantime, will be of interest in bumpers for Tom Lacey.

He looks a nice type, as does the runner-up **Adjournment**, who is by Court Cave, and did little wrong on debut for Francesca Nimmo. His dam – who is out of Champion Hurdle winner Alderbrook – is a half-sister Noble Emperor and Streams Of Whiskey, so he will probably need a trip in time, but is worth monitoring. It is likely that he will have another start in a Point-to-Point for his current connections, after which I would expect to see him go through the sales ring.

GUARDINO *(Ben Pauling)*

RUNNER-UP in a 2m4f maiden at Oldtown in February – in a race that was won by Asterion Forlonge in 2018 – Guardino is a good-looking son of Authorized, who was purchased by Ben Pauling at Cheltenham (£170,000) six days after that racecourse debut. The winner was given an easy lead that day and although he was unable to claw back **Supreme Jet** (who is also worth monitoring going forward) it was a highly promising debut. He came clear of the remainder, having travelled well throughout, and he looks to have the requisite pace to win a bumper for his new connections. Although he only saddled two winners in that division last season, Ben Pauling is a trainer who tends to do well in bumpers, and Authorized – as a sire – has a fine strike-rate in such events.

LORD ACCORD *(Neil Mulholland)*

OWNER Lynne McLennan has plenty to look forward to this season, with *Leading Prospect* Nada To Prada and David Pipe's Martinhal among her team, and she now has a horse in training with Neil Mulholland. That horse is Lord Accord, who finished third at Moig last November. A Yeats half-brother to the high-class Monksland (three times a winner at Grade 2 level for Noel Meade), he had made a serious error with a circuit to run, and he was far from fluent at the two fences down the far side, when just working his way back into the race.

The fact that he was able to get upsides two out – where he again lacked fluency – suggests that he has plenty of natural ability, and he showed a good attitude to keep on for third. The form of the race is mixed, with the winner disappointing on debut for Henry de Bromhead and Robcour, whilst the runner-up wasn't beaten far by the exciting Keskonrisk, and if his new trainer can iron out his jumping, he looks a promising type. Before he goes hurdling, I suspect that we might see Lord Accord in a bumper, and I don't envisage him having a problem in handling better ground.

ONLY THE BOLD *(Evan Williams)*

EVAN WILLIAMS has purchased several expensive Irish Point-to-Point winners in recent years, and he was at it again in February, when paying £215,000 to secure Only The Bold, who had won at Tyrella, for Warren Ewing, the previous month. A half-brother to Westerner Lady (won 10 races for Willie Mullins, including a Grade 2 novice chase), he had unseated his rider on debut at Borris House, before running out an easy winner on good ground. Having taken up the running four fences from home, the Jeremy five-year-old thinned a packed field out over the next couple, and was never headed thereafter, eventually winning by nine lengths. He looks to have more than enough pace to contest a bumper, but it could be that he heads straight over hurdles. Interestingly, the same connections (he will represent the stable's long-standing owners, Mr & Mrs Rucker) have introduced similar types – Quoi de Neuf and Coconut Splash – over 2m4f at Aintree in the past couple of years, so it is clearly a track which his trainer likes as a starting point.

REALITY CHEQUE *(Willie Mullins)*

AN early faller at Dromahane over Christmas, Reality Cheque ran out a five-length winner at Kilfeacle, on his second start for Pat Doyle. The son of Getaway jumped up stylishly into third place, three fences from home, and travelled like the winner from that point. Asked to take over in between the final two fences, he readily brushed aside the runner-up, to win with plenty in hand. There was a yawning gap back to an experienced performer in third, and this five-year-old has reportedly joined the Willie Mullins stable. A half-brother to Famous Saying (winner of a decent four-year-old Point-to-Point bumper for Noel Meade in May 2018) he looks to have the pace to win a bumper, despite being bred to appreciate a longer trip once sent jumping. He is very much one to be look forward to.

SIR GERHARD *(Gordon Elliott)*

ONE of the more high-profile winners from the 2019-2020 season, Sir Gerhard showed a fine turn of foot to break away from the field, when winning at Boulta for Ellmarie Holden. Briefly challenged three out, he quickly accelerated when Derek O'Connor gave him a squeeze, and he was in complete control by the second last. Ears pricked, he jumped the final fence really well, so it wasn't surprising that he proved popular when going through the ring at Cheltenham, the following month, where he fetched £400,000. Purchased by Gordon Elliott, the son of Jeremy is the latest acquisition of leading owners Cheveley Park Stud, and it is likely that we would have seen him in a bumper in the spring, had the season not ended prematurely. Jamie Codd gives the five-year-old a very positive mention in this year's *A View From The Saddle* section, and he is likely to be difficult to beat in a bumper on his first start under Rules. Elliott likes to target the bumper at Down Royal's big meeting – winning it for the past five years (including with Malone Road for Cheveley Park in 2018) – so that could be an option, if he is ready in the early part of the season. It is likely that his performance on debut will dictate which route is then taken, but he could conceivably be the horse that attempts to provide the owners with their third straight win in the Weatherbys Champion Bumper. Alternatively, given that he is already five, he might be sent hurdling after one run. Either way, he looks to be a very exciting prospect.

STAR GATE *(Evan Williams)*

A WINNER of the four-year-old maiden at Bellharbour in which Petibonome took a heavy-fall, Star Gate showed a fine turn of foot to put the race to bed on the run to last, appearing to idle in the closing stages. The Imperial Monarch gelding was making a winning debut for Colin Bowe and Rob James, in what was the first four-year-old maiden of 2020, and a race that was won 12 months earlier by Fado des Brosses. Like that winner, Star Gate was subsequently purchased by Evan Williams, and he looks to have the pace to start off in a bumper, should his new connections wish (although that is something which his owners don't always tend to do). He was purchased for £140,000 at Cheltenham in February, and looks to be another nice young prospect for leading owners, the Rucker's.

TALLOW FOR COAL *(Jamie Snowden)*

WINNER of the St Leger in 2010, Arctic Cosmos had three winners as a sire during the 2019-2020 Irish Point-to-Point season (to the date when racing was suspended), one being Tallow For Coal, who won over 2m4f at Knockanard in mid-February. Despite making a serious error three out (James Hannon did well to retain the partnership), he was soon left clear as there was carnage in behind, eventually winning as he liked. A half-brother to four winners, he was picked up for £50,000 at Cheltenham just five days after making that winning debut, and he is now in training with Jamie Snowden, for whom he will carry the colours of Apache Star Racing. Whilst he wouldn't be one of the higher-profile horses to feature in this section, he has the potential to do well under Rules, for his new connections.

SIR GERHARD

OLIVER SHERWOOD
RACING

With over 30 years experience Oliver Sherwood has trained in excess of 1100 winners including 6 at the Cheltenham Festival, 2 Hennessy's and a Grand National plus a whole host of listed races.

Oliver has a string of no more than 60 horses which allows to him to get to know them well and each horse is treated as an individual, most of them will be turned out in the extensive paddocks every day.

Rhonehurst is a picturesque yard set in the heart of Upper Lambourn, situated close to the Jockey Club run gallops which boasts facilities that are second to none.
It is a warm, friendly place and we look forward to welcoming you to meet the team.

Rhonehurst, Lambourn. Hungerford, Berkshire. RG17 8RG
EMAIL: info@oliversherwood.co.uk | TELEPHONE: +44(0)1488 71411
FAX: +44(0)1488 72786 | MOBILE: +44(0)797 959 1867
www.oliversherwood.co.uk

ABACADABRAS LEADS SHISHKIN OVER THE LAST IN THE SUPREME NOVICES' HURDLE

Top-Class
PERFORMERS

AGAIN, as with last year, I thought I would take a look at the leading performers – and those hoping to break through – in each of the main divisions, starting with the two-mile hurdlers.

With dual Champion Hurdle winner Buveur d'Air injured in the Fighting Fifth at Newcastle, it was left to the same connections' **Epatante** to take up the mantle, and despite beginning the campaign in handicap company, she rounded off her season by providing owner JP McManus with a fourth successive win in the Champion Hurdle. The six-year-old made a winning reappearance – incidentally on the same day that Buveur d'Air suffered his injury – at Newbury, winning from a mark of 137 under Aidan Coleman. Her progression from there saw her land the Christmas Hurdle in taking fashion, before justifying favouritism in the feature on day one at Cheltenham.

GOSHEN

EPATANTE

The daughter of No Risk At All travelled with ease in the Champion, and was delivered with a perfectly-timed challenge, by the now-retired Barry Geraghty. Whilst she clearly sets the standard in the division, she is rated just 162, a rating which is not insurmountable for those hoping to take the step into open company. In fairness, Epatante has herself had just the six starts over hurdles, so could well be open to further improvement this season, and she is certainly the one who the second-season hurdlers have to beat. Given the route often taken by Nicky Henderson, I would expect her to head up to Newcastle to contest the Fighting Fifth on reappearance, after which she will, no doubt, be aimed at Kempton, a track which clearly suits her potent turn of foot.

Second in the betting for the Champion Hurdle at this stage is **Goshen**, who would have run out a facile winner of the Triumph but for parting company with Jamie Moore after the final flight. The winner of his first three starts over hurdles,

Gary Moore's four-year-old ended the campaign with an official rating of 157, leaving him with just 5lbs to find with the current Champion Hurdle winner, according to the handicapper. Having been a bit wayward in his earlier races, personally I was concerned about him handling the occasion and the track at Cheltenham, but he really would have destroyed the field if he would have successfully negotiated that final obstacle. Even allowing for the fact that it might not have been the strongest of Triumph Hurdles, it would have been a deeply impressive performance. Expected to return to the Flat through the summer, he hadn't been seen under that code at the time of going to print, and the Masterson Holdings Hurdle – back at Cheltenham in October – would appeal as a good starting point, giving him one more opportunity to take on his own age group, before being forced into open company.

It will be fascinating to see if he can take that step, and his first chance to attempt to bridge the gap is likely to come in either the International Hurdle (Cheltenham, December) or in the Christmas Hurdle on Boxing Day. Despite the victory of Espoir d'Allen two years ago, the record of five-year-olds in the Champion Hurdle remains pretty desperate, with just two winning in the past 34 years, from 104 who have taken their chance. Despite the division appearing to lack any real strength-in-depth, his current price to win the Champion Hurdle next March (5-1 best, and generally a 9-2 shot) looks a little on the skinny side at this stage.

With Shishkin and Envoi Allen – respective winners of the Supreme and Ballymore – expected to go novice chasing, the novice from last season who looks most likely to make an impact in this division is **Abacadabras**, who was beaten by just a head in the festival opener back in March. Fourth in the Champion Bumper the previous season, he quickly developed into a high-class novice, beating subsequent Grade 1 winner Latest Exhibition on his second start, and giving stable-mate Envoi Allen a race in the Royal Bond. A Grade 1 winner over Christmas, he travelled like a dream in the Supreme, and looked all over the winner coming down the hill. Perhaps if he had been asked to kick clear on the home-bend the result might have been different, but he was still in front jumping the final flight, and might well have been beaten by a top-class performer in what looked to be a very strong renewal of the race. Already rated 158 in Ireland (I.H.R.B. Ratings) he doesn't have too much to find with Epatante, and would make more appeal than Goshen at the prices (currently a general 7-1 chance) for the Champion Hurdle.

He could return in the WKD Hurdle at Down Royal – a meeting that Gordon Elliott likes to target – after which the Morgiana would be the obvious race before Christmas, followed by the Irish Champion Hurdle. Given the lack of a real standout two-miler over in Ireland, his price could contract considerably throughout the season, should he take control of the division on home soil.

Following his victory in the County Hurdle (from a mark 137), **Saint Roi** has an I.H.R.B. Rating of 151, so is only 7lbs behind Abacadabras, according to the Irish handicapper, and given that he has had just the four starts over hurdles, it wouldn't be inconceivable to think that he could make up into a Champion Hurdle contender. I have included him amongst this year's *Leading Prospects* in the hope that he goes chasing, but Willie Mullins and JP McManus might just consider starting him off in a conditions hurdle, especially when considering that the leading owner doesn't appear have anything else to run in the division (in Ireland) this season. The form of his Cheltenham success was given a boost during the summer, when runner-up and stable-mate **Aramon** won the Grimes Hurdle, then

followed up under top-weight in the Galway Hurdle. Having won that handicap off 155 (now rated 163 in Ireland), the seven-year-old is another who could enter the equation for Grade 1s this season.

Last year's Morgiana Hurdle was won by **Saldier** who was forced to miss the Champion Hurdle, and has actually only been sighted once in each of the past two seasons. He picked up an injury when winning the Punchestown Grade 1 last November, and that kept him off the track over Christmas, after which his recovery took longer than expected. At the time of being ruled out of the festival, it was mentioned that he could be back for Punchestown, so you would like to think that he will be ready to return this autumn, and he remains unexposed after just the six starts (same as Epatante) over hurdles. At a general 25-1, he could be the 'forgotten horse' in the Champion Hurdle picture.

With Saldier an absentee, last season's Irish Champion Hurdle went the way of **Honeysuckle**, who battled on strongly to beat Darver Star (subsequently third in the Champion Hurdle). Henry de Bromhead and Kenneth Alexander then resisted the temptation of taking on the boys at Cheltenham, instead stepping their mare back up in distance to face her own sex. She, of course, got the better of Benie des Dieux in what was a fantastic tactical-battle, to maintain her 100% record, and it would seem that – should she remain over hurdles (and that is reported to be the case) – following up in the same race would be the main aim. Her first big target will again be the Hatton's Grace at Fairyhouse, a course where she has won five of her eight races over hurdles. Personally, being a wide margin Point-to-Point winner, I would have loved to have seen her sent chasing. She certainly has the physique for it and I think she would make a top-class novice if her connections have a re-think; she would have numerous Grade 1 options between 2m and 2m4f.

SAINT ROI (CENTRE)

HONEYSUCKLE

Looking at the three-mile division, the pre-season Stayers' Hurdle market is headed by **Paisley Park**, with last season's winner Lisnagar Oscar a general 16-1 shot. The former, who had of course won the race in 2019, was sent off at 4-6 to retain his crown in March, following victories in Newbury's Long Distance Hurdle, and in the Cleeve on trials day. His dominance over the division warranted such a short-price, and following his seventh place, he was subsequently found to have an issue with his heart. When he returns to action, he will wear a heart monitor in his work, and we should learn plenty from his reappearance, which will probably again come at Newbury. Whilst I sincerely hope that he returns to his best this season, I will be waiting until seeing him on the track again before making any sort of conclusive judgement.

On the day, **Lisnagar Oscar** run out a worthy winner, but he was officially rated just 146 going into the festival, and the division has a wide-open feel to it at present. Now rated 160, he has the option of going chasing again, but I suspect that he will remain over hurdles, with the aim being for him to return to Cheltenham to defend his crown.

Of the potential new blood in the division, Latest Exhibition would be of interest in Ireland – although he is believed to be going chasing along with Monkfish and Fury Road – so it could be that **Thyme Hill** is the second-season hurdler, with the potential to make a big impact. Already rated 151 after just four starts over hurdles, he raced exclusively in Graded events last season, winning the Persian War, Hyde, and Challow before the turn of the year. Third behind Envoi Allen in the 2019 Champion Bumper (finished one place in front of the aforementioned Abacadabras), he was sent off favourite for the Albert Bartlett, and didn't get much luck in running. Having been kept wide throughout, he looked to go between Latest Exhibition and Monkfish on the run to the final flight, and was short of room between Monkfish and Fury Road after the last. The front four were 10 lengths clear of the remainder, and on another day, the result might well have been different. If the three Irish-trained runners who finished in front of him – as well as the main protagonists from the Ballymore – do indeed go chasing, he looks to be the one who could step forward. Expected to return to action in the West Yorkshire Hurdle at Wetherby, Philip Hobbs' six-year-old looks a fair price (16-1 best) in an open-looking year.

Hobbs could have another potential player in the division, should JP McManus opt not to go chasing with **Sporting John**. Prior to the festival, he had looked a high-class novice last season, and the Coral Hurdle at Ascot would appeal as a good starting point in November. He won over course-and-distance on his third start for Hobbs in mid-February, and it would be a good stepping-stone before attempting 3m at some stage. The Relkeel Hurdle – staged over an extended 2m4f at Cheltenham on New Year's Day – would be another option over an intermediate trip, and there would certainly be worse 40-1 shots than him, should he be committed to remaining over hurdles.

The past two renewals of the Coral Hurdle were won by **If The Cap Fits**, who wasn't seen after finishing only fifth in the Cleeve, in which Lisnagar Oscar finished only third incidentally (in receipt of 3lbs from Paisley Park). He will be carrying the colours of Simon Munir and Isaac Souede when he does return to action and is a high-class performer on his day, with his victory at Aintree in 2019 his first start over 3m. Unexposed as a stayer, he is still only eight and with relatively low-mileage on the clock, having had just the 10 starts over hurdles. However, it is believed that he could go novice chasing this season.

Unless we are dealing with a multiple-winner (which can happen in this race) the Stayers' Hurdle is a race which tends to favour second-sea-

LISNAGAR OSCAR

THYME HILL

MINELLA INDO, CHAMP (CENTRE) AND ALLAHO

son hurdlers (12 of the past 20 winners fall into this category), and one more who might enter the fray is **McFabulous**. Being a novice until the end of November, he could well reappear in the Persian War at Chepstow, and an impressive display there could tee up a crack at the Long Distance Hurdle at Newbury, or the Long Walk at Ascot.

Over in Ireland, there doesn't appear to be too much strength-in-depth in the staying hurdle division, especially if the main protagonists from the Albert Bartlett (in particular Latest Exhibition) do indeed go chasing, as expected. Given the manner in which she won the Galmoy Hurdle in January, it would be fascinating to see **Benie des Dieux** aimed

AL BOUM PHOTO

at the Stayers' Hurdle this season. The Frank Ward Memorial Hurdle at Leopasrdstown over Christmas would be another option for the top-class mare over a staying trip, which would mean that she could avoid Honeysuckle, at least until Cheltenham. A re-match in the Close Brothers Mares' Hurdle is an exciting prospect (and is probably a race that will materialise), although given the open feel to the Stayers' Hurdle picture at present, that could be the easier option come next March. The versatile nine-year-old – who remains unexposed as a stayer – could certainly dominate the division domestically, beforehand.

Moving onto the chasers, and starting with the stayers, two-time Gold Cup winner **Al Boum Photo** is the obvious place to start. Given that he followed an identical path back to Cheltenham last season, it is safe to assume that he will once again be given a light-campaign, with the hat-trick bid in mind. Expect to see him return to Tramore on New Year's Day (if it isn't broke, why fix it?) and he obviously sets the standard, in terms of looking at the Gold Cup itself. He perhaps didn't travel quite as well as he did in 2019 (kept a shade wider than the previous year), but he kept on all the way to the line, just holding off the late-challenge of Santini. With a decent-looking crop of staying novices coming through, he might need to improve upon last year's form, if he is to make it three-in-a-row.

Runner-up **Santini** run a huge race, and would have got up in another stride or two. He hadn't really impressed in his victories earlier in the campaign, and did just get caught out for tactical speed on the run to two-out. Despite being eight, he has only had the six chase starts, and he showed a fine attitude to claw back three or four lengths in the final half-furlong. Again, the Cotswold Chase at Cheltenham on trials day would appeal as the most suitable mid-season race for him, with the likes of Kempton and Haydock tighter than ideal. He is a thorough stayer.

Third home in March, **Lostintranslation** also run a big race, especially when you consider how most of the stable's runners performed during the week. He travelled with purpose and looked a huge threat turning in, only really giving way in the dying strides. Given how impressive he was at Haydock earlier in the season, he will surely be aimed at the Betfair Chase once again, after which it will be interesting to see if his connections opt to have another crack at the King George. Pulled-up last year, that clearly wasn't his running, and the wind-operation prior to Cheltenham clearly worked. Although horses beaten in the Gold Cup don't have a particularly good record when returning, the one anomaly on that statistic in recent years was Native River, who finished third in 2017, before winning it the following year. He, too, was of course trained by Colin Tizzard, and in comparison to the front two in the betting (who are half the price or less), Lostintranslation could represent the each-way value from last season's contest (14-1 at present).

Clan des Obeaux finished only eighth in the Gold Cup, and as I stated in last year's book, the King George will once again offer him the best chance to land another Grade 1. He was hugely impressive at Kempton on Boxing Day, although you do have to factor in that Lostinstranslation clearly failed to give his running, and his stable-mate Cyrname was a blatant non-stayer on the day. His season will likely be geared around winning the festive showpiece, as he doesn't get the trip in the Gold Cup.

Nicky Henderson might well have two bullets to fire come next March, with RSA winner **Champ** currently third best in the Gold Cup market. A two-time Grade 1 winning novice hurdler, the eight-year-old was far from foot-perfect in his first three starts over fences, culminating in a heavy-fall in the Dipper on New Year's Day. Henderson was unable to get a prep-run into Champ ahead of the festival (ruled out of the Reynoldstown due to concerns about him racing right-handed, then he was due to run at Kelso only for that to be abandoned) and he, again, didn't jump especially fluently. Watching the

race back, it is still hard to believe he gets up and wins, given his position when pecking two out, but he really will need to jump much better this season in open company. He clearly has an awful lot of natural ability, and is a horse that I am a huge fan of, but he can't win a Gold Cup – in my opinion – unless he improves, in that respect. With that in mind, I imagine that he will be kept relatively low-key to begin with and expect him to be considered for the Future Stars Intermediate Chase at Sandown, a race which Henderson has won with both Might Bite and Santini in the past three seasons. This will also confirm whether or not there really is an issue with him racing on a right-handed track, a theory which I'm not convinced by, as he has run well at Kempton, Ascot and Perth – albeit against lesser opposition – in the past. Should Henderson wish to keep Champ to a left-handed track, the Grade 2 Many Clouds Chase at Aintree would be another possible starting point.

I really hope he does prove me wrong and develops into a leading contender for the Gold Cup, but for now, I'm happy to watch him during the first half of the season. If – and I am purely only playing devil's advocate here – things didn't go to plan early on in the campaign, I wonder if Champ might just end up reverting back to hurdles for a crack at the Stayers'. In fairness to him, his jumping – on the whole – is quite safe, it just lacked fluency last season, but that could still come after just four chase starts.

The placed horses in the RSA are even less-exposed as chasers, as both had run just twice before the festival. In terms of developing into a Gold Cup contender, **Minella Indo** would be the more obvious of the pair, as he appears to have plenty of stamina in reserve. The winner of the Albert Bartlett in 2019 (also went on to win the Grade 1 at Punchestown, again beating Allaho), Henry de Bromhead's seven-year-old might well have prevailed in the RSA, had he not paddled his way through the last fence. He will need to relax a little more this season (was quite keen in the RSA), but he appeals as the type of horse to progress with experience, and he looks to be a potential major player in the big Irish staying races this season, such as the Savills Chase and the Irish Gold Cup, although the same connections also have **Monalee** (fourth in the Gold Cup) for such events. A nice problem to have, I'm sure.

Just one place further back in the Gold Cup was **Delta Work**, who struggled to get involved at Cheltenham, with a couple of untimely errors (notably the one seven fences from home) probably proving quite costly. He had earlier won the aforementioned Savills Chase and Irish Gold Cup, and will again be aimed at such races, no doubt. He is still only seven and has had just the nine chase starts.

Back to the English challenge and **Topoftthegame** – who beat both Santini and Delta Work in the 2019 RSA – is expected to return to action in late-November, with Newbury's Ladbrokes Trophy pencilled in as his likely starting point. He travelled beautifully that day and won what turned out to be the race of the festival that year. Ahead of last year's festival, I was slightly concerned about his stamina, so it will be interesting to see how he fares at Newbury over an extended 3m1f, as that will give us a good indication to his Gold Cup prospects. Evidently not the easiest to train, there is no doubt that he has the ability to mix it at this level, and if all went well at Newbury, I would imagine that he would return there for his Gold Cup-prep in the Denman Chase next February.

Before we 'drop in trip', I wanted to briefly touch upon **Burrows Saint**, who won the Irish Grand National in 2019. I thought he had the ideal profile for Aintree last season, with the one exception being that he was only seven (the last seven-year-old winner of the National was in 1940). Willie Mullins' seven-year-old remains very-lightly raced over fences (had just the eight starts) and ran out a ready winner of a hurdle race at Punchestown on New Year's Eve last year. I would expect him to be campaigned similarly this time around, with Aintree firmly to the forefront of Mullins' mind. It could be that the Bobbyjo Chase is an option in the build-up to the National (staged after the weights are announced, of course) and last year – with Tiger Roll set to race off a mark of 170 – he was set to carry 10-10 from a mark of 156. Something similar would be just fine come next April, and although it isn't a race that I tend to look at in advance as a rule, the 25-1 on offer with several firms about Burrows Saint seems more than fair at this stage, as does the 20-1 (Non-Runner-No Bet) with SkyBet.

Let's go back to this year's RSA, whilst moving forward to look at the middle-distance division. The horse in question is **Allaho**, who finished third behind Champ, whilst leaving the impression that he would have gone very close in the Marsh. Like the runner-up Minella Indo, he had only had the two previous chase starts, winning emphatically at the second attempt. Although it is difficult to say that he 'doesn't stay' as he has finished placed in an Albert Bartlett and the RSA, given his positive way of racing, allowing him to bowl along over 2m4f – 2m5f might be the best way forward. Cheveley Park Stud also have A Plus Tard for similar races, but he can operate over even shorter, and I would like to see Allaho trained with the Ryanair in mind,

as opposed to the Gold Cup. There are plenty of good races over intermediate trips earlier in the campaign – with the John Durkan and Ascot Chase two Grade 1 options – and if he were ready in time, the Grade 2 at Down Royal would be the ideal starting point, being for second-season chasers only. The Horse & Jockey Hotel Chase (or the Kinloch Brae as it was formerly known) at Thurles would be another good option for him in the New Year.

Willie Mullins also has **Min** for the John Durkan (won it for the past two years) and Ryanair, and keeping them apart would be advisable, with both horses wanting to get on with things. He gained a much-deserved festival success in the Ryanair last season and he is at his best when able to dictate (as he did when winning with 2019 Melling Chase in imperious fashion). However, he is nine turning 10 this season, whilst Allaho – being only six – is clearly open to significantly more improvement as a chaser. Min certainly begins the season as the one who sets the standard over this sort of trip.

Following his narrow victory in the Marsh, **Samcro** (and runner-up **Melon**) are another pair to note in this division. Following his defeat at Limerick over Christmas, it was a fantastic training performance from Gordon Elliott to bring him back to his best, winning at the festival for a second

SAMCRO (NEARSIDE) AND MELON

time in three years. Given that he won at the fixture last year – and the fact that we know Elliott likes to target the meeting – he is likely to reappear in the aforementioned Grade 2 event at Down Royal.

It certainly looks to be a strong division over in Ireland, with A Plus Tard and Fakir d'Oudairies another pair, who might end up in the Ryanair. I will touch upon both of those shortly, but in England, there wouldn't appear to be as much strength-in-depth. Ryanair runner-up **Saint Calvados** probably sets the standard at present, and the fact that he has now seen out two races over 2m4½f, offers his connections more options going forward. The same

DEFI DU SEUIL

set of connections also have **Simply The Betts** to call upon, and he will now be forced into Graded company, having been rated 157 by the assessor. He started last season rated just 125, so will need to take another big step forward this season.

Similarly, fellow festival handicap winner **Imperial Aura** will have to step up, having also been rated 157. Given that neither horse has raced in a Graded event (with the exception of graded handicaps) to date, their ratings appear somewhat excessive. If there is a second-season chaser to breakthrough at the top-level over this sort of trip in England, it could well be **Brewin'upastorm**, who was having just his third chase start when unseating Richard Johnson in the Arkle. He wasn't really seeing his races out the previous spring, so came back in distance following a wind-operation. It is likely that his optimum will end up being around the 2m4f mark, and Olly Murphy's seven-year-old remains a horse of considerable potential. As I have stated elsewhere in this year's book (see *Around The Yards*) he could reappear in the Haldon Gold Cup, or more likely the Colin Parker at Carlisle, after which races such as the Peterborough Chase and/or the Silviniaco Conti will be suitable mid-season options. He is currently a 33-1 shot for the Ryanair (whereas the other pair are 25s) and I could see that contract-

ing through the winter. I actually think the Melling Chase at Aintree – where he ran so well as a novice hurdler – could be the ideal spring target for him.

Ascot Chase winner **Riders Onthe Storm** was well-purchased ahead of last season, and could return to action in the Old Roan at Aintree, from a lofty mark of 162. He wasn't far away when falling three out in the Ryanair, a race in which I thought he might struggle, having had such a tough race at Ascot. I would imagine that the Ascot Chase will once again form part of his schedule, although I think he would stay 3m on a sharp track (if ridden with a bit more restraint), which could open up more options.

Cyrname – who was touched upon earlier – was beaten when taking that very heavy fall at the final fence. It is quite possible that his battle with Altior from the beginning of the season took a lot out of him, but if anyone can get him back to his very best it is Paul Nicholls. It seems that his trainer is preparing to give him another chance to prove his stamina over 3m – with a trip to Down Royal mentioned as a possible starting point – after which I wouldn't be at all surprised to see him aimed at the Ascot Chase once again.

The 2018 Ascot Chase was won by **Waiting Patiently** who only saw the track once last term,

PUT THE KETTLE ON

when running a big race in the Tingle Creek. He was put in his place by Cyrname the following year, but didn't appear at his best that day, nor when well-beaten by Min at Aintree. It was, therefore, nice to see Ruth Jefferson's stable-star post such a positive effort on his reappearance last season, something which promised much for when he was stepped back up in trip. Sadly, that didn't materialise (met with another setback), and he is another who I really hope returns to action this winter. Despite being nine, he has raced sparingly in recent seasons and has still only had 10 starts over fences.

Another horse who was in Grade 1-winning form at Ascot last season was **Defi du Seuil** who is a good place to start when assessing the two-mile chase division. He had already won the Shloer Chase at Cheltenham and the Tingle Creek at Sandown by the time he impressively beat Un de Sceaux in the Clarence House in January. With the opposition falling by the wayside (even on the day), he was sent off at 2-5 to win the Queen Mother Champion Chase, but simply never travelled. Having beaten the winner twice earlier in the campaign, it is evident that he didn't perform on the day. Assuming he returns to his best this autumn, I would expect him to be campaigned similarly, although there is the chance that he could go back up in distance, with much of his novice chase form coming around 2m4f.

Altior was one of those non-runners in the Champion Chase, having earlier returned to winning ways in impressive fashion in Newbury's Game Spirit Chase. Having appeared not to get home behind Cyrname at Ascot, he recorded a 15th win from 16 starts over fences, when winning at Newbury, and is now likely to remain over the minimum trip. The Tingle Creek and Kempton's Desert Orchid Chase are options in the first half of the season, after which the Game Spirit could tee up another tilt at the Queen Mother. It should be remembered that he is 10 turning 11 this season, and Moscow Flyer (when regaining his crown in 2005) is the only 11-year-old winner of the Champion Chase in the past 43 years.

Another late withdrawal from the race in March was **Chacun Pour Soi**, who had earlier finished runner-up to A Plus Tard over Christmas, before running out an impressive winner of the Dublin Chase. Despite being eight, he has only had five runs over fences (and only three runs over hurdles) and they looked to go a proper gallop when he beat the same connections' Min (had won the race the previous two seasons and franked the form in the Ryanair Chase). His jumping is assured and he looks a worthy favourite at this stage for the Queen Mother, given that he is probably capable of further improvement. It hasn't been a good race for Willie Mullins to date, but I would expect Chacun Pour Soi to enjoy another successful campaign, and head to Cheltenham as a leading contender. The Dublin Chase will, again, likely be the main objective prior to the festival.

A Plus Tard had match-fitness on his side when beating him at Leopardstown's Christmas Festival, then was pulled-out – due to the drying ground – in February. I was slightly disappointed with his effort in the Ryanair, and it could be that he ends up contesting that race again come the spring, but given that his biggest success to date came in that

2m1f contest over Christmas, I thought he should feature in this division. He could follow a similar path – starting off in the Fortria Chase at Navan – or, the John Durkan would be the obvious early-season target, should Henry de Bromhead want to keep him to 2m4f or thereabouts. Still only six, he remains a top-class prospect, and there certainly appears to be more depth to this division in Ireland than in England.

Indeed, de Bromhead also has **Notebook** and Put The Kettle On to consider for similar races. The former was sent off favourite for the Arkle in March, having won a brace of Grade 1s at Leopardstown. He didn't look totally comfortable coming down the hill at Cheltenham, and might be more suited back on a more galloping track this season, whilst it could also be that he had a much tougher race than first thought in the Irish Arkle, with **Cash Back** also well-beaten when he falling two out at Cheltenham. Returning to Leopardstown will suit Notebook, although he will need to relax in the prelims if he is to build on a fine novice campaign (was worked up and bolted to the start before the Irish Arkle).

Stable-companion **Put The Kettle On** landed the Arkle, fending off the challenge of Fakir d'Oudairies under Aidan Coleman. That was her first start since winning the Grade 2 at the November meeting, and her jumping is a huge asset. Whilst she would need to take another big step forward, she will have the option of stepping up to 2m4f (a multiple winner at that distance) for the new mares' only race, which would appeal as the obvious spring target.

Arkle runner-up **Fakir d'Oudairies** is another to add further depth to the 2m – 2m4f chase division in Ireland, as his form was solid throughout the whole of last season, and he might well have prevailed at the festival, but for making a shuddering error two out. He made the most of the weight he received from Melon to win on debut, and then was upsides Samcro when that rival fell two out in the Drinmore. Mark Walsh lost an iron on the home turn when beaten by Notebook over Christmas, and he could be in for a fruitful campaign, given his versatility. He jumped really well in the main last season, and is quite experienced for his age (five) given that he ran over fences in France as a three-year-old, before joining Joseph O'Brien. Whilst it wouldn't be a huge surprise to see him stepped back up in distance eventually, I would expect him to be campaigned over the minimum trip whilst the ground is soft.

To conclude, it is back to England and the winner of the Champion Chase **Politologue**. Despite the obvious disappointment of Defi du Seuil, there was no denying that the grey was the worthy winner on the day. It was a fantastic training performance from Paul Nicholls, who had freshened him up following a below-par run in the Tingle Creek. He had earlier attempted to give Defi du Seuil 3lbs when runner-up in the Shloer Chase, and his jumping was exceptional in the Queen Mother. Being nine, it is hard to imagine that he will be an improver this season and it is difficult to believe that the Champion Chase won't be a stronger race next March. His win at Cheltenham was actually his first since November 2018 and I suspect that his races might now be spaced apart.

GOOD BOY BOBBY HAS THE RIGHT KIND OF PROFILE FOR THE BETVICTOR GOLD CUP

Big-Race
TRENDS

BETVICTOR GOLD CUP

Cheltenham (Old course) - 2m4f 44y (Grade 3 handicap)

Saturday 14th November 2020

OVERVIEW

CHELTENHAM'S November meeting signifies the switching of codes for many, with it being the first major fixture in the National Hunt season, and the BetVictor Gold Cup is the feature race of the three-day meeting.

Although last year's winner was in her third season over fences, it tends to be a race which favours an unexposed (often a second-season) chaser. That is actually the case with many of the feature handicaps in the early part of the season, so looking for horses with scope for improvement is hugely important around this time.

WEIGHTS AND OFFICIAL RATINGS

LAST year's winner *Happy Diva* became the ninth winner in the past 15 years to be rated in the 140s, whilst a further three winners won off a mark of 139. Therefore, 12 out of the past 15 winners were rated between 139 and 149, with only one winner (*Splash Of Ginge*) winning from a rating below that 139 marker during this same period. The two horses to have won from in the 150s during this time – *Al Ferof* (159) and *Taquin du Seuil* (156) – were Grade 1 winners as novices, so clearly possessed a lot of class.

In terms of weight carried, last year's winner became just the fourth horse in 13 years to carry 11-stone (or more) to victory, but perhaps more significantly, the third winner to do so in the past five years. Like Happy Diva, 2015 winner *Annacotty* carried exactly 11-stone, so the only two to shoulder more were the aforementioned high-class pairing, *Al Ferof* and *Taquin du Seuil*.

Unless you are looking at a genuine Grade 1 performer, I would be inclined to focus on those rated in the 140s and those carrying no more than 11-stone.

PREP RUN OR FRESH?

LAST year I highlighted that 10 of the previous 20 winners had run earlier in the season (one of which being in July in the Galway Plate), so there was no real evidence to suggest whether there was any benefit in having had a prep-run. However, *Happy Diva* became the fourth successive winner to arrive at Cheltenham with a recent run under her belt, so perhaps it is becoming a more significant trend. She

actually finished runner-up in the **bet365 Handicap Chase** – a Listed race at Wetherby's Charlie Hall fixture – and *Splash Of Ginge* had used the same race as a springboard to victory two years earlier.

Another northern-based race which was a good guide to the BetVictor Gold Cup not so long back was the **Colin Parker Memorial Intermediate Chase** from Carlisle. *Exotic Dancer* (2nd) and *L'Antartique* (1st) were back-to-back winners of this (2006 and 2007) to have run in that race, whilst *Little Josh* dead-heated in it prior to winning this race. Last year's Colin Parker representative in the BetVictor was the same stable's Count Meribel, who could finish only sixth, but it still proved to be a strong event, with Betfair Chase winner Lostintranslation successful, whilst Kildisart (later finished runner-up at the festival) was back in third. Pay close attention to that contest on Sunday 1st November, although there is only that 13-day gap between the two races.

The other pair of recent winners to have had a run already – *Taquin du Seuil* and *Baron Alco* – had run at Chepstow's two-day October meeting. That fixture continues to grow so could continue to offer a springboard to the BetVictor, especially this season as it would seem likely that trainers/owners will be keen to get their horses out nice and early, following the prolonged summer break.

LIGHTLY-RACED OVER FENCES

AS touched upon in the *Overview*, this has – in the main – been a race which has favoured second-season / lightly-raced chasers, since the turn of the century. However, *Happy Diva* became the fourth 'more-experienced' winner in the past five years, winning this race on her 15th start over fences.

2018 winner *Baron Alco* was a second-season chaser, who had raced only seven times over fences previously, whilst all 11 winners between 2004 and 2014 had raced no more than nine times over fences, with several also falling into the second-season category. Last year's result might have been so different had Slate House not fallen two out, as he was travelling ominously well at the time, and was in that second-season bracket. He had won a novice chase at the track the month previous, and previous course form is arguably the strongest trend on offer for this race.

PREVIOUS COURSE FORM

HAPPY DIVA was still travelling well when brought-down in the 2018 renewal, and she returned to the track to finish a sound second behind Aso on the New course on New Year's Day in 2019. She also finished runner-up in a mares' only event at the April meeting that year, and those placed efforts made her the ninth straight winner to have won or placed at Cheltenham previously.

Since the turn of the century, 13 of the 20 winners had won over fences at the course previously, whilst another four had placed. *Caid du Berlais* hadn't actually run at the course as a chaser (the only winner during this period to fall into that category), but he had twice finished placed in handicap hurdles at the festival, so was hardly devoid of course form.

Course form is almost essential when looking at this race.

A couple of this year's festival winners – **Imperial Aura** and **Simply The Betts** – would normally fit the ideal profile for this race, but both have since been hammered by the handicapper, and could find life tough this year from their revised marks. Both are now rated 157, and could, therefore, be forced into open company.

GRADE 1 CLASS

ALONG with the Ladbrokes Trophy at Newbury, several of these early-season handicaps offer younger horses the chance to win a big handicap before going on to better things, and several recent winners of this ended up as genuine Graded-class performers. And, as highlighted last year, 14 winners since the turn of the century had already contested a Grade 1 race at some stage, with four – *Tranquil Sea*, *Al Ferof*, *Annacotty* and *Taquin du Seuil* – having already won at the very highest level.

Last year's winner didn't enhance this record, but again, had Slate House stood up, he had contested Grade 1 novice hurdles and went on to win the Kauto Star Novices' Chase on Boxing Day, so it is something to take seriously.

AGE

NINE of the past 17 winners were aged seven, which again hints at the younger up-and-coming horse. During the past 13 years, only *Johns Spirit* (aged six) and *Caid du Berlais* (five) have won at a younger age than seven.

The record of five-year-olds is an interesting one, with only Paul Nicholls running a horse of that age during the past seven years. *Caid du Berlais* was successful for that age group and there is every chance that the ill-fated Granit Jack would have done the same back in 2007, as he was cruising

KEY TRENDS

- ⭐ 12 of the past 15 winners were rated between 139 – 149
- ⭐ 17 of the past 20 winners had won or placed over fences at Cheltenham
- ⭐ 12 of the past 16 winners had 9 or less chase starts
- ✓ 14 winners this century had contested a Grade 1
- ✓ The past 4 winners had run already this season
- ✓ 9 of the past 17 winners were aged 7
- ✓ 12 winners this century were sent off at single-figures
- ✓ The past 9 winners had won (6) or placed (3) at Cheltenham previously (over fences or hurdles)
- ✓ Respect Nigel Twiston-Davies' runners
- ✓ Respect Jonjo O'Neill's runners
- ✗ Only 1 winner this century had not run over fences at Cheltenham
- ✗ Only 1 winner in the past 15 years rated below 139
- ✗ Only 2 winners in the past 13 years carried more than 11-0
- ✗ Only 1 winning 5yo since 1999 (and 2 in total)
- ✗ Only 4 winners this century rated 150 or higher
- ✗ Nicky Henderson is 0/25 since winning the race in 2003

when taking a fatal fall two out. Nicky Henderson is the only other trainer to saddle a five-year-old in the past decade, with that season's King George and Gold Cup winner Long Run finishing third on his reappearance in 2010 (also saddled Triolo d'Alene two years later). The record during the past decade stands at just the one winner from nine who have tried, and *Cyfor Malta* (1998) was the only other five-year-old winner.

MARKET FORCES

12 WINNERS this century were sent off at single-figure odds, with five outright favourites winning, although none since *Tranquil Sea* in 2009. A further four winners were priced between 10-1 and 14-1 (*Happy Diva* returning at this price last year) so it can pay – in general – to focus on the top-end of the market.

TRAINERS TO NOTE

HAVING first won it with *Tipping Tim* in 1992, **Nigel Twiston-Davies** has won this on four occasions in total, with his other trio coming in the past 12 years. Subsequent Gold Cup winner *Imperial Commander* (2008) got the ball rolling for this fine recent record, with *Little Josh* (2010) and, more recently, *Splash Of Ginge* making it three winners from 13 runners during the past 12 years. Backing all of the Twiston-Davies runners during this time would have yielded a healthy profit of £41.50 to a level-stake of £1.

It could be that Twiston-Davies relies on **Good Boy Bobby** this year, and he would be a fascinating contender. Runner-up when trying to concede 5lbs to Mister Fisher at Cheltenham last December, he has yet to be really tested in a big-field event, but from a mark of 146, he would appeal as one of the more well-treated second-season chasers. He will be sporting the double green silks of Simon Munir and Isaac Souede this season and he looks an ideal candidate based on several of the key trends. A former *Leading Prospect* in this publication, he has Grade 1 form to his name, he has placed form at the track, and he is an unexposed chaser, rated in the 140s. What's not to like?

Another local trainer with a fine record in the race is **Jonjo O'Neill**, who has saddled three winners from 14 runners during the past 14 years. Backing them all would have yielded a profit to the tune of £20 (LSP £1) and since 2013, O'Neill's record stands at two winners from just five runners. He has been without a runner in each of the past three years.

Paul Nicholls has won the race twice in the past eight years, and he has had a horse finish in the first three for the past three years, most recently with Brelan d'As (runner-up) last year. During the last 10 years, Nicholls has saddled 23 runners, so it is clearly a race which he likes to target, and it could be that he runs **Saint Sonnet** this year. He won easily on his British debut at Catterick and shaped better than the bare result in the Marsh at the festival, travelling well for a long way. He is only five, but as we have already seen, his trainer is more than happy to run horses of that age in this race.

The most successful trainer in the history of this race is Martin Pipe, who saddled a remarkable eight winners between 1987 and 2005. Since he retired and handed over the reins at Pond House to **David Pipe**, his son has had just the one winner (*Great Endeavour*) from 20 runners. Several of his runners have been sent off prominently in the market, so it is a record worthy of a degree of caution, although Warthog did run a huge race for him at big odds last year. The grey returned to win the Caspian Caviar the following month, before sadly suffering a fatal injury on trials day.

However, this meeting remains one which the Pipe stable likes to target, and the trainer enjoyed a Sunday double last year, when the well-backed Duc de Beauchene won the opening conditional jockeys' handicap hurdle, and Israel Champ book-ended the card in the Listed bumper. Pipe has actually won that conditional jockeys' race four times in the past nine years (three of which were sent off 13-2 or shorter), so take note if he has a fancied runner in that event – apologies for digressing a little.

Back to matters in hand, and even more of a concerning record is that of **Nicky Henderson**, who is 0/25 since *Fondmort* provided him with his sole win in the race, back in 2003. He was without a runner last year, and whilst I am not saying that he will not win the race again, Henderson does tend to get his horses rolling slightly later than many of the other big yards. As a rule, Newbury's Winter Carnival (a couple of weeks later) tends to be when he really gets going, although he might well have his horses out earlier this year, due to the truncated 2019-20 season.

ROLL OF HONOUR

Year	Form	Winner	Age	Weight	OR	SP	Trainer	Runners	Last Race (No. of days)
2019	2	Happy Diva	8	11-0	143	14/1	K Lee	17	2nd Listed Wetherby Chase (15)
2018	2	Baron Alco	7	10-11	146	8/1	G Moore	18	2nd Chepstow Chase (34)
2017	4	Splash of Ginge	9	10-6	134	25/1	N Twiston-Davies	17	4th Listed Wetherby Chase (15)
2016	6	Taquin du Seuil	9	11-11	155	8/1	J O'Neill	17	6th Gr.3 Chepstow Hurdle (35)
2015		Annacotty	7	11-0	147	12/1	A King	20	fell Gr.3 Topham (218)
2014	7	Caid du Berlais	5	10-13	143	10/1	P Nicholls	18	7th Galway Plate (108)
2013	1	Johns Spirit	6	10-2	139	7/1	J O'Neill	20	1st Cheltenham Chase (28)
2012		Al Ferof	7	11-8	159	8/1	P Nicholls	18	3rd Gr.1 Manifesto (219)
2011		Great Endeavour	7	10-3	147	8/1	D Pipe	20	6th Listed Aintree Chase (217)
2010	1	Little Josh	8	10-5	146	20/1	N Twiston-Davies	19	1st Carlisle Chase (13)

LEADING TEN-YEAR GUIDES

bet365 Handicap Chase 2 (*Splash Of Ginge 4th, Happy Diva 2nd*)

UNIBET GREATWOOD HANDICAP HURDLE

Cheltenham (Old course) - 2m 87y (Grade 3)

Sunday 15th November 2020

OVERVIEW

NOT so long ago, the Greatwood was beginning to have an impact as a Champion Hurdle trial, with *Rooster Booster* completing the double in the same season (2002-03) and five years later *Sizing Europe* won this before winning the Irish Champion Hurdle, resulting in him being sent off 2-1 favourite for the Champion itself. *Khyber Kim* finished runner-up in the Champion Hurdle four months after winning this, whilst 2010 winner *Menorah* won the International Hurdle on his next start (as did *Khyber Kim* 12 months earlier) before finishing fifth in the Champion.

Detroit City (2006) and, more recently, *Old Guard* both also won the International on their next start, so it has been certainly a stepping-stone to Graded success. It is another early-season event in which second-season / lightly-raced hurdlers have a fine record, so look for those unexposed types. Usually strongly-run, the ability to travel comfortably at such a pace tends to be key in all races over the minimum trip around Cheltenham, especially on the Old course.

WEIGHTS AND OFFICIAL RATINGS

LAST year's winner *Harambe* became the seventh winner in the past eight years to have carried 11-stone or less. Alan King's charge carried exactly 11-0 (as did *North Hill Harvey*), whilst only *Garde la Victoire* carried more during this period (11-9). Five of the previous six winners carried 11-4 or more, which again hints that in recent years the race has started to go the way of a top-end handicapper, rather than a horse with aspirations of making an impact at the top-level over hurdles.

As touched upon in the *Overview*, the Greatwood had earlier been won by some very smart hurdlers, and the likes of *Space Trucker* (11-11), *Grey Shot* (11-5), *Rooster Booster* (11-12), *Rigmarole* (11-12) and *Khyber Kim* (11-9) all carried big weights to victory, so it can be done.

Since 2003, 10 of the 17 winners won from a mark in the 140s. Only three winners during this time won from a mark in the 120s, whilst three more – including last year's winner and *Sizing Europe* – won from 136 or 137. Therefore, the percentage play is to focus on those rated from the mid-130s to 149.

Menorah (2010) is the only winner during this 17-year period to win from a mark in the 150s (151), whilst the same stable's *Rooster Booster* won off 155, although as stated above, he won the Champion Hurdle just four months later.

LIGHTY-RACED HURDLERS

HARAMBE became the 16th winner this century to have run nine times or less over hurdles, prior to their Greatwood success. A dozen of those 16 winners had run no more than six times over hurdles, so it really is a race that favours the lightly-raced type.

Again, including last year's winner, 13 of the past 16 winners were second-season hurdlers. Those of you who have read the *Cheltenham Festival Betting Guide* in recent years will be well aware than I am a keen advocate of backing novices in handicaps during the second half of the season, and this is the next step really. Still unexposed and open to more improvement than their older opponents, it is a good time of year for the second-season hurdler/chaser in many of these early-season handicaps.

It should be said, such horses (falling into the 'nine starts or less' category) made up a high proportion of the field last year, with only one of the first seven home being more-exposed, and these did include subsequent Coral Cup winner Dame de Compagnie. She was having her first start in 19 months when running encouragingly in the Greatwood, and won her next two starts, latterly when landing a gamble at the festival. The lightly-raced theme can continue throughout the season, with Pic d'Orhy winning the Betfair Hurdle on just his 10th start; more of that race later.

AGE

RATHER in-keeping with the previous subsection, only two winners this century were older than six. Both *Rooster Booster* (the only winning eight-year-old of this race) and *Khyber Kim* were late-maturing horses, who finished first and second in the Champion Hurdle later the same season, whereas every other winner this century (and since 1992, in fact) were aged six or younger. *Shu Fly* in 1991 was the only other seven-year-old winner.

PREVIOUS COURSE FORM

HARAMBE became just the third winner in the past 14 years to have not run at Cheltenham previously. The other pairing during this time were *Sizing Europe* (trained in Ireland) and *Dell 'Arca* (first run in the UK having been trained in France previously), so despite last year's result, course form would seem advantageous. The second and third from last year had run at the track previously, whilst the fifth home – the aforementioned Dame de Compagnie – was a winner at the track, against her own sex, as a novice.

Six of the 11 recent winners with course form had already won at Cheltenham, whilst three winners during the past 11 years had contested the **Supreme Novices' Hurdle** the previous March. *Menorah* was able to complete the double, whilst the other pairing finished only mid-division in the festival curtain-raiser. It is also worth noting that *Elgin* had also contested the Supreme, albeit a couple of seasons prior to his Greatwood win. Of those who ran in last season's race, fifth and sixth **Allart** and **Edwardstone**, would appeal as a couple of potential candidates for this. Both rated in the low-140s, the pair shaped well in defeat at the festival and are likely to head down the handicap hurdle route.

OTHER 'KEY RACES'

ANOTHER notable guide from the previous season has been Aintree's **Top Novices' Hurdle**, with three of the past nine winners having contested the 2m event at the Grand National meeting. Obviously, last season's meeting was cancelled, so it won't have an impact this year, whilst the **Sodexo Handicap Hurdle** (staged this season on Saturday 31st October) from Ascot has thrown up a couple of winners in the past nine years. Both *Brampour* and *Elgin* were successful in both races, and last year Gumball came within a neck of becoming the third horse to complete the early-season double in nine years. Pay healthy respect to the winner of that race, if turning up at Cheltenham just a couple of weeks later.

PREP RUN OR FRESH?

AGAIN, rather like the previous day's BetVictor Gold Cup, the Greatwood has a fairly even split of horses winning on reappearance or those who have had a run, since the turn of the decade. However, also like the BetVictor, a prep-run is seemingly becoming more significant, with only one winner in the past six (*North Hill Harvey*) winning this on their first start of the season. *Nietzsche* was having his first run over hurdles since the previous May, but had run on the Flat at Newmarket just 16 days earlier.

Last year's front four had all run earlier in the

season, with *Harambe* and Quio de Neuf (4th) also hailing from Chepstow's two-day meeting in mid-October. Respect those with a recent run in the book.

CURRENT FORM

IF using the most recent Flat run of *Nietzsche*, only two winners (*Olofi* and *Harambe*) in the past decade failed to record a first four finish on their previous start. The former was having his first start of the season, so if looking solely at those who had run recently, a prominent showing is a positive. Obviously, last year's winner bucked this trend somewhat, but – in hindsight – probably didn't want the stamina test over 2m3½f on soft ground at Chepstow, which he got in the Persian War.

TRAINERS TO NOTE

HAVING saddled two winners in the past three years **Alan King** seems the logical starting point. King had previously had placed efforts in between

2007 and 2010, when his five runners had all finished third or fourth, after which he only ran three horses over the next five years. In the past four years, he has seen Winter Escape go off a short-priced favourite, after which his fortunes have taken an upturn. His record in the past decade stands at two winners from nine runners, and backing those blindly would have yielded a profit of £19 to a level-stake of £1.

Supreme Novices' sixth **Edwardstone** appeals as the type who could land a valuable handicap this season, so it could be that he represents the Barbury Castle team this year. A keen-going sort, he should be well-suited by strongly-run handicaps, and is very much one to take seriously if we have a dry autumn.

Philip Hobbs has saddled four Greatwood winners since 2002, and went mighty close to winning it for a fifth time, as Gumball was denied by just a neck last year. Hobbs saddled two in the race last year, but only had one runner between *Garde la Victoire* winning in 2010 and then, so is clearly

becoming more selective. Since 2000, Hobbs has saddled 26 horses in the Greatwood in total, although his record in the past 10 years stands at two winners and a second from just 10 runners.

Paul Nicholls has won this race on three occasions since 2003, so again his runners warrant respect. Interestingly, his last two winners were only four, and he has also seen four of his runners since 2013 finish either second (2) or third (2).

Former assistant to Nicholls, **Dan Skelton** has a fine record in 2m-handicap hurdles in general, and he won this race with *North Hill Harvey* in 2016. Blue Heron (4th) and Superb Story (2nd) went close for the stable prior to their winner, and it is a race that Skelton seems to target.

In contrast to those with good records in the race, this is another early-season contest which has so far eluded **Nicky Henderson**. As I alluded to when looking at the BetVictor Gold Cup, Henderson only gets going around this time and his record in the Greatwood since 2003 stands at 0/14. Of those 14 runners, nine were sent off at single-figure odds, and these include four seconds – Caracciola, Aigle d'Or, Cash And Go and Vaniteux – whilst his two runners last year finished fifth and seventh, respectively. His two runners were the only pair in the first 10 home who hadn't had a recent run (either over hurdles or on the Flat) and the aforementioned Dame de Compagnie clearly benefited for the outing.

As I touched upon earlier **Allart** is a horse who could be of interest in handicap hurdles this season, but Henderson's record would have to be slightly concerning if he were to turn up, especially if turning up without a run under his belt.

EDWARDSTONE

ROLL OF HONOUR

Year	Form	Winner	Age	Weight	OR	SP	Trainer	Runners	Last Race (No. of days)
2019	7	Harambe	6	11-0	137	16/1	A King	14	7th G2 Persian War Novices' Hurdle (37)
2018	6	Nietzsche	5	9-7 (3oh)	126	20/1	B Ellison	18	6th Warwick Hurdle (179)*
2017	41	Elgin	5	10-8	145	10/1	A King	13	1st Listed Ascot Hurdle (15)
2016		North Hill Harvey	5	11-0	141	6/1	D Skelton	16	4th Aintree Nov. Hurdle (219)
2015	1	Old Guard	4	10-10	145	12/1	P Nicholls	17	1st Cheltenham Hurdle (23)
2014	3	Garde La Victoire	5	11-9	144	10/1	P Hobbs	15	3rd Aintree Hurdle (22)
2013	212	Dell' Arca	4	10-5	128	12/1	D Pipe	18	2nd Auteuil Hurdle (157)
2012		Olofi	6	10-11	136	8/1	T George	18	16th Gr.3 County Hurdle (247)
2011	1	Brampour	4	11-4	149	12/1	P Nicholls	24	1st Listed Ascot Hurdle (15)
2010		Menorah	5	11-12	151	6/1	P Hobbs	17	2nd Gr.2 Aintree Nov. Hurdle (219)

LEADING TEN-YEAR GUIDES

Previous season's Supreme Novices' Hurdle 2 *(Menorah 1st, North Hill Harvey 9th)*
Previous season's Top Novices' Hurdle 3 *(Menorah 2nd, Brampour 9th, North Hill Harvey 4th)*
Sodexo Handicap Hurdle 2 *(Brampour 1st, Elgin 1st)*

* *Nietzche had two Flat runs, at Ayr (23rd June) and Newmarket (2nd November), prior to the Greatwood*

BETFAIR STAYERS' HANDICAP HURDLE

Haydock - 3m 58y (Grade 3)

Saturday 21st November 2020

OVERVIEW

STILL referred to by many as the 'Fixed Brush Hurdle' those obstacles were used between 2007 and 2016, after which the track stopped using the portable hurdles and returned to standard flights for all hurdle races. The distance of the race has changed on more than one occasion, but the race is currently staged over an extended 3m, although you do need a horse who has the speed to hold their position around the tight inside track. Again, this is a race in which lightly-raced hurdlers boast a fine recent record.

LIGHTLY-RACED HURDLERS

THE banging of the 'lightly-raced hurdler' drum continues here, with last year's winner *Stoney Mountain* becoming the tenth winner in the past 11 years to have had seven or less starts over hurdles. Eight of those 10 winners were second-season hurdlers, so once again, this is the obvious place to start.

Given that the first 10 horses home last year were aged five or six, it goes without saying that trainers tend to target the race with their less-exposed young stayers. Clearly the prize money helps in that respect, and as a consequence, it tends to be a very competitive race.

CLASS ANGLE

PREDICTING the future is never easy (you don't say), but on four occasions during the past decade, the winner of this race has gone on to win a Grade 1. *Sam Spinner* and *Paisley Park* are the most recent examples, both of whom won the Long Walk Hurdle at Ascot on their very next start, with the latter, of course, going on to win the Stayers' Hurdle less than four months after winning this race. And, last season's Stayers' Hurdle winner was also lurking down the field in this event, with Lisnagar Oscar finishing only ninth on his return from chasing. Clearly, this race can be a catalyst for future success at a higher level.

AGE

AGAIN, in-keeping with the lightly-raced theme, it shouldn't be a huge shock that *Kruzhlinin* is the only winner of the race who was aged older than seven (he was nine). 10 of the past 11 winners were aged five or six, again strongly suggesting that we should focus on the up-and-comers, rather than the exposed stayers.

One youngster who would be an intriguing contender this year, would be Ballymore fifth **Mossy Fen**. He is expected to go chasing this season, but we have seen previously horses can run in this race before switching to fences (*Diamond Harry* being a prime example) and his owners are local to the track, being from Liverpool. A winner over 2m7f on his Rules debut, he is a Grade 2 winner who ran well for a long way at the festival, and will be suited by going back up in distance. If he were mine, a mark of 143 might tempt me towards this race, before considering sending him over the larger obstacles.

WEIGHT AND OFFICIAL RATINGS

THERE has been a wide range of weights carried to success in this event since its inception in 2005, with four winners shouldering top-weight (11-12), those being *Millenium Royal* (the only winner to be rated above 149), *Diamond Harry*, *Trustan Times* and *Paisley Park*.

The last-named won off a mark of 147, but aside from the future Stayers' Hurdle winner, eight of the past nine winners were rated between 136 and 143. Only six of last year's 17-strong field fell into this 8lbs bracket, including the 16-1 winner.

Another lightly-raced, second-season hurdler, who would fit the mould (currently rated 140) is *Leading Prospect*, **Imperial Alcazar**, who reportedly has this as an option, ahead of a novice chase campaign. As stated previously in this year's book, he really does appeal as a horse who will improve once getting 3m, and this could be a good starting point.

MARKET FORCES

STONEY MOUNTAIN became the biggest-priced winner of the race since 2007 and, in general, it has been fairly 'punter-friendly' in recent years, despite the competitiveness of the race. Prior to last year's race, nine of the previous 11 winners were sent off at single-figures, with eight winners of the race in total starting at 7-1 or shorter. The last outright favourite to win, however, was the well-handicapped *Grands Crus*, who was sent off at 6-4 on the back of an impressive win at Cheltenham just six days earlier.

PREP RUN OR FRESH?

SIMILARLY to the first two races featured in this section, there was a fairly even split in the informative years between those arriving fresh, or those who had run in the early weeks of the season. During the first nine years, five winners had a recent run to their names, with the other four winning on their seasonal reappearance. However, also like the two Cheltenham handicaps already covered, it seems that a prep-run is becoming more significant, with five of the past six winners having run during or October (4) or November (1), and this includes the past four winners. An extended 3m on (what is usually) soft ground at Haydock can be quite testing, so a fitness edge must offer some sort of advantage.

CURRENT FORM

ALL five of those recent winners who had already had a run all finished first, second or third last-time-out. In addition to this, the earlier winners of the race who had run earlier in the season, four of the five were arriving at Haydock on the back of a win. Therefore, a bold showing seems almost essential, for those who have had a run.

Grands Crus won this race under a penalty in 2010 (won at Cheltenham six days earlier), but since then the likes of Volnay de Thaix and, more recently, First Assignment (sent off 11-10 two years ago) have been beaten when carrying a penalty for a very recent success. Therefore, tread carefully with those who won after the weights for this early-closing event were published.

KEY RACES

BOTH *Aubusson* and *Sam Spinner* had finished runner-up in the **Silver Trophy Handicap Hurdle** at Chepstow the previous month, so that is an obvious race of interest. Last year's Silver Trophy winner, Flash The Steel, ran well for a long way in this event, before appearing not to get home, and it was a race that worked out very well, so is worth noting in general for the months ahead. Two subsequent festival winners contested last year's Silver Trophy (Imperial Aura and Indefatigable), whilst Bold Plan (won a handicap on this same Haydock card) and Greaneteen (won his next three starts once switched to fences) also advertised that form.

The past two winners of this race arrived at Haydock on the back of having won the same 2m4f

Best Odds Guaranteed At Virgin Bet Handicap Hurdle at Aintree in late-October. Obviously, there will now be a fair bit of a focus on the winner of that race, should they head down the 'East Lancs Road' to Haydock some four weeks later.

Both *Paisley Park* and *Stoney Mountain* had contested the **Albert Bartlett Novices' Hurdle** the previous March, with neither making any sort of impact. From this year's Albert Bartlett, Olly Murphy's **The Wolf** and Colin Tizzard-trained **Harry Senior** are a couple who could be well-suited to this event, if they don't go chasing straight away. From a mark of 143, the latter would be particularly interesting, given his earlier novice form, which included a Grade 2 success at Cheltenham on trials day.

PROVEN STAMINA NOT ESSENTIAL

AS I touched upon in the *Overview*, despite the distance of this race, tactical speed is required to hold a position around what is a very tight inside hurdles track. Nine of the past 11 winners had run over a trip around 2m4f – 2m5f on their previous start, so respect those who are stepping up (or back up, in some cases) in distance.

Last year's winner *Stoney Mountain* had run over 3m as a novice, whilst *Paisley Park* had only had the one attempt at the trip, in the aforementioned Albert Bartlett. Six of the previous nine winners before that pair were having their first start beyond 2m5f, so form in the book over 3m isn't essential.

TRAINERS TO NOTE

DAVID PIPE enjoyed a very successful run in this race between 2010 and 2013, winning it three times in that four-year period. *Grands Crus* got the ball rolling, quickly followed by *Dynaste* and *Gevrey Chambertin*, with the first-named pairing amongst the group of winners who were trying the trip for the first time. Pipe has only saddled two runners in the race during the past four years, with Umbrigado coming home in fifth last year, when looking a likely type on paper.

Pipe is sure to have one or two earmarked for this race again, with *Leading Prospect* **Brinkley** one who I hope he considers for the trip north. The five-year-old is very lightly-raced, so might want a run beforehand, but gave the impression when winning at Newbury that he will stay a longer trip, and he could well be ahead of his mark (130). Plus, like Pipe's past three winners of the race, he is a grey – what bigger trend could you want (said with tongue firmly in cheek, of course)?

The record of **Nick Williams** was also highlighted last year and he was again without a runner. Nick or Jane Williams (under whose name several of the yard's horses now run) have only had one representative in the past four years, so they are clearly selective in the horses that they target at this event. To date, they have saddled two winners from just five runners, with Tea For Two (beaten favourite in 2015) another who went on to bigger and better

things, so it is clear that they like to target the race with a future Graded performer. If he doesn't go chasing, it could be that the lightly-raced **One For The Team** is aimed at this race, following his wide-margin victory at Newbury back in February.

In contrast, three high-profile trainers have yet to strike in this race, starting with **Paul Nicholls** whose record stands at 0/11 following the eighth placing of Highland Hunter last year. Several of Nicholls' runners were sent off fairly short, too, and they include three favourites (or joint-favourites).

Jonjo O'Neill once again had a runner hit the frame last year (Tedham), but he is now 0/10 in this event, although he has had four horses finish in the first four. Interestingly, those placed horses include subsequent Gold Cup winner Synchronised (won the blue-riband event later that same season) and subsequent dual-festival winner Holywell. Again, this hints at the *Class Angle* which was highlighted earlier.

And, without a runner last year, **Nicky Henderson** remains at 0/8, although he has now gone five years without a runner in the race. He, too, has had four horses finish in the first four, but it seems that this is now a race which (in recent years at least) he is less focused on.

BRINKLEY

ROLL OF HONOUR

Year	Form	Winner	Age	Weight	OR	SP	Trainer	Runners	Last Race (No. of days)
2019	1	Stoney Mountain	6	11-3	138	16/1	H Daly	17	1st Aintree Hurdle (27)
2018	1	Paisley Park	6	11-12	147	4/1	E Lavelle	7	1st Aintree Hurdle (27)
2017	2	Sam Spinner	5	10-9	139	6/1	J O'Keefe	16	2nd Gr.3 Chepstow Hurdle (42)
2016	P3	Kruzhlinin	9	10-13	136	9/1	P Hobbs	13	3rd Aintree Hurdle (14)
2015		Baradari	5	11-2	136	12/1	D Skelton	16	15th Gr.3 Aintree Hurdle (225)
2014	2	Aubusson	5	10-13	141	9/1	N Williams	16	2nd Gr.3 Chepstow Hurdle (28)
2013		Gevrey Chambertin	5	11-7	143	6/1	D Pipe	17	6th Gr.1 Sefton Hurdle (232)
2012	1	Trustan Times	6	11-12	142	10/1	T Easterby	16	1st Wetherby Hurdle (21)
2011		Dynaste	5	10-13	141	7/1	D Pipe	20	6th Sandown Nov. Hurdle (252)
2010	1	Grands Crus	5	10-10 (6 ex)	132	6/4F	D Pipe	18	1st Cheltenham Hurdle (6)

LEADING TEN-YEAR GUIDES

Silver Trophy Handicap Hurdle 2 (*Aubusson* 2nd, *Sam Spinner* 2nd)
Best Odds Guaranteed At Virgin Bet Handicap Hurdle 2 (*Paisley Park* 1st, *Stoney Mountain* 1st)
Previous season's Albert Bartlett Novices' Hurdle 2 (*Paisley Park* 13th, *Stoney Mountain* P.U.)

RACING GIFTS

UNIQUE HORSE RACING GIFTS FROM ARTIST **DARREN BIR**

At **birdieracinggifts.co.uk** you will find a huge range of fu
unique, horse racing gifts designed by Horse Racings cartooni
of choice Darren 'Birdie' Bird.

We have gifts for friends and family of all ages at fantastic value f
money prices. Choose from our huge product range including Mug
Greeting Cards, Mousemats, Keyrings, Framed Prints, Cushions an
much more.

| MUGS | FRAMED PRINTS | CUSHIONS | GREETING CARDS | MOUSEM |

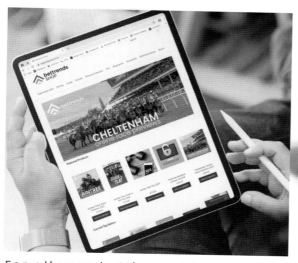

LADBROKES TROPHY CHASE

Newbury - 3m1f 214y (Grade 3 handicap)

Saturday 28th November 2020

OVERVIEW

STILL referred to by many – myself included – as the 'Hennessy' Newbury's Ladbrokes Trophy is arguably the most prestigious staying handicap chase in the calendar, with the exception of the Grand National. With a roll of honour which includes the greats such as *Mill House* and *Arkle*, as well as the likes of *Burrough Hill Lad* and *One Man*, and more recently *Denman, Bobs Worth* and *Native River*, it really is a highlight in the early months of the season. This is yet another early-season handicap which favours the unexposed, whilst proven stamina is also a positive.

LIGHTLY-RACED CHASERS

LAST year's winner *De Rasher Counter* ticked plenty of boxes, none more so than the fact that he was a second-season chaser, winning this race on just his seventh start over fences. In doing so, he became the 14th second-season chaser * to win the Ladbrokes Trophy since 1999, and the 15th during this period to have had nine or less chase starts, prior to the race. Incidentally, 14 of those 15 had run no more than seven times over fences.

* *correct if using Be My Royal (first past the post, later to be disqualified) as the 2002 winner*

2018 winner *Sizing Tennessee* was in his third season over fences, but he had spent two seasons in novice company, whilst *Strong Flow* won this as a novice back in 2003. Looking solely at the past decade, six of the last 10 winners were second-season chasers.

PREP RUN BECOMING A REAL POSITIVE

DE RASHER COUNTER became the seventh successive winner of this race to have run earlier in the campaign. We had an eight-year spell between 2005 and 2012, when six of the eight winners were successful on their seasonal reappearance, but rather like some of the earlier races touched upon, a prep run is seemingly becoming more significant once again.

Overall, 14 of the past 21 winners had run earlier in the campaign. Of those 14, only two (including last year's winner) failed to record a top three finish on their previous start, therefore a prominent showing is ideal when it comes to those who had a prep. The performance of *De Rasher Counter* in a hurdle race at Uttoxeter 43 days earlier actually put me off his chances, but he was clearly blowing away the cobwebs with this race in mind. Again, if using *Be My Royal* as the 2002 winner, 12 of the past 21 winners won last-time-out. Only four of the past 21 winners failed to record a top three finish last time.

As highlighted already – in both this section and other areas of this year's publication – it seems likely that trainers will want to have their horses ready fairly early (ground permitting) this year, due to the enforced prolonged break. Therefore, I would suggest it even more likely that we will see horses having a prep for the likes of this race, wherever possible.

PREVIOUS SEASON'S CHELTENHAM FESTIVAL FORM

DE RASHER COUNTER might not have run at the Cheltenham Festival as a novice, but plenty of recent Ladbrokes Trophy winners did. Both *Native River* and *Sizing Tennessee* had hit the frame in the **National Hunt Chase** the previous March, whereas going back a little further will highlight that five winners in the space of 10 years (between 2005 and 2014) contested the **RSA Insurance Novices' Chase** just over seven months earlier. *Trabolgan, Denman* and *Bobs Worth* had all won the RSA, whilst *Diamond Harry* was pulled-up and *Many Clouds* was brought down.

Interestingly, *Many Clouds* was the only horse to have run after the RSA, with the other four winning this race on their very next start. Oliver Sherwood's future Grand National winner ran in the **Mildmay Novices' Chase** at Aintree (also thrown up a couple of winners in the past decade), a race which obviously won't be a factor this year. However, respect Graded novice chase form from last season.

It is worth pointing out that two of Nicky Henderson's three winners of this race – *Trabolgan* and *Bobs Worth* – defied lofty marks, following victory in the RSA Chase on their previous start. Therefore, it is not beyond the realms of possibility, that he could saddle **Champ** here, off a mark of 161. Quite whether this test is what he requires is another matter, but he did demonstrate reserves of stamina that I wasn't sure that he possessed at the festival, and he does have a fine record at the track. Four from four at Newbury, he has twice won at this two-day fixture, and also won the Grade 1 Challow Novices' Hurdle the season before last. As stated elsewhere in the book (see *Top-Class Performers*) I suspect that he might be handed a quieter introduction this season.

COURSE FORM
THAT leads us on nicely to the next sub-section, course form. No fewer than 10 of the past 15 winners had won at Newbury previously. Again, *De Rasher Counter* added his name to this list, becoming the first in three years to do so. One recent winner – Willie Mullins' *Total Recall* – had never travelled to England prior to his victory, so overall, it is a fairly strong recent trend. Pay healthy respect to winning form at the track.

Last year's winner had won a novices' handicap chase at the festive meeting the previous December, and on that card last year, **Copperhead** was successful in the Madarin Handicap Chase. He went on to win the Grade 2 Reynoldstown Novices' Chase, before falling when beaten in the RSA. Again, as well documented earlier in this year's book, plenty of Colin Tizzard's runners appeared to fail to run to form at the festival, so he could easily leave that behind, and he certainly has the right profile for this race.

PROVEN STAMINA
AS you would expect from a race of this nature, form over 3m or thereabouts is almost essential. Only three winners this century had failed to win over that trip (or further) earlier in their careers, one of those being *Triolo d'Alene*, who had been successful over an extended 2m7f. The other pair – *Madison du Berlais* and *Many Clouds* – had placed form over 3m.

Horses with a 'proper' National Hunt background have a fine record in the Ladbrokes Trophy, with 14 winners this century having won a bumper or a Point-to-Point at the beginning of their careers. Although not always the case, this background tends to point towards a horse with stamina, and last year's winner was successful under both disciplines when trained in Ireland. A runaway winner in 1998, *Teeton Mill* was a serial winner in Points and Hunter Chases before racing under Rules, and whilst he wouldn't have the profile of many a 'Hennessy' winner, he certainly boasted plenty of stamina.

BACK-CLASS
GRADED novice chase form has already been

KEY TRENDS
- 15 of the past 21 winners had 9 or less chase starts (14 of them had 7 or less)
- 10 of the past 15 winners had won at Newbury previously
- The past 15 winners were rated 145 or higher
- 14 of the past 21 winners were second-season chasers
- 14 of the past 21 winners (including the past 7) had a prep run
- 14 winners this century had won a bumper and/or P2P
- 10 of the past 21 winners were aged 7
- 11 of the past 17 winners started at 8-1 or shorter
- 7 of the past 15 winners ran in either the RSA or NH Chase
- Respect Graded novice hurdle form
- Only 4 of the past 21 winners were not in their first three seasons over fences
- Only 4 of the past 21 winners did not record a top 3 finish last-time-out
- Only 3 winners this century had failed to win over 3m
- Only 2 of the past 21 winners were not aged 6-8
- Only 2 of the past 17 winners returned greater than 12-1

covered, but plenty of winners of this race had Graded novice hurdle form in the book, when going back through their form. Again, last year's winner ticked this box, having contested the Grade 2 Classic Novices' Hurdle, on trials day in 2018 (was in third when falling at the last, behind Santini). All bar one of the past 11 winners contested either a Grade 1 or 2 as a novice hurdler, or ran in the Weatherbys Champion Bumper even earlier in their career.

OFFICIAL BHA RATINGS
NINE of the past 10 winners were rated between 146 and 156, with the last eight winners falling into the slightly narrower bracket between 147 and 155. Since 2005, every winner has been rated 145 or higher.

Two horses have won from marks above 155 this century, those being *Denman* (twice – off 161 and 174) and *Bobs Worth* (160). Both went on to win the Gold Cup later that season (after his first success in the case of *Denman*) which indicates the calibre of horse required to win from such a lofty rating. But, it can be done.

AGE
RATHER in-keeping with the up-and-coming, improving second-season chaser trends, it is unsurprising that the only two winners this century were not aged between six and eight. Those were *Denman* (who won his second 'Hennessy' at the age of nine) and *Sizing Tennessee*, who didn't fit with many trends two years ago. In hindsight, he probably won a below-par renewal, with only 12 horses going to post that year, a figure that was doubled 12 months later.

During the past 21 years, 19 winners were aged six (5), seven (10) or eight (4).

MARKET FORCES
12-1 SHOTS have won the past two renewals of the race, but prior to that 11 of the previous 15 winners were sent off at single-figure prices. In fact, all 11 returned with a starting price of 8-1 or shorter, with six favourites (one being joint-favourite) successful during this period. During those past 17 years, only two winners were sent off at odds greater than 12-1, so generally, the top end of the market has dominated.

TRAINERS TO NOTE
WITH two wins in the race in the past four years, and a further four placed horses since 2013, **Colin Tizzard** is the obvious place to start. He went mod-handed last year, saddling no fewer than four runners, with Elegant Escape (runner-up in 2018) again hitting the frame. Mister Malarky was another of his runners last year, and he went on to win the Betway Handicap Chase (formerly the Racing Post

Chase) later in the season, so his runners in such events clearly warrant considerable respect. As already touched upon, it could be that **Copperhead** is the main hope for the Tizzard stable this year.

Paul Nicholls and Nicky Henderson have both won the race three times since 2003, with the novice *Strong Flow* and *Denman* (twice) providing Nicholls with success in a race in which he rode the winner, back in 1986 and 1987. It is clearly a race that means a lot to him, and it could be that he runs **Topofthegame** in this year's renewal, having missed the whole of last season. The winner of the 2019 RSA Chase, it will be interesting to see how the handicapper rates him, after his lay-off. He still has the potential to go to the very top as a chaser, so would be a fascinating contender, although it is worth noting that Nicholls has gone 10 years (and 20 runners) since his last win in the race.

Like Colin Tizzard, **Nicky Henderson** also saddled four runners last year, with Beware The Bear faring best, finishing in fourth. He has had three horses hit the frame since winning back-to-back renewals in 2012 and 2013.

TOPOFTHEGAME

ROLL OF HONOUR								
Year	Form	Winner	Age	Weight	OR	SP	Trainer	Runners	Last Race (No. of days)
2019	6	De Rasher Counter	7	10-10	149	12/1	E Lavelle	24	6th Uttoxeter Hurdle (43)
2018	1	Sizing Tennessee	10	11-3	148	12/1	C Tizzard	12	1st Fontwell Chase (57)
2017	1	Total Recall	8	10-8	147	9/2F	W Mullins (IRE)	20	1st Gr.3 Munster National (55)
2016	2	Native River	6	11-1	155	7/2F	C Tizzard	19	2nd Gr.2 Wetherby Hurdle (28)
2015	1	Smad Place	8	11-4	155	7/1	A King	15	1st Kempton Chase (26)
2014	1	Many Clouds	7	11-6	151	8/1	O Sherwood	19	1st Listed Carlisle Chase (27)
2013	13	Triolo d'Alene	6	11-1	147	20/1	N Henderson	20	3rd Gr.3 Ascot Chase (28)
2012		Bobs Worth	7	11-6	160	4/1F	N Henderson	19	1st Gr.1 RSA Chase (262)
2011	3	Carruthers	8	10-4	146	10/1	M Bradstock	18	3rd Gr.3 Cheltenham Chase (14)
2010		Diamond Harry	7	10-0	156	6/1	N Williams	18	p.u. Gr.1 RSA Chase (255)

LEADING TEN-YEAR GUIDES
Previous season's RSA Insurance Chase 3 *(Diamond Harry p.u., Bobs Worth 1st, Many Clouds b.d.)*
Previous season's National Hunt Chase 2 *(Native River 2nd, Sizing Tennessee 3rd)*
Previous season's Mildmay Novices' Chase 2 *(Many Clouds 4th, Native River 1st)*

RANDOX HEALTH BECHER CHASE

Aintree (Grand National course) - 3m1f 188y (Grade 3 handicap)

Saturday 5th December 2020

OVERVIEW

FIRST run in 1992, the Becher Chase is now a Grade 3 handicap, and is staged over a similar trip to the previous race covered, the Ladbrokes Trophy at Newbury. One of two races contested over the famous fences on the same card, this is a race where previous course experience is a big positive. Often run on testing ground, stamina is also a key attribute.

COURSE FORM

WALK IN THE MILL has now won back-to-back renewals of the Becher, becoming the second dual-winner in the past decade (and the third overall), with *Hello Bud* successful in both 2010 and 2012. When winning the race for the first time (2018), *Walk In The Mill* became the first winner since 2009 to have not previously run on the Grand National track. Of the past nine winners, six had previously recorded a first five finish in a race on this course.

Overall, 20 of the past 26 winners had experience of some sort on the course, of which 11 had finished in the first five in a race over the big fences. Although the fences are not as big and stiff as they were several years ago, they do still offer a rather unique test, so previous course experience seems highly advantageous. *Walk In The Mill* went on to finish fourth in the 2019 Grand National, so clearly relishes the test that the track brings.

Six of the past 10 winners (and three of the past four winners) had contested the previous season's **Randox Health Grand National.** Obviously, this has no impact this year, but it seems a growing trend, which should be monitored moving forward. The recent trio who are included in this statistic – *Vieux Lion Rouge* (7th), *Blaklion* (4th) and *Walk In The Mill* (4th) – had all run sound races in the 'big one' around eight months earlier.

At the beginning of the decade, *Hello Bud* (twice) and *West End Rocker* had also contested the Grand National in the same calendar year, whilst back in 1998 *Earth Summit* won the Becher on his first start after winning the National. The following year *Feels Like Gold* won the Becher, having finished fifth in the National the previous April. *Oscar Time* had also hit the frame in a National, but 20 months prior to his Becher win.

FOCUS ON EXPERIENCED CHASERS

AS well as Aintree experience being a positive, this race – in contrast to the other handicaps already covered in this section of the book – tends to go the way of a chaser with plenty of experience. 23 of the 28 winners to date had already run at least 13 times over fences, whilst 13 of those had already had at least 20 chase starts.

As highlighted last year, of the five 'lesser experienced' winners of the Becher, three were trained by **Paul Nicholls**, who saddled *Silver Birch*, *Eurotrek* and *Mr Pointment* to win this race in the space of four years, between 2004 and 2007. They had run six, six and four times, respectively, over fences. He also saddled *Join Together* to finish runner-up on his seventh start in 2012, so he clearly doesn't mind running an unexposed type in this race.

Generally, however, focus on those with more experience.

STAMINA ASSURED

IT can also pay to focus on horses with proven stamina. During the past decade, eight of the 10 winners had already won (6) or placed (2) in a race over 3m1½f or further. Given that the ground tends to be soft at this fixture, stamina really does come into play, with the field often well strung out. Also, the fact that the Grand Sefton is staged on the same card means that any horses with stamina doubts do have the option of running in that contest over 2m5f.

TAKE FRENCH-BREDS SERIOUSLY

I HAVE written plenty about the precociousness of French-bred horses in the past couple of editions of the *Cheltenham Festival Betting Guide*, and this is another feature handicap chase in which they are beginning to have a real influence. During the past seven years, four winners were French-bred (admittedly, *Walk In The Mill* has won it twice) and all from less than 23% representation during this period. Just 31 of the 137 runners during the past seven years were French-bred horses, so four winners is a fine return. Backing every French-bred runner blindly during this period would have yielded a profit of £15 to a level-stake £1.

MORE TRADITIONAL BACKGROUND

PRIOR to the back-to-back victories of *Walk In The Mill*, 10 of the previous 11 winners had won either (or both, in the case of *Blaklion*) a Point-to-Point or a bumper (National Hunt Flat race) at the start of their careers.

In terms of breeding, GB-bred horses did well in the early days of the Becher, but Irish-bred horses dominated prior to the 'French takeover'. In total, 11 of the past 16 winners were bred in Ireland. During those 16 years, *Blaklion* is the only winner who wasn't bred in either France or Ireland.

AGE

ONLY three seven-year-olds have won the Becher, and only two in the past 26 years. Again, this kind of falls in line with the 'experienced' statistic. It is worth noting that three seven-year-olds took their chance last year, including beaten favourite Mulcahys Hill (pulled-up). Runner-up, Kimberlite Candy, and the previous season's National Hunt Chase winner Le Breuil were the other pair.

11 of the 28 winners to date were aged 10 or older, with *Hello Bud* winning this at the age of 14, and *Oscar Time* as a 13-year-old. Three 12-year-old winners also suggest that we shouldn't overlook any veterans. However, during the past 13 years, nine of the winners were aged eight (3) or nine (6) so it could be that, as the race has improved in Grade, we have seen a pattern emerge pointing towards that age group. It is certainly worth noting that the four French-bred winners were all aged nine or less, but that probably shouldn't come as a surprise, with *Walk In The Mill* (for example) jumping fences at the age of four.

WEIGHTS AND OFFICIAL RATINGS

THERE have been some fine weight-carrying performances over the years in the Becher, but since *Vic Venturi* shouldered 11-12 in 2009, only one winner (*Blaklion*) has carried more than 10-12. Overall, only seven of the 28 winners carried more than 10-12, with all of them shouldering 11-5 or more.

The ground is invariably soft on Becher Chase day at Aintree, so carrying a low-weight, over a long distance, is clearly advantageous. In fact, seven winners to date were racing from 'out of the handicap' – I'm not usually in favour of supporting such horses, but if there is ever a time to consider it, it is mid-winter over a marathon trip.

In terms of official BHA Ratings, *Blaklion* is the only winner to race off a mark higher than 148 in the past 21 years. 15 of those 21 winners were rated 142 or lower (again, nine of the past 10 winners fit this criteria).

MARKET FORCES

NO fewer than 20 of the 28 winners of the Becher Chase were sent off at 10-1 or shorter, with 18 of them sent off at single-figure odds. Between 2012 and 2015, the four winners were priced between 14-1 and 25-1, but normal service has been resumed of late, in a race which is invariably won by a horse towards the top of the market.

Six outright favourites have been successful, most recently *Vieux Lion Rouge* and *Blaklion*, the latter being the shortest-priced winner in the race's history, when returning at 7-4 three years ago.

PREP-RUN COUNTS

WALK IN THE MILL was pulled-up in the Badger Beers Silver Trophy at Wincanton on his reappearance last year, but it was clearly enough to leave him spot on for his repeat bid in the Becher, and he became the tenth winner in the past 13 years to have had a prep run beforehand. During this period, only *Hello Bud, Chance du Roy* and *Vieux Lion Rouge* were successful in this race, on their first start of the campaign. Overall, 21 of the 28 winners had run earlier in the season.

KEY RACES

THE previous season's Grand National has already been highlighted in an earlier sub-section, whilst *Blaklion* became the fourth winner of the race to have run in the **Charlie Hall Chase** at Wetherby on their previous start. It should be said, however, that the other trio came in the early days of the race, and he is the only winner in the past 19 years to have contested the early-season Grade 2.

Four more recent winners had run at Cheltenham's November meeting, with both *Oscar Time* and *Walk In The Mill* contesting the **Markel Insurance Amateur Riders' Handicap Chase** over 3m1f. That race was lost last season, when the opening day of the three-day fixture was abandoned.

TRAINERS TO NOTE

AS already touched upon, **Paul Nicholls** won the race three times in the space of four years between 2004 and 2007, but with six wins to his name, the most successful Becher Chase trainer is, without doubt, **Nigel Twiston-Davies**. His record in the race was well-documented last year, and although Ballyoptic (carried top-weight, off a mark of 159) couldn't enhance that record, his runners warrant utmost respect. His six winners span back to 1993, when *Indian Tonic* won the second renewal of the race, whilst 1998 winner *Earth Summit* was having his first start since winning the Grand National earlier in the year. His three latest victories were achieved during the past decade, and his overall record stands at six winners from 27 runners. Backing all of his runners would have landed you a profit of £14.25 to a level-stake of £1.

WALK IN THE MILL

ROLL OF HONOUR

Year	Form	Winner	Age	Weight	OR	SP	Trainer	Runners	Last Race (No. of days)
2019	PU	Walk In The Mill	9	10-8	141	8/1	R Walford	18	P.U. Wincanton handicap chase (28)
2018	3	Walk In The Mill	8	10-3	137	10/1	R Walford	18	3rd Cheltenham Chase (22)
2017	2	Blaklion	8	11-6	153	7/4F	N Twiston-Davies	15	2nd Gr.2 Charlie Hall Chase (35)
2016		Vieux Lion Rouge	7	10-9	142	8/1F	D Pipe	20	7th Gr.3 Grand National (238)
2015	72	Highland Lodge	9	10-7 (7oh)	132	20/1	J Moffatt	17	2nd Sedgefield Chase (54)
2014	11U	Oscar Time	13	10-12	136	25/1	R Waley-Cohen	20	u.r. Cheltenham Chase (22)
2013		Chance du Roy	9	10-6	135	14/1	P Hobbs	20	8th Cheltenham Chase (233)
2012	35	Hello Bud	14	10-0 (5oh)	130	14/1	N Twiston-Davies	16	5th Cheltenham Cross-Country (22)
2011	P	West End Rocker	9	10-10	137	10/1	A King	14	p.u. Gr.3 Cheltenham Chase (21)
2010		Hello Bud	12	10-5	133	15/2F	N Twiston-Davies	17	p.u. Gr.3 bet365 Gold Cup (211)

LEADING TEN-YEAR GUIDES

Previous season's Grand National 6 *(Hell Bud 5th & 7th, West End Rocker b.d., Vieux Lion Rouge 7th, Blaklion 4th, Walk In The Mill 4th)*
Market Insurance Amateur Riders' Handicap Chase 2 *(Oscar Time u.r., Walk In The Mill 3rd)*

CASPIAN CAVIAR GOLD CUP

Cheltenham (New course) - 2m4f 127y (Grade 3 handicap)

Saturday 12th December 2020

OVERVIEW

A SIMILAR event, in many ways, to the BetVictor Gold Cup – which is unsurprisingly a fine trial for this – in that it is Grade 3 handicap over an intermediate trip, although a bit more stamina is usually required to win the Caspian Caviar Gold Cup. Staged on the stiffer New course, it is run over an additional 83 yards and often attracts a smaller field, and the prize money (and prestige) in this event is slightly less.

BETVICTOR GOLD CUP – KEY TRIAL

PREVIOUS course form is again a strong positive when assessing this race, none more so than the **BetVictor Gold Cup** from the previous month. Last year's winner *Warthog* became the fourth successive winner of the race (and the sixth in 11 years) to have run in the BetVictor on his previous start. Four of the six had recorded a top five finish (ranging from 2nd to 5th) whilst going back a little further, *Exotic Dancer* completed the big-race double back in 2006. *Monkerhostin* (2004) had also finished third in the BetVictor, although he did have time to run over hurdles at Windsor in between races. Given that there was no race in 2008, that means that no fewer than nine of the past 15 winners had contested the BetVictor, with seven of them recording a top-five finish.

No winner this century had failed to run at Cheltenham previously, with only one (*Niceonefrankie*) failing to record a victory, or at least finish in the first three, at the track. Good course form seems almost essential in this race, and the BetVictor should be the first race to review, when assessing it.

FRENCH-BRED WINNERS

AS well as placing in the 'key trial' *Warthog* also met with another very strong trend, in that he became the third French-bred to win the race in the past four years, and the 11th in the past 17 renewals. From just 36% of the fields during this period, French-bred horses have now won 65% of renewals of this race since 2002. Just four went to post last year, with favourite *Cepage* also finishing in the first four, and backing every French-bred runner since 2002 would have yielded a profit of £27 to a level-stake of £1. The record stands at 11 winners from 85 runners during this period (the total number of runners during this time amounts to 234).

LIGHTLY-RACED CHASERS

AGAIN, this is yet another handicap which favours the unexposed. *Warthog* – who sadly suffered a fatal-injury on his very next start, back at the same track on trials day – became the 13th winner in the past 17 renewals to have won the Caspian Caviar on the back of nine chase starts or less. He was having just his sixth run over fences, and after we had a couple of more exposed winners in 2017 and 2018, it was a case of reverting to type last year.

AGE

NO horse over the age of eight has been successful since *Fragrant Dawn* back in 1993. All bar two of the winners since were aged either six (6), seven (8), or eight (7). Again, this fits the mould of an improving young horse.

At the other end of the scale, be wary of five-year-olds, who don't have a great record. There weren't any five-year-old runners last year, but the record of that age group in the previous decade stood at 0/7, with six of them being trained by Paul Nicholls. Dual King George winner *Clan des Obeaux* finished runner-up in this race as a five-year-old (off a mark of 155, under top-weight), so it is worth considering should **Saint Sonnet** turn up. He looks more than capable of winning a valuable handicap this season, but the age statistic would be against him in this particular event.

Nicholls has, however, saddled two four-year-olds in this race during the past eight years, and both won. *Unioniste* and *Frodon* (both French-bred horses) were the pair, so take note if there is another four-year-old deemed precocious enough to represent the powerful stable. The weight-allowance (currently 7lbs) for such horses is a healthy one, whereas the five-year-olds are forced to race against their elders off their genuine handicap marks.

WEIGHTS AND OFFICIAL RATINGS

WARTHOG became the lowest rated winner of this race (132) since 2005, when *Sir Oj* won from out of the handicap, and there hasn't really been a steady pattern, in terms of weights carried, or winning BHA ratings. During the past 11 years, only four horses won from a mark greater than 145, and all four were trained by Paul Nicholls. The other seven winners were rated between 132 – 145, with six of them carrying less than 10-10. *Niceone-frankie* carried 11-5 when winning in 2014, but he was racing off a mark of just 142, so it was clearly a below-par renewal. Again, there is no clear pattern here, although perhaps we should focus on those below the 145 mark, unless trained by Nicholls. In fact, Nicholls is the only trainer to have a won the race with a horse rated above 150 this century.

MARKET FORCES

OF the 19 winners since 1999, 14 of them (including the last three, and seven of the past nine winners) were sent off at single-figure odds. Only one favourite has obliged during this period – that being *Poquelin* in 2009 – and it, generally, pays to focus on those just in behind the market leader.

PAUL NICHOLLS

I HAVE touched on **Paul Nicholls** in a couple of subsections already, and such is his record in this race, he deserves one of his own. He has saddled six winners in the past 11 years, from 20 runners, and backing them all would have produced a profit of £33 to a level-stake of £1. Brelan d'As was unable to enhance his fantastic record last year, but this is clearly a race that he takes very seriously, and any Ditcheat representatives warrant serious consider-

KEY TRENDS

- ⭐ 9 of the past 15 winners contested the BetVictor Gold Cup (7 of them finished in the first five)
- ⭐ 11 of the past 17 winners were French-bred
- ⭐ Paul Nicholls has saddled 5 of the past 11 winners
- ✓ 21 of the past 23 winners were aged 6-8
- ✓ 14 of the past 19 winners were sent off at single-figures
- ✓ 13 of the past 17 winners had run 9 times or less over fences
- ✓ Every winner this century had run at Cheltenham previously
- ✓ 4yo's are 2/2 this decade (both trained by Paul Nicholls)
- ✗ Only 3 winners this century rated higher than 150 (all trained by Paul Nicholls)
- ✗ Only 1 winner this century had failed to win or place at Cheltenham previously
- ✗ No winner older than 8 since 1993
- ✗ Be wary of 5yo's

FRODON – WINNING THE RACE FOR A SECOND TIME IN 2018

ation. A 25% strike-rate in a race of this nature over 11 years is very healthy indeed, and he went close several times prior to winning it for the first time in 2009. In the four previous renewals he saddled either the runner-up or the third. He is the first name to look for, when assessing this race, either at entry stage, or on the day, and in general November and December is a period during the season when Nicholls invariably does very well.

OTHER TRAINERS TO NOTE

THE records of both **Jonjo O'Neill** (two wins, both of whom went on to perform at a higher level) and **Nicky Henderson** (three winners from 15 runners since 2000) were well covered last year, and neither trainer had a runner in last year's renewal.

David Pipe won the race for a second time last year, and he has saddled 15 runners since 2007, when he first won the race with *Tamarinbleu*. He saw subsequent BetVictor winner Great Endeavour finish runner-up in 2010, and he has actually only saddled two horses in the past four renewals, the other being Starchitect. He was clear, and looked to have the race at his mercy, when sadly breaking down on the approach to two out. Pipe is clearly more selective in what he runs in this race nowadays, and his record would read even better, only for that dreadful incident three years ago.

WARTHOG WINS LAST YEAR'S RENEWAL

ROLL OF HONOUR

Year	Form	Winner	Age	Weight	OR	SP	Trainer	Runners	Last Race (No. of days)
2019	3	Warthog	7	10-3	132	7/1	D Pipe	13	3rd BetVictor Gold Cup (28)
2018	12	Frodon	6	11-12	164	7/1	P Nicholls	12	2nd Gr.3 BetVictor Gold Cup (28)
2017	22219	Guitar Pete	7	10-2	134	9/1	N Richards	10	9th Gr.3 BetVictor Gold Cup (28)
2016	1110	Frodon	4	10-10	149	14/1	P Nicholls	16	10th Gr.3 BetVictor Gold Cup (28)
2015	11	Village Vic	8	10-0	136	8/1	P Hobbs	14	1st Musselburgh Chase (23)
2014	1	Niceonefrankie	8	11-5	142	16/1	V Williams	12	1st Ascot Chase (22)
2013	6132	Double Ross	7	10-8	133	7/1	N Twiston-Davies	13	2nd Ascot Chase (22)
2012	113	Unioniste	4	9-9 (6oh)	143	15/2	P Nicholls	14	3rd Cheltenham Nov. Chase (29)
2011	02	Quantitativeeasing	6	10-7	145	6/1	N Henderson	17	2nd Paddy Power Gold Cup (28)
2010	25	Poquelin	7	11-7	163	16/1	P Nicholls	16	5th Paddy Power Gold Cup (28)

LEADING TEN-YEAR GUIDES

BetVictor Gold Cup 6 *(Poquelin 5th, Quantitativeeasing 2nd, Frodon 10th & 2nd, Guitar Pete 9th, Warthog 3rd)*

BETFAIR EXCHANGE TROPHY

Ascot - 1m7f 152y (Grade 3 handicap)

Saturday 19th December 2020

OVERVIEW

FIRST run in 2001, the Betfair Exchange Trophy was run as 'The Ladbroke' until 2015, and is yet another handicap in the first half of the season in which lightly-raced hurdlers have a fine record. Upgraded from Listed to Grade 3 status in 2013, it is a race which has grown in quality in the past few years, and it often attracts runners from Ireland, although they don't have a particularly strong record in the race.

It should be noted that the 2004 and 2005 renewals were run the following January (2005 and 2006, respectively) at Sandown.

LIGHTLY-RACED HURDLERS

LAST year *Not So Sleepy* became the second horse to win this race after just four runs over hurdles (the other being second-season novice *Chauvinist* back in 2002). Overall, 11 of the 17 winners had run nine times or less over hurdles previously, with a further three winners successful on their 11th hurdles start. Five of the seven winners between 2002 and 2008 had run between four and six times over hurdles, and like so many of these feature handicaps, the unexposed are the first horses to focus on.

11 of the 17 winners were in their second season over hurdles, with five of them (if using *Sternrubin* as the 2015 winner (dead-heated with *Jolly's Cracked It*, who himself was a second-season hurdler)) second-season novices.

IN-FORM HORSES

AGAIN, if using *Sternrubin* as the 2015 winner, no fewer than nine winners of this race had won on their previous start. Arriving at Ascot in good form seems almost essential, as only two of the 17 winners had failed to record a first-three finish last-time-out. One of those – *Tamarinbleu* – was having his first start of the season, having contested the Top Novices' Hurdle at Aintree on his previous start, whilst *Mohaayed* finished only seventh in the Greatwood Hurdle, before winning this race in 2018.

Tamarinbleu is the only horse to (officially) win this race on reappearance, although *Acambo* was having his first start since winning the Swinton Hurdle in May. Therefore, don't be put off by a David Pipe-trained runner who hasn't been in action for a while. *Bayan* had finished runner-up in the Galway Hurdle the previous August, whilst

Hunters Call was also having his first start since August, when winning this on his stable-debut for Olly Murphy.

COURSE FORM

THIS time, if we use *Jolly's Cracked It* as the 2015 winner (won two novice hurdles at the track) four of the past 10 winners had won at the track previously. *Not So Sleepy* added his name to this list, having won over course-and-distance on his previous start, running away with a handicap just 29 days earlier. Both *Jolly's Cracked It* (3rd) and *Sentry Duty* (1st) had contested the Listed **Sodexo Handicap Hurdle** at Ascot's first National Hunt meeting. * note: the previous 10 winners span back to 2008, as there was no race in either 2009 or 2010, with the meeting abandoned due to the weather on each occasion.

KEY RACES

THREE winners in the past eight years had contested the **Greatwood Hurdle** at Cheltenham earlier in the campaign, two of which on their previous start. *Cause Of Causes* finished third in the Greatwood prior to winning this race, whilst *Brain Power* – who had time to win at Sandown in between – and *Mohaayed* both finished unplaced.

Both *Raya Star* (3rd) and *Sternrubin* (1st) arrived at Ascot on the back of running in Newbury's **Ladbrokes Intermediate Hurdle** (known as the Gerry Feilden to many of us), and being a competitive handicap for second-season hurdlers, the right kind of horse for this race ought to be involved in the finish at Newbury. Last year's race was won by subsequent Champion Hurdle winner, *Epatante*, who could easily have run here off a mark of 150, but instead went to Kempton, where she won the Christmas Hurdle in impressive fashion.

Interestingly, the first three winners of this race all contested races at the same Newbury fixture – the 'Hennessy meeting' as it was then – so pay healthy respect to form-lines from their Winter Carnival, which clearly fits in well, time-wise, with this race. *Thesis* was one of those winners, and he also ran at Cheltenham in December, a meeting at which three winners in the space of five years ran, between 2003 and 2007. Pay healthy respect to form from the big early-season fixtures at the Grade 1 tracks.

AGE

NO horse older than seven has won this race, which is rather in-keeping with the improving up-and-coming type. Four seven-year-olds have been successful, although one of those was *Desert Air* in January 2006, when the race was run after the New Year. Focus on those aged seven and – predominantly – under.

OFFICIAL BHA RATINGS

THERE has been no real pattern with regards to either official ratings or weight carried in this event, although only one winner in the past 10 was rated in the 120s. Three horses won from a mark in the 120s during the first seven years of the race, but more recently – coinciding with the rise in quality – only *Hunters Call* (128) has managed that feat. And, at the other end of the scale, only *Brain Power* (149) has been successful from a mark higher than 146. Focus on the horses rated in the 130s and low-mid 140s.

MARKET FORCES

FOUR of the first seven winners were sent off at single-figure odds (ranging from 9-4F to 7-1) and the pattern has returned of late, with four of the past seven winners priced between 9-2 and 9-1. Last year's winner *Not So Sleepy* was joint-favourite, as was *Jolly's Cracked It* when dead-heating five years ago, but only one outright favourite (*Jack The Giant* in 2007) has been successful to date.

THE IRISH CHALLENGE

THE excellent record of **Gordon Elliott** was highlighted last year, with the trainer responsible for two winners – *Cause Of Causes* and *Bayan* – from just six runners. He has also had a second (Roman Villa in 2007) and a third (Flaxen Flare in 2013) so his runners warrant utmost respect. Elliott has only saddled two runners in the past five years, however, but backing all six of his runners would have produced a healthy profit of £35, to a level-stake of £1.

ARAMAX

Boodles winner **Aramax** could be one option for Elliott this year, although he did disappoint when well-supported for the Galway Hurdle. The way he won at Cheltenham suggested that he could win another handicap, whilst **Grand Roi** (bought for £400,000) could be another. He is rated 140 in England following victories at Fakenham and Warwick, and would be a fascinating runner if lining up in one of the early-season feature handicaps.

Aside from Elliott, the Irish have a very poor record in this event. The record of Irish-trained (non-Elliott) runners currently stands at 0/34, with the likes of **Willie Mullins**, Tony Martin and Noel Meade all having had several runners in the race. In fact, Mullins' record alone stands at 0/11, so be wary of the Irish challenge.

Incredibly, leading owner JP McManus won four of the five handicap hurdles at the Cheltenham Festival in March, with Dame de Compagnie (Coral Cup), Aramax (Boodles Juvenile Handicap Hurdle), Sire du Berlais (Pertemps Final) and Saint Roi (County Hurdle) all successful in the green and gold hoops. However, this is one race that he has yet to win, and it is not for the want of trying. Three times he has been responsible for the runner-up (all three of those were trained in England, incidentally) but his record currently stands at 0/20, with 17 of those runners coming in the past 10 renewals. Given the ammunition at his disposal, he is likely to hit the target at some stage, but for now, his record is a poor one. The aforementioned Aramax could be one who attempts to end the run this year.

OTHER TRAINERS TO NOTE

LAST year's winner was trained by **Hughie Morrison**, who is more commonly known for his exploits as a Flat trainer, but boasts a fantastic record under National Hunt rules, something which I highlighted earlier on in the publication (see *Around The Yards*). *Not So Sleepy* was his first runner in the race since 2003 – when Tom Paddington fell three out – whilst his only other runner was *Marble Arch*, who won the inaugural running of the race in 2001. Unless last year's winner returns, I'm not sure that Morrison will have anything for this year's race. Nevertheless, it is an excellent strike-rate (67%) that he boasts, and any horse who he does run in the race would warrant plenty of consideration. It is also noteworthy that all three of his runners started at 7-1 or shorter, so he is clearly very selective, a comment which also applies to his National Hunt runners as a whole; he is a shrewd operator under both codes.

Nicky Henderson is the most successful trainer in this race, having saddled four winners, going back to 2002 when *Chauvinist* ran out a facile winner. *Jack The Giant* and *Sentry Duty* won back-to-back renewals (2007 and 2008) for the Seven Barrows team, whilst *Brain Power* is Henderson's most recent winner. He has also been responsible for a further five horses who finished in the first three, and although Countister couldn't improve that record last year, it remains a race which he clearly likes to target. Overall, he has had 26 runners in the race, and backing his horses blindly would have produced a profit of £11.75 to a level-stake of £1.

From just eight runners, **Dan Skelton** has had two winners in this race since 2013, and his record in valuable 2m handicap hurdles, in general, is very good. This has already been highlighted when looking at the Greatwood Hurdle, and three victories in the Country Hurdle during the past five years confirms that he is very adept at targeting such contests. As well as his winners – *Willow's Saviour* and *Mohaayed* – he saw Shelford finish fourth in 2014, and any runners from his Lodge Hill stable should be noted.

Skelton's former boss **Paul Nicholls**, on the other hand, doesn't have a great record in this race, and again saddled two unplaced horses last year, taking his overall record to 0/22. Plenty have been sent off at single figures, too, including Sud Bleu (7-1), Monte Cristo (3-1F), Prospect Wells (11-4F) and Brampour (6-1) in the same season, and the enigmatic Modus (6-1). Interestingly, during the past seven years he has run 11 horses, of which five were owned by Johnny de la Hey, so it would appear to be a race that he wants to win. Mont des Avaloirs (5-1F) and Tamaroc du Mathan (7-1) have represented the owner in the past two renewals, with the former meaning that Nicholls has been responsible for three outright beaten favourites.

ROLL OF HONOUR

Year	Form	Winner	Age	Weight	OR	SP	Trainer	Runners	Last Race (No. of days)
2019	1	Not So Sleepy	7	10-3	127	9/2JF	H Morrison	13	1st Ascot Handicap Hurdle (29)
2018	47	Mohaayed	6	11-10	145	16/1	D Skelton	21	7th Gr.3 Greatwood Hurdle (34)
2017	9453	Hunters Call	7	10-3	128	9/1	O Murphy	17	3rd Sligo Hurdle (135)
2016	381	Brain Power	6	11-11	149	12/1	N Henderson	19	1st Listed Sandown. Hurdle (14)
2015	DEAD-HEAT								
	1	Sternrubin	4	10-10	134	9/1	P Hobbs	21	1st Newbury Hurdle (23)
	3	Jolly's Cracked It	6	11-3	141	7/1JF	H Fry		3rd Listed Ascot Hurdle (67)
2014	124	Bayan	5	11-5	146	14/1	G Elliott (IRE)	18	4th Leopardstown Handicap (98)
2013	11	Willow's Saviour	6	10-5	130	10/1	D Skelton	20	1st Musselburgh Hurdle (43)
2012	12613	Cause of Causes	4	10-13	142	25/1	G Elliott (IRE)	21	3rd Gr.3 Cheltenham Hurdle (34)
2011	213	Raya Star	5	10-1	134	12/1	A King	16	3rd Newbury Hurdle (21)
2010	NO RACE								

LEADING TEN-YEAR GUIDES

Greatwood Hurdle 3 *(Cause of Causes 3rd, Brain Power 8th, Mohaayed 7th)*
Ladbrokes Intermediate Hurdle 2 *(Raya Star 3rd, Sternrubin 1st)*

LADBROKES KING GEORGE VI CHASE

Kempton - 3m (Grade 1)

Saturday 26th December 2020

OVERVIEW

THE highlight of the festive period, the King George is one of three Grade 1s on the card at Kempton on Boxing Day, and is one of the most prestigious races in the National Hunt calendar. The roll of honour includes some all-time great staying chasers, and since *Pendil* won back-to-back renewals in 1972 and 1973, we have seen a further dozen horses win the race more than once. *Clan des Obeaux* added his name to this list when winning a second successive King George last Christmas, and in doing so, provided his trainer Paul Nicholls with a remarkable 11th win in the race. He did, of course, saddle *Kauto Star* to win five King George's in the space of six years, toppling of the record of *Desert Orchid* who won the race four times between 1986 and 1990.

STAMINA

I LED with this sub-section last year and it proved pivotal. Kempton is perceived – by many – as being a speed course, and in many respects, that is correct. In races over shorter distances on this track, pace is essential, and this is possibly why we have seen many a good two-mile chaser have a crack at the King George. In recent years, the likes of Azertyuiop and Master Minded have failed to get home in this race, and Cyrname suffered the same fate last year. All three of those were trained by Paul Nicholls, of course.

Two years ago *Clan des Obeaux* became just the third winner this century to win the King George having not previously won over 3m. He had run twice over slightly further, when third in the previous season's Betway Bowl and fourth in the Betfair Chase on reappearance, but an extended 2m5½f was previously as far as he had won. Prior to that, *Edredon Bleu* and *Kicking King* won back-to-back renewals in 2003 and 2004, and although the former was well-known for his exploits over shorter, the latter had finished runner-up over 3m at Down Royal on his reappearance and did appeal as a horse who would develop into a genuine stayer. Proven stamina is a positive.

GRADE 1 CLASS

WHEN winning his first King George two years ago,

Clan des Obeaux also broke another key-trend, in that he hadn't previously won at the top level. He was the only winner this century to fall into this category, with *Teeton Mill* (1998) the last before that. This is a staying chase of the highest calibre, and as such, proven form in this grade is almost a necessity. In fairness, most of the horses contesting a King George will have been successful at Grade 1 level, with only Aso (the outsider of last year's five-strong field) failing in that regard in the latest renewal.

KING NICHOLLS

AS already touched upon in the *Overview*, trainer **Paul Nicholls** has won the King George on 11 occasions, with *See More Business* providing him with his first success in 1997. Those 11 wins were provided by just four horses, with *Kauto Star* winning five. His other three winners – the other (not mentioned thus far) being *Silviniaco Conti* – have now all won the race on two occasions, all of which again highlights the talents of the trainer, in terms of maximising longevity out of his top-class chasers. Since 1997, Nicholls has saddled 32 horses in the King George (only twice during the 23 years has he been without a runner), meaning his 11 winners give him a remarkable strike-rate of 34% and backing all of his runners would have yielded a profit of £20.20 to a level stake of £1.

As well as saddling the winner, Nicholls was also responsible for the runner-up last year (albeit beaten by 21 lengths) and the CSF paid £13.65. Nicholls has also been responsible for five third placed horses, including Azertyuiop and another

KAUTO STAR

non-stayer, Al Ferof. The latter was another who was going up in distance, and is another example of a horse who lacked the stamina for the race. It is clear that Nicholls likes to chance his speedier horses in the King George, and his strike-rate (and LSP) would be much healthier if you focused on his proven stayers. Master Minded was pulled-up in 2011, last season's Champion Chase winner Politologue finished a well-beaten fourth in 2018, and Cyrname looked a non-stayer last year (although that could, in part, be due to the tough race he had on reappearance), so be wary of his horses going up in trip.

With Topofthegame set to return in the Ladbrokes Trophy, it would seem unlikely that he will be rushed back out four weeks later for this, so it seems more likely that **Clan des Obeaux** will be the main hope of the stable once again this season. He will be bidding to become the fourth horse to win the race three times, following on from *Wayward Lad*, *Desert Orchid* and, of course, *Kauto Star*.

Nicholls is one of just three trainers to have won the race in the past 14 years, a statistic that is mainly due to the fact that he has won nine of those 14 renewals.

COURSE FORM

GIVEN that we see plenty of horses winning more than one King George, form in **last year's renewal** is often key, and is a good starting point. As well as the recent multiple winners *Cue Card* had run three times in the race prior to winning it (including a second two years earlier), whilst going back a bit further, both *Florida Pearl* and *Best Mate* had finished runner-up in the race prior to winning it.

Kempton form in general is important and the previous season's **Kauto Star Novices' Chase** (formerly the 'Feltham' and now named after the five-time winner) – staged on the same card – is often a good guide. *Long Run* had won that event as a four-year-old, whilst *Silviniaco Conti* finished runner-up, and *Might Bite* was a final fence faller, when having the race at his mercy. A prominent showing in that Grade 1 contest can often lead to a bold showing in the King George, and last year's race was won by the Colin Tizzard-trained **Slate House**. Despite the fact that his form tailed off afterwards, it wouldn't be surprising to see him return to form in the autumn and then being aimed at this. He is a 33-1 shot at the time of writing, and – at this stage – is a good way off the usual required standard, however.

Thistlecrack is the only King George winner in the past 13 years, who had failed to win or finish

second at the track previously. Still a novice, he was having his first start at the track when winning the race four years ago.

OFFICIAL BHA RATINGS

I BRIEFLY mentioned the 'required standard' in the previous subsection, and as highlighted last year, horses rated 170 or over are a good starting point, although both Cyrname (177) and Lostintranslation (173) failed to add to that last year. *Clan des Obeaux* was rated 169 before last year's race (only third highest), and although it hasn't been the case in recent seasons, the top-rated horse was successful on no fewer than eight occasions between 2002 and 2014. Considering that two of those winners (*Kicking King* twice) hadn't been given a rating by the English handicapper, it was a strong trend at the time. Despite recent results, respect those rated in the 170s.

AGE

ONLY twice in the past 29 years has the winner been older than nine. Those two were *Edredon Bleu* and *Kauto Star* (2011) who won the King George at the age of 11. The spread of the other 27 winners were six (6), seven (10), eight (6) and nine (5), although *Long Run* was effectively a five-year-old when successful for the first time. The 2010 renewal took place on 15th January 2011, following the abandonment on Boxing Day 2010.

KEY RACES

SINCE the introduction of the **Betfair Chase** in 2005, the Haydock Grade 1 has been used by no fewer than 11 King George winners as the stepping-stone to Kempton. Clearly, the £1m bonus on offer (for any horse who can win the Betfair, King George and Gold Cup in the same season) helps persuade owners to follow that certain path, although in truth, there aren't too many races for genuine Grade 1 staying chasers to contest. Once horses reach the top level, their season often maps itself out. **Lostintranslation** ran out a hugely impressive winner at Haydock last year, only to pull-up in the King George, when clearly under-performing. He returned to form in the Gold Cup, however, and I would still expect to see him sent down a similar path this winter. If Colin Tizzard can get him back to the form he showed when winning at Haydock last November, he could easily be a major player in this year's King George, as the way he travelled through the Gold Cup would suggest that a track like Kempton really ought to suit.

It could be that he reappears in the **Charlie Hall Chase** at Wetherby, should his trainer think that he needs a prep-run prior to Haydock, as that was the route he often took with *Cue Card*, who provided him with a first King George in 2015. The Charlie Hall was also used as a starting point for the season for *Silviniaco Conti* (beaten before winning the Betfair Chase), although they are the only two King George winners this century to have run at Wetherby, with *See More Business* the last before those.

Clan des Obeaux started the last campaign in Northern Ireland, contesting the **Ladbrokes Champion Chase** (formerly the JNWine.com Champion Chase) at Down Royal, where he finished runner-up behind Road To Respect. Subsequent Savills Chase and Irish Gold Cup winner Delta Work was back

in fourth that day, so don't write off the beaten horses from that contest in terms of the rest of the season, and both *Florida Pearl* (2001) and *Kicking King* (2004) were also beaten in that race on reappearance, before winning the King George two months later. *Kauto Star* was successful at Down Royal in 2008, before unseating Sam Thomas in the Betfair, then winning his third King George.

Although it is a race which won't have an impact this year *Clan des Obeaux* became the fifth winner in the past seven years to have finished in the first three in the **Betway Bowl** at Aintree, the previous April. He had finished runner-up to Kemboy at the 2019 Grand National meeting, and (normally) this race and the Gold Cup (more of which shortly) are the two obvious races from the spring to look at. As highlighted in previous editions of both the *Cheltenham Festival Betting Guide* and the *Aintree & Punchestown Festivals Betting Guide* (before they merged), Aintree isn't too dissimilar to Kempton – despite the fact that they race the opposite way around – and often form translates from one course to the other.

THE GOLD CUP

SIX of the past 11 winners of the King George had contested the previous season's **Gold Cup**, with only *Kauto Star* (2009) successful in the same calendar year. Since then – and whilst horses beaten at Cheltenham have proven successful at Kempton – only two Gold Cup winners (in the past 10 years) have taken their chance. That pairing were both beaten, but since 1999 the record of the winner of the Gold Cup in the King George reads 1111123. Five winners from seven runners is a fine strike-rate, although it would seem unlikely that **Al Boum Photo** will be aimed here, with his season likely to start at Tramore once again. He would have

LOSTINTRANSLATION

the tactical speed to cope with the track at Kempton, should his connections have a re-think in the early weeks of the season.

The only runner in last year's five-strong field who had contested either the Gold Cup or the Betway Bowl was *Clan des Obeaux*, who had run in both events.

FRENCH-BRED WINNERS

FRENCH-BRED horses have won 15 of the 20 runnings of the King George this century. *First Gold* got the ball rolling in 2000 and *Edredon Bleu* sprung a 25-1 surprise three years later. *Kauto Star, Long Run* and *Silviniaco Conti* then won nine renewals between them (2006 – 2014) and that huge winning run could well have been extended either end, with Monkerhostin beaten a neck in 2005 and Vautour going down by just a head in 2015.

After three successive non-French-bred winners, *Clan des Obeaux* has won the last two renewals, making it 11 in the past 14 years. Admittedly, four of last year's five runners were bred in France, but that certainly isn't the case in most years. In fact, during the 20 runnings this century, only 41% of the fields (75 of the 181 runners) were made up of French-bred horses, so a 75% strike-rate is well-above what could be expected. During the past 14 years, French-bred horses have made up 44% of the fields (53 of the 120 runners) yet have won 79% of those renewals.

Of those three recent non-French-bred winners, two of them – *Cue Card* and *Thistlecrack* – were bred in Britain, so *Might Bite* is the only Irish-bred winner of the King George during the past 14 years. This is slightly unusual for a staying chase of such quality.

MARKET FORCES

17 OF THE 20 winners this century came from the top three in the market, with 16 of the 17 being sent off at 9-2 or shorter. Last year's winner was the biggest of the 17 (returned 11-2) and it is a race which rarely throws up a shock. *Edredon Bleu* was a 25-1 winner in 2003, whilst *Clan des Obeaux* was the next biggest price, when winning at 12-1 two years ago. *Florida Pearl* returned at 8-1 in 2001, and they are the only trio to win from outside the top three of the betting. Of the 17 winners, 11 were sent off as outright favourite.

OTHER TRAINERS TO NOTE

THE case for Paul Nicholls has been well-documented in an earlier subsection, whilst **Nicky Henderson** and Colin Tizzard are the only other winning trainers of the race in the past 14 years. During the past decade, Henderson has had 11 runners, so three winners is a decent return, and he was without a runner in three of those past 10 runnings, including last year.

Colin Tizzard won back-to-back King Georges thanks to *Cue Card* and *Thistlecrack*, and he, too, has had 11 runners during the past decade. However, those 11 runners are actually only made up of five individual horses.

ROLL OF HONOUR

Year	Form	Winner	Age	Weight	OR	SP	Trainer	Runners	Last Race (No. of days)
2019	2	Clan des Obeaux	7	11-10	169	11/2	P Nicholls	5	2nd Gr 1 Down Royal (54)
2018	4	Clan des Obeaux	6	11-10	160	12/1	P Nicholls	10	4th Gr.1 Betfair Chase (32)
2017	1	Might Bite	8	11-10	162	6/4F	N Henderson	8	1st Listed Sandown Chase (44)
2016	111	Thistlecrack	8	11-10	-	11/10F	C Tizzard	5	1st Newbury Nov. Chase (30)
2015	11	Cue Card	9	11-10	172	9/2	C Tizzard	9	1st Gr.1 Betfair Chase (35)
2014	51	Silviniaco Conti	8	11-10	174	15/8F	P Nicholls	10	1st Gr.1 Betfair Chase (34)
2013	3	Silviniaco Conti	7	11-10	173	7/2	P Nicholls	9	3rd Gr.1 Betfair Chase (31)
2012	2	Long Run	7	11-10	172	15/8F	N Henderson	9	2nd Gr.1 Betfair Chase (34)
2011	P1	Kauto Star	11	11-10	174	3/1	P Nicholls	7	1st Gr.1 Betfair Chase (37)
*2010	3	Long Run	6	11-10	162	9/2	N Henderson	9	3rd Gr.3 Paddy Power Gold Cup (63)

LEADING TEN-YEAR GUIDES

Betfair Chase 7 (*Kauto Star 1st, Long Run 2nd, Silviniaco Conti 3rd & 1st, Cue Card 1st, Clan des Obeaux 4th*)

Last season's Cheltenham Gold Cup 5 (*Long Run 3rd, Silviniaco Conti fell & 4th, Clan des Obeaux 5th*)

Last year's renewal 5 (*Long Run 2nd, Silviniaco Conti 1st, Cue Card 5th, Clan des Obeaux 1st*)

Last season's Betway Bowl 5 (*Silviniaco Conti 3rd & 1st, Cue Card 2nd, Clan des Obeaux 2nd*)

Last year's Kauto Star Novices' Chase 3 (*Long Run 2nd, Silviniaco Conti 2nd, Might Bite fell*)

Charlie Hall Chase 2 (*Silviniaco Conti 5th., Cue Card 1st*)

* Run in January 2011

BETWAY CHALLOW NOVICES' HURDLE

Newbury - 2m4f 118y (Grade 1)

Tuesday 29th December 2020

OVERVIEW

THE first Grade 1 novice hurdle of the season in England, the Challow often attracts a small field, and is invariably run on soft ground. That is, perhaps, the reason that winners of this race have an appalling record in the Ballymore at Cheltenham (a race in which tactical speed is required), and this can be won – at times – by a hardened, experienced novice. That wasn't the case last year, as *Thyme Hill* proved a class above his rivals (although he, perhaps, needed to work harder than may have been expected), and some high-class horses have won this race down the years. The roll of honour includes *Wichita Lineman, Diamond Harry, Bindaree* and, subsequent Gold Cup winner, *Denman*, who won a re-routed renewal at Cheltenham on New Year's Day in 2006.

GRADE 2 FORM

HAVING won twice in Grade 2 company earlier in the season, *Thyme Hill* made it nine winners in the past 12 years to have won at that level, prior to winning the Challow. Of the nine, eight had won a Grade 2 over hurdles, whilst *Barters Hill* had won the Grade 2 bumper at Aintree the previous spring. Of last year's five runners, only the winner and Enrilo (3rd) had even contested a race at that level.

Going back even further, *Cornish Rebel* was another Grade 2 bumper winner (although that Newbury race is now Listed) and both *Brewster* and *Bindaree* had also won Grade 2s over hurdles. Pay healthy respect to those with winning form at this level.

KEY RACES

THIS leads us on nicely to the *Key Races*, and without doubt, the best guide to the Challow is Cheltenham's Grade 2 **Hyde Novices' Hurdle** in November. *Thyme Hill* won that event, and became the eighth winner of the Challow since 2004 to have won or been placed in the race earlier in the campaign. Of the eight, five horses completed the double, so pay close attention to that event, with the Challow in mind.

Thyme Hill actually made his debut over hurdles in Grade 2 company, when beating Fiddleronth-

eroof in the **Persian Warn Novices' Hurdle** at Chepstow. This, too, has proven to be a good guide to the Challow, with Philip Hobbs' earlier winner – *Fingal Bay* – also winning both contests. Since 2009, when *Reve de Sivola* won the early-season event at Chepstow, only six Persian War winners have contested the Challow, and four have won; the other pair being Timesremembered and Blaklion, who both finished placed.

Fingal Bay also had time to win the **Winter Novices' Hurdle** at Sandown prior to his Challow success, and that is third key form race to note. Three Challow winners in the past nine years had also won that race, the other pair being *Taquin du Seuil* and *Messire des Obeaux*. Enrilo was unable to enhance the record of the Winter winner in the Challow last year, and in all, seven of the past nine winners attempted to follow up at Newbury, so the strike-rate wouldn't be quite as strong as that of the Persian War winner. Nevertheless, it remains a piece of form to take seriously, and going back a little further, *Coolnagorna* is another who won both races (2002).

COURSE FORM

FIVE of the past 17 winners boasted winning form at Newbury from earlier in their careers, however, only *Champ* had won a hurdle race at the Berkshire track. The other quartet had won bumpers the previous season, with *Cornish Rebel* and *Barters*

CHAMPAGNESUPEROVER

Hill successful in the Listed event on Betfair Hurdle day. The winner of that race last season wouldn't appeal as a horse who is certain to go on over hurdles (Flat-bred) and the race was certainly run to suit his finishing speed. Those directly in behind him could, however, make their marks over hurdles this season, so don't be surprised if one of those were to turn up here come Christmas time, perhaps **Champagnesuperover** being the pick. He ploughed through bad ground on debut at Ayr, and ought to relish a stiffer test of stamina once sent jumping.

Wichita Lineman and *Diamond Harry* both won two bumpers at the track, the latter winning back-to-back renewals of the valuable sales bumper. Due to last season being cut short, that race – along with another late-season bumper – was lost, so this particular trend might not have as much of an impact this year.

BUMPER FORM

STRONG bumper form – in general – has also been a good pointer, with *Captain Cutter* a Listed winner in that sphere on his racecourse debut (Ascot), whilst *Backspin* was a winner at the Punchestown Festival, when trained by Mags Mullins. More recently, *Poetic Rhythm* was also Listed bumper winner (won two bumpers), whilst *Thyme Hill* finished third in the Champion Bumper at Cheltenham, so strong bumper form is also a positive.

SECOND-SEASON/EXPERIENCED NOVICES

PRIOR to last year, the previous three winners were all second-season novices, and in all six winners during the past 18 years fell into this category. To be precise, *Brewster* was actually a third-season novice, but you can see where I am going here, experience can often count for plenty, in a race that can be a stamina test at times. In addition to the second-season novices, both *Souffleur* and *Parlour Games* had already run six times over hurdles.

At the other end of the scale, *Backspin* and *Barters Hill* – who only faced two opponents, and was quite experienced from bumpers – are the only pair to have won the Challow on the back of just one run over hurdles, in the past 16 years. Soon after the turn of the century, both *Classified* and *Cornish Rebel* managed to achieve this, but it is something that has proven more difficult in recent years. During the past decade, 15 horses have contested the Challow on the back of just the one start, and only the two have won.

Since *Barters Hill* managed it five years ago, seven horses have tried this without success, two of which were owned by Barbara Hester, who saw

Robin Roe fall when going well in 2016 and Brew-in'upastorm finish fourth two years later. This appears to be a race which she likes to target with her brightest young prospects.

During the past nine years, both *Captain Cutter* and *Thyme Hill* won the Challow on their third start (both unbeaten at the time over hurdles), but the average number of hurdles starts comes out of 3.5 over the past decade.

AGE

NINE of the past 10 winners were aged five or six (as you would expect for a novice hurdle), with *Messire des Obeaux* a winning four-year-old in 2016. Like 2009 winner *Reve de Sivola*, he had been contesting juvenile hurdles the previous season, so boasted plenty of hurdles experience. So, if looking at a youngster, that kind of background is favourable, and it is also worth noting that Politologue and Native River were both beaten in this race at the age of four, before going on to much bigger and better things as chasers.

BRITISH-BRED SUCCESS

THERE are a couple of staying novice races in the spring – namely the RSA at Cheltenham and the Sefton Novices' Hurdle at Aintree – in which British-bred horses have a decent record (from limited representation), and four have also won the Challow in the past 13 years. *Souffleur* started the trend in 2007, with *Diamond Harry, Parlour Games* and *Thyme Hill* making it four wins from just 13 runners during that period. Restless Harry also finished runner-up (at 40-1 in 2009) for the British-bred contingent, whilst Kateson finished third two years ago. As I have highlighted in the *Cheltenham Festival Betting Guide* previously, British-bred horses seem to do well in races which require a degree of stamina, and this is beginning to become another good example.

MARKET FORCES

THYME HILL became the third successive – and the 11th this century – winning favourite, when justifying odds of 4-6 last year. Given that the classier types – with proven form in the book – tend to come to the fore, it is hardly surprising that the race tends to be dominated by those towards the head of the betting. Of those 19 winners this century, only three were sent off greater than 5-1, with the biggest of all being *Captain Cutter* at 8s. It isn't really a race in which we see a shock.

OFFICIAL BHA RATINGS

THE past four winners had already obtained the highest official BHA Rating (or joint-top in the case of *Poetic Rhythm*) which ties in with proven form, and often experience, shining through. The past three winners were rated either 147 or 150, which gives you an indication of the level often required. Looking further back, *Diamond Harry* was rated 147 going into the 2008 renewal (although he wasn't top-rated) whilst *Fingal Bay* was already rated 149 before winning this race nine years ago. Respect

any horse rated in the high 140s.

CONNECTIONS TO NOTE

AS highlighted last year, owner **JP McManus** has won this race on no fewer than four occasions since 2006, and he has only had five runners in the race. *Wichita Lineman, Backspin, Captain Cutter* and *Champ* have all carried the famous green and gold hoops to victory in the Challow, whilst *Baltazar d'Allier* finished runner-up in 2016. Without a runner last year, the level-stake profit (to £1) stands at £15.75 for the McManus runners.

The first two of McManus' four winners were trained by **Jonjo O'Neill**, who boasts an unblemished record of four-from-four in the Challow, with his other pair of winners being *Coolnagorna* and *Taquin du Seuil*. Without a runner in the race during the past seven years, be sure to take note if the trainer considers one good enough to take their chance.

Bonanza Boy provided **Philip Hobbs** with the first of three wins in the Challow back in the 1986-87 season, with *Fingal Bay* and *Thyme Hill* adding to that tally much more recently. Hobbs has actually only saddled that pair in the past decade, so he is another who is clearly very selective, and isn't a trainer who runs horses in Graded races for the sake of it. Rather surprisingly, Hobbs was without a bumper winner during the whole of last season, so it remains to be seen as to whether he will have a runner this year.

A further three trainers have won the race twice this century, those being **Nicky Henderson** (twice in the past seven years), **Nick Williams** (who won back-to-back renewals with *Diamond Harry* and *Reve de Sivola*) and **Paul Nicholls,** although he hasn't won it since *Denman* was successful.

ROLL OF HONOUR								
Year	Form	Winner	Age	Weight	OR	SP	Trainer	Runners	Last Race (No. of days)
2019	11	Thyme Hill	5	11-7	147	4/6F	P Hobbs	5	1st G2 Cheltenham Nov Hurdle (42)
2018	111	Champ	6	11-7	150	EvensF	N Henderson	7	1st Newbury Hurdle (28)
2017	13	Poetic Rhythm	6	11-7	147	15/8F	F O'Brien	6	3rd Gr.2 Cheltenham Nov. Hurdle (43)
2016	11	Messire des Obeaux	4	11-7	143	100/30	A King	8	1st Gr.2 Sandown Nov. Hurdle (29)
2015	1	Barters Hill	5	11-7	-	4/11F	B Pauling	3	1st Huntingdon Nov. Hurdle (58)
2014	21021	Parlour Games	6	11-7	145	6/1	J Ferguson	6	1st Gr.2 Cheltenham Nov. Hurdle (45)
2013	11	Captain Cutter	6	11-7	130	8/1	N Henderson	6	1st Market Rasen Nov. Hurdle (23)
2012	121	Taquin du Seuil	5	11-7	137	13/8F	J O'Neill	6	1st Gr.2 Sandown Nov. Hurdle (22)
2011	111	Fingal Bay	5	11-7	149	1/4F	P Hobbs	5	1st Gr.2 Sandown Nov. Hurdle (29)
2010	1	Backspin	5	11-7	-	5/1	J O'Neill	9	1st Bangor Nov. Hurdle (14)

LEADING TEN-YEAR GUIDES

Hyde Novices' Hurdle 4 *(Fingal Bay 1st, Parlour Games 1st, Poetic Rhythm 3rd, Thyme Hill 1st)*
Winter Novices' Hurdle 3 *(Fingal Bay 1st, Taquin du Seuil 1st, Messire des Obeaux 1st)*
Persian War Novices' Hurdle 3 *(Fingal Bay 1st, Poetic Rhythm 1st, Thyme Hill 1st)*

UNIBET TOLWORTH NOVICES' HURDLE

Sandown - 1m7f 216y (Grade 1)

Saturday 2nd January 2021

OVERVIEW

SHORTLY after the Challow comes the second domestic Grade 1 novice hurdle, the Tolworth is staged over the minimum trip, at Sandown, on the first Saturday of the year. Despite the distance, it is a race which tends to favour genuine National Hunt types – with bumper and Point-to-Point winners boasting a fine recent record – which is probably to do with the combination of the stiff uphill finish and the customary soft ground.

The race has a good record of producing subsequent festival winners, with *French Holly, Monsignor, Noland, Yorkhill* and *Summerville Boy* all winning this race since 1998, then going on to win either the Supreme or the Ballymore. The 2000 renewal was a particularly strong one, as *Monsignor* beat Best Mate (runner-up in the Supreme) with Triumph Hurdle winner Snow Drop back in fourth.

The race was lost in 2009 and 2010, and has been staged at other tracks on four occasions – due to the weather – since the turn of the century; Kempton (2014), Wincanton (2003), Warwick (2002) and Ascot (2001).

EXPERIENCE VS THE UNEXPOSED

IN recent years, we have seen both *Yorkhill* and *Finian's Rainbow* win the Tolworth on the back of just one start over hurdles. That pair went on to prove themselves high-class, both later than season and over fences, and it was probably their natural class that allowed them to win a Grade 1 with limited experience. They are actually the only two horses to win this race on their second start this century, with the previous one being *Behrajan* who won as a juvenile in 1999. Again, he would finish third in the Stayers' Hurdle just 14 months later. If you are considering backing a horse on the back of just one run over hurdles in this race, you should be asking yourself if you believe they have the potential to reach that kind of level. Last year, both Son Of Camas and Silver Hallmark were well-beaten in this race, on their respective second starts.

Six winners since 2005 – when *Marcel* was successful – were second-season novices. Along with *Captain Conan* and *L'ami Serge*, he boasted

plenty of experience from France, whilst *Minella Class* had ran once over hurdles in Ireland, before joining Nicky Henderson. *Breedsbreeze* and *Elixir de Nutz* were the other pair, so don't dismiss the so-called 'more-exposed'. Rather like in the Challow, experience can tell in novice hurdles at this time of year.

Subsequent Supreme Novices' winner *Summerville Boy* was a maiden when he won this race three years ago, but he is the only maiden to do so in recent memory. He had run three times over hurdles, however, the same number as last year's winner *Fiddlerontheroof*, who had won a heavy-ground novice hurdle, over course-and-distance, some four weeks earlier. Before joining Colin Tizzard, the giant six-year-old had run in two Irish Point-to-Points, and three bumpers, so certainly wasn't lacking in racecourse experience.

BUMPER & POINT-TO-POINT BACKGROUND

DESPITE not winning between the flags, last year's winner did win the third of his three starts in the bumper division, when trained by John J Walsh. In doing so, he became the eighth winner in the past decade to have won either a bumper, or an Irish Point-to-Point, at the beginning of their careers. *Minella Class* – who won this race on his third start over hurdles, and his second start for Nicky Henderson – had a similar profile to *Fiddlerontheroof*. He failed to win in three starts in Point-to-Points, before winning one of his two bumpers in Ireland, again gaining considerable racecourse experience in the process.

Of those eight winners, only *Yorkhill* had won both a Point and a bumper (won two), whilst the pair who didn't meet this criteria – *Captain Conan* and *L'ami Serge* – were both French recruits. *Elixir de Nutz* was another import from France, but he had won an AQPS race (French bumper) before joining the Philip Hobbs, for whom he he ran twice, before being switched to Colin Tizzard.

Going back a little further, *French Holly* (6th) and *Monsignor* (1st) had contested the Weatherbys Champion Bumper the previous March, and both *Thisthatandtother* (5th) and *Noland* (6th) ran in the Grade 2 at Aintree, so strong bumper form has been evident. Overall since the turn of the century, 13 of the 19 winners had won either (or both in the case of *Yorkhill*) a bumper (10) or a Point-to-Point (4).

You will see from that breakdown that bumper winners have fared better over a longer-spell, but it is worth noting that the Point-to-Point horses are making more of an impact of late. During the past seven years, four of the winners started life in Irish Points, and given the quality on show in that sphere nowadays, it is something which is high-ly-likely to continue to rise.

KEY RACES

RATHER like with the Challow, early season form from Cheltenham has proven to be a good guide towards the Tolworth in recent years. Both *Summerville Boy* and *Elixir de Nutz* had contested the Grade 2 **Sharp Novices' Hurdle** at Cheltenham in November, a race which was won last season by the Emma Lavelle-trained Hang In There, who disappointed in this race. In fairness (and, in hindsight), it didn't look a particularly strong 'Sharp' – or Supreme Trial as it is now, officially, known – at the time, but it is clearly a race that should be respected as a piece of form. Interestingly, the likes of the Sharp – and both the Persian War and

Hyde, which were covered under the Challow – could have a bit more depth to them this year, with the extension to the novice ruling, meaning horses

FIDDLERONTHEROOF PROVIDES COLIN TIZZARD WITH A THIRD TOLWORTH IN FOUR YEARS

who won for the first time in February or March will be eligible. They won't, however, be eligible for this race, nor the Challow.

Both *Summerville Boy* and *Elixir de Nutz* returned to Cheltenham in the December to contest the **British EBF "National Hunt" Novices' Hurdle**, a race that *Melodic Rendezvous* also won before he landed his Tolworth. Although it didn't have an impact on this race last season, it was still a quality renewal, with Chantry House beating subsequent Grade 2 winner Stolen Silver, with Pileon back in fourth. That race is staged over 2m1f on the New course at Cheltenham, so also often requires stamina in the finish, rather like the Tolworth.

Ascot's Grade 2 **Kennel Gate Novices' Hurdle** has also thrown up three winners this century, with both *Monsignor* and *L'ami Serge* winning both races. *Lingo* finished runner-up at Ascot prior to winning this race, although the two races are fairly close in the calendar these days.

MARKET FORCES

SINCE the turn of the century, 13 of the 19 winners were either favourite or second-favourite. 10 of the 13 – and four of the past six winners – were outright favourite, so this is another race in which the top-end of the market tends to dominate. Last year's winner *Fiddleronroof* justified favouritism, returning at 5-4, whilst only four winners this century were sent off at odds greater than 5-1.

TRAINERS TO NOTE

AS highlighted last year, this is clearly a race which **Colin Tizzard** is beginning to target, and target with great effect. *Fiddleronroof* made it three winners in the past four years for the

Dorset-based trainer. His only 'loser' in the race was Russian Doyen (2018), who lacked the experience of his other winners, taking his chance on just his second start over hurdles. He had also failed to win in two bumpers (didn't run in Points) so didn't really fit the profile of the recent winners of this race.

Interestingly, none of his three winners had run for the stable prior to that current season, so don't be surprised if one of his expensive Point-to-Point recruits ends up being aimed here. Given the pace that he showed when winning at Borris House, I wouldn't be shocked to see **Amarillo Sky** campaigned over shorter, and if he were to win early in the season, he could enter the picture for this race. Whoever Tizzard deems good enough to represent his ever-burgeoning yard should be given utmost respect.

Paul Nicholls won the Tolworth on four occasions during six years (between 2003 and 2008), although his record in the past decade is 0/7. Five of those seven did finish second or third, however, so he has been knocking on the door.

In contrast, **Nicky Henderson** won four renewals of the race in the space of five years between 2011 and 2015, and of his three runners since, O O Seven chased home *Yorkhill* in 2016. Henderson has actually won the race five times in all, with his first winner coming back in 1992, when Johnny Kavanagh partnered *New York Rainbow* to victory.

It is also worth noting that **Willie Mullins** boasts a 100% record, with *Yorkhill* his sole runner in the Tolworth to date. There are lots of options in Ireland over the festive period, so it isn't a great surprise that this isn't really a race which the Irish tend to target.

ROLL OF HONOUR								
Year	Form	Winner	Age	Weight	OR	SP	Trainer	Runners	Last Race (No. of days)
2020	221	Fiddleronroof	6	11-7	140	5/4F	C Tizzard	7	1st Sandown Nov Hurdle (28)
2019	F211	Elixir de Nutz	5	11-7	140	3/1	C Tizzard	5	1st Cheltenham Nov. Hurdle (22)
2018	1223	Summerville Boy	6	11-7	142	8/1	T George	5	3rd Cheltenham Nov. Hurdle (22)
2017	1	Finian's Oscar	5	11-7	-	11/10F	C Tizzard	6	1st Hereford Nov. Hurdle (19)
2016	11	Yorkhill	6	11-7	-	4/9F	W Mullins (IRE)	5	1st Punchestown Hurdle (27)
2015	11	L'Ami Serge	5	11-7	149	4/9F	N Henderson	4	1st Gr.2 Ascot Nov. Hurdle (15)
2014*	31	Royal Boy	7	11-7	138	9/1	N Henderson	6	1st Ascot Hurdle (22)
2013	1231	Melodic Rendezvous	7	11-7	135	7/2	J Scott	7	1st Cheltenham Nov. Hurdle (22)
2012	341	Captain Conan	5	11-7	-	9/1	N Henderson	5	1st Auteuil Hurdle (198)
2011	1	Minella Class	6	11-7	-	6/4F	N Henderson	5	1st Newbury Hurdle (24)

LEADING TEN-YEAR GUIDES
British EBF "National Hunt" Novices' Hurdle 3
(Melodic Rendezvous 1st, Summerville Boy 3rd, Elixir de Nutz 1st)
Sharp Novices' Hurdle 2 (Summerville Boy 2nd, Elixir de Nutz 1st)
* Run at Kempton Park

UNIBET LANZAROTE HANDICAP HURDLE

Kempton - 2m5f (Listed)

Saturday 9th January 2021

OVERVIEW

WHEN the Lanzarote Hurdle returned to Kempton in 2007 – following a year at Carlisle – the distance of the race was increased from 2m to 2m5f, so for the basis of (the majority of) these statistics, it makes sense to focus on those past 13 renewals (no race in 2009, due to the weather). This is yet another handicap in which lightly-raced hurdlers do well, and being in the second half of the season, this is the time of year when novices begin to make an impact in such races. Winning form on right-handed tracks also appears to be a huge positive in this event.

RIGHT-HANDED FORM

ALL 13 winners, since the distance of the race was increased, had won on a right-handed track previously. Of the 13, 11 had won racing right-handed over hurdles, with *Big Time Dancer* a three-time winner on the Flat (all of his wins on the level came on right-handed tracks) and *William Henry* was a bumper winner at this track. He was one of four previous course winners to feature among the 13, whilst last season's winner *Burrows Edge* had twice hit the frame over course-and-distance, so Kempton form is also a positive.

Whilst in certain instances it can be true, I feel that there is often a lot made of whether a horse prefers to race one way around or the other. However, it is clear from the statistics that the Lanzarote has been a race in which form on right-handed tracks is indeed beneficial. Last season's result would probably have been different had Debestyman not unseated Michael Nolan at the final flight, and although Suzy Smith's runner had not won when racing this way around under Rules, he had won his Point-to-Point on a right-handed track (Ballindenisk).

In fairness, two-thirds of last year's field had won racing right-handed previously, but it is a notable trend all the same.

NOVICES

FOUR of the past nine winners were novices. *Swincombe Flame* and *Tea For Two* – both trained by Nick Williams – were the first pairing, soon followed by *Yala Enki* and *Big Time Dancer*, who were both second-season novices. Three of the four – with the exception of *Yala Enki* – won on their previous start.

Only four of the 13 runners last season were novices, with market leader Notre Pari (a second-season novice, having just his fifth run over hurdles) being one, and he was in the process of running a big race, when coming down at the final flight.

As the season progresses towards the spring festivals, novices increasingly begin to make an impact in open handicap company (by this time, many will have had time to have recorded the required three runs to qualify) and, personally, I'm a big advocate of siding with unexposed novices in handicaps. Looking back at this year's Cheltenham Festival, five of the eight handicap winners – The Conditional (Ultima), Simply The Betts (Plate), Milan Native (Kim Muir), Saint Roi (County Hurdle) and Chosen Mate (Grand Annual) – were novices, so it is always a good starting point.

LIGHTLY-RACED HURDLERS

DURING the past nine years – when novices have been successful on four occasions – the other five winners were second-season hurdlers. And, the past 11 winners, were all lightly-raced, in that they had all had nine or less starts over hurdles. Eight of those 11 had run seven times or fewer over hurdles, with *Swincombe Flame*, *Oscara Dara* and *Tea For Two* all winning the Lanzarote on just their fourth start over hurdles.

Going back to 2007, and the first running of the race over 2m5f, *Verasi* had run 16 times over hurdles previously, whilst 2008 winner *Nycteos* was having his 11th start when successful, so only just missed out on further enhancing this pretty strong statistic.

Of last year's 13 runners, eight could be classed as 'lightly-raced' having raced between three and seven times over hurdles previously. But for the final flight carnage, the race would have been fought out by three of them. Again, focus on the unexposed.

In terms of winning experience, all bar one of the past 12 winners – that being *Yala Enki* who had won just the once – had recorded two previous career wins over hurdles.

AGE

IN-KEEPING with the past two subsections, it shouldn't come as a surprise that the past 13 winners were all aged eight or younger. *Oscara Dara* and *William Henry* – both trained by Nicky Henderson – were the only eight-year-old winners during this period, and both were lightly-raced for their age.

Going back even further – before the race distance was increased – the Lanzarote was still a race which tended to go the way of a younger horse, and you have to go back to 1988 to find an 'older' winner, in the shape of 12-year-old *Fredcoteri*. Since 1989, the 30 winners were aged eight or younger, with only the Henderson-trained pair striking for the eight-year-olds. During those last 30 renewals, only five of the winners were aged five, meaning 23 were aged six (16) or seven (7). Perhaps more significant is that only one five-year-old (*Saphir du Rheu*) has won since the distance of the race was increased.

MARKET FORCES

11 of the past 12 winners were sent off at single-figure odds, with four favourites (three outright, and *Tea For Two* a joint-favourite) successful during this time. A further four – including *Burrows Edge* last season – were sent off second (or joint-second) in the betting, with another pair third (or joint-third). So, it really has paid to focus on the top-end of the market in recent seasons, with the one big-priced winner being *Big Time Dancer*.

HENDERSON RUNNERS REVERTING TO HURDLES

NICKY HENDERSON has won the Lanzarote Hurdle four times in all, with *Non So* providing him with the first of those back in 2003. His three more recent winners – which have all come in the past eight years – have one notable thing in common, that they had run over fences on their previous start. *Burrows Edge* had fallen on his first start over fences at Ludlow the time before; *William Henry* had pulled-up in the Steel Plate And Sections Novices'

Chase on what was his one and only attempt at chasing; and *Oscara Dara* had been beaten at Plumpton in a novices' chase the previous month.

As stated elsewhere in the book, Henderson tends to start his horses a little later than many of the other yards, which means if things don't go to plan with a novice chaser on debut, it could be Christmas-time (or the New Year) before they are ready to go again. Perhaps that is often behind his thinking to switch a horse back to hurdles, possibly retaining their novice status for the following

NICKY HENDERSON

BIRCHDALE

season. I thought that **Birchdale** might have been a candidate to follow suit last season, but we didn't see him return until the Cheltenham Festival (following a disappointing chasing debut) when he shaped reasonably well in the Coral Cup. He is only six and has the option of going chasing again, but if not, he has the right kind of profile for this race, in that he remains very lightly-raced. I wouldn't be at all surprised if he were to win a nice handicap at some stage this season.

CONDITIONAL JOCKEYS

THIS is something which I flagged up last year – and it could just be coincidental – but five of the past seven winners were ridden by a conditional jockey. Harry Derham, Lizzie Kelly, Charlie Deutsch, James Bowen and Jonjo O'Neill Jnr were the successful riders, and it could just be with big meetings elsewhere in the country (Classic Chase day at Warwick and racing from Wetherby, too) that there are more rides to share around on this particular day in the calendar. Only one jockey claimed weight last year, that being the amateur Lucy Turner.

KEY RACES

THERE aren't too many races which stand-out in terms of a guide towards the Lanzarote, but both *James de Vassy* and *Yala Enki* ran in the **Betfair Stayers' Handicap Hurdle** at Haydock on their previous start, before dropping back in distance. Last season's third – the Nigel Twiston-Davies' trained Echiquier – had finished sixth in the extended 3m Grade 3 on his penultimate start.

And, two winners in the past 11 years – *Micheal Flips* and *Modus* – both finished third in the Listed **Sodexo Handicap Hurdle** at Ascot, in the early weeks of the season. That race is over the minimum trip, so in contrast to the above named-pairing, they were stepping up in distance.

OFFICIAL BHA RATINGS

THERE has been a varied range of both weights carried and official ratings of winners, although since the distance of the race was increased, only two horses have been successful from a mark in the 120s. The average rating of the winners during this period is 135, although five winners in the past decade have won off 140 or higher, suggesting the race is – in general – improving quality-wise. *Saphir du Rheu, Modus* and *William Henry* all won from a mark of 145.

OTHER TRAINERS TO NOTE

THE case for Nicky Henderson has already been well made, whilst **Paul Nicholls** has won the race three times since 2008. Nicholls was without a runner last year, and although it is three years since his last winner, Topofthegame ran a cracker in 2018, before going on to win the Heroes Handicap Hurdle at Sandown.

The trainer with the best win-to-run ratio in the race, however, is **Nick Williams** who has saddled three winners from just five runners (a remarkable 60% strike-rate). *James de Vassy, Swincombe Flame* and *Tea For Two* were Williams' first three runners in the race, and his other pair – who both ran in 2018 – were 25-1 shots. His three winners were sent off at 8-1, 9-2 and 9-2 respectively, and the last-named pairing were last-time-out novice winners.

Dan Skelton has yet to win the Lanzarote, and had two unplaced horses in last season's renewal, but he had previously been responsible for the runner-up in both 2018 and 2019, and he also had the third back in 2014. Therefore, three of his eight runners to date have hit the frame, and given his record in several other major handicap hurdles – admittedly, over 2m – his runners should be noted.

ROLL OF HONOUR								
Year	Form	Winner	Age	Weight	OR	SP	Trainer	Runners	Last Race (No. of days)
2020	F	Burrows Edge	7	11-4	132	5/1	N Henderson	13	Fell Ludlow Beginners' Chase (24)
2019	36421	Big Time Dancer	6	10-10 (5)	125	16/1	J Candish	14	1st Doncaster Hurdle (42)
2018	P	William Henry	8	11-7 (5)	145	7/1	N Henderson	16	p.u. Cheltenham Nov. Chase (57)
2017	327	Modus	7	11-4	145	7/1	P Nicholls	13	7th Gr.3 Ascot Hurdle (28)
2016	15	Yala Enki	6	9-12 (5)	130	11/4F	V Williams	9	5th Gr.3 Haydock Hurdle (49)
2015	131	Tea For Two	6	9-12 (7)	134	9/2JF	N Williams	13	1st Towcester Nov. Hurdle (15)
2014	541	Saphir du Rheu	5	11-7 (5)	145	6/1	P Nicholls	13	1st Sandown Hurdle (35)
2013	12	Oscara Dara	8	11-0	140	5/1	N Henderson	18	2nd Plumpton Nov. Chase (26)
2012	211	Swincombe Flame	6	10-4	123	9/2	N Williams	19	1st Wincanton Nov. Hurdle (19)
2011	0	James de Vassy	6	11-2	144	8/1	N Williams	19	13th Listed Haydock Hurdle (56)
LEADING TEN-YEAR GUIDES								
Betfair Stayers' Handicap Hurdle 2 *(James de Vassy unplaced, Yala Enki 5th)*								

BETFAIR HURDLE

Newbury - 2m 69y (Grade 3 handicap)

Saturday 6th February 2021

OVERVIEW

FORMERLY known as the 'Schweppes' then the Tote Gold Trophy, the Betfair Hurdle has had its current sponsor since 2012, and is – arguably – the most prestigious handicap hurdle of the season, away from the Cheltenham Festival. A full field of 24 took their chance last year, in a race which was used as a springboard to Champion Hurdle success in 1997 when the novice *Make A Stand* won for Martin Pipe. Novices have a fine recent record in this event.

NOVICE DOMINATION

THE recent stranglehold of novices in the Betfair Hurdle might have been broken last year, although favourite Ciel de Niege was less than a length away from further enhancing their fine record in the race. Prior to last year, eight of the previous 10 winners were novices, with six of them having had just the three runs needed to qualify. The recent statistic might have been even better had Darlan not fallen in the 2012 renewal, as he was cruising at the time. Given what he achieved afterwards – prior to taking a fatal fall at Doncaster just a year later – he would have surely gone very close. He was another who had only had the three runs beforehand and had been kept relatively low-key (out of Graded company).

Darlan's owner **JP McManus** has been responsible for two winners (both novices after three runs) and four seconds during the past 11 years, so it is a race which he clearly likes to target. During the past 11 years, McManus has had 22 runners in the race and granted a shade more luck, he might have been looking at three or four winners during this period. It should be noted that his two winners were English-trained novices, who were sent off at 6-1 and 5-1, respectively, whereas several of his runners were much bigger prices. Respect any lightly-raced youngsters representing the leading owner, especially if prominent in the betting.

LIGHTLY-RACED HURDLERS

LAST year's winner might have been a novice, but *Pic d'Orhy* had only had the nine starts over hurdles previously. Going back to 2005 (inclusive), all 14 winners of the Betfair Hurdle (no race 2006 or 2009) had raced 10 times or less over hurdles, with nine of them having had no more than four starts previously.

Agrapart was one of the winning novices with four runs to his name, whilst the most recent Irish-trained winner of the race – *Essex* in 2005 – had also only had the four starts. He had shown smart form in juvenile hurdles the previous season, whilst *Zarkandar* won this race on his belated reappearance, having won the Triumph and Anniversary Hurdle as a juvenile. Paul Nicholls' runner won this race on just his fourth start over hurdles.

Going back a bit further, *Sharpical, Decoupage, Geos* and *Landing Light* were four successive winners – between 1998 and 2001 – who had also run eight times or less over hurdles. Landing Light, who later developed into a high-class dual-purpose performer, justified favouritism on his fourth start as a hurdler.

Since 1997 when *Make A Stand* won, 19 of the 22 winners had run 10 times or less over hurdles, so focus on the lightly-raced, even if looking outside of novice company. And, in terms of winning experience, only one of the past 21 winners – that being *Geos* when winning his second Betfair in 2004 – had previously won more than three times over hurdles.

REPEAT OFFENDERS

GEOS was one of the winners during a three-year spell (2002 – 2004) when 'more exposed' horses won the Betfair, and he, of course, was repeating his victory from four years earlier. *Copeland* had finished runner-up to *Geos* in 2000 and himself went one place better in 2002, so if looking for a different angle (away from the lightly-raced types), it is worth considering those who have run well in the race previously.

More recently, 2010 winner *Get Me Out Of Here* returned to finish runner-up two years later, whilst Cheltenian finished fourth in 2014 (as a second-season novice) before finishing runner-up 12 months later.

CURRENT FORM

PIC D'ORHY arrived at Newbury on the back of finishing unplaced at Ascot (2m3½f) and became the first winner in the past 12 to have failed to record a top-three finish last time out. The previous 11 winners had either won (5), finished second (3) or finished third (3) on their previous start. Going back even further, only two more winners this century failed to finish first, second or third on their previous start, so respect those arriving in good form.

AGE

SINCE the second victory of *Geos* in 2004, all 14 winners were aged either five (8) or six (6), which again ties in with the recent record of novices and lightly-raced horses. At the other end of the scale, *Geos* – when winning the race for the second time – is the only winner since 1993 (when *King Credo* won at the age of eight) aged above seven.

WEIGHT AND OFFICIAL RATINGS

SIX of the past nine winners – and this includes the past four winners – carried 11-1 or more, with *Al Dancer* carrying the biggest weight to victory this century (11-8). It should be said, however, that he faced only 13 rivals in a weakened rescheduled renewal at Ascot, whereas the 2018 and 2020 renewals saw full fields of 24 take their chance.

Following the victories of *Heathcote* and *Wingman* – who are the only pair this century to win from a mark in the 120s – eight of the 11 winners have won from a mark between 132 and 141. The lowest of those being *Violet Dancer*, who like the other-named pairing, represented the Gary Moore stable. The three 'higher-rated' winners in recent years were *Zarkandar* (151), *My Tent Or Yours* (149) and last year's winner *Pic d'Orhy* (146).

MARKET FORCES

GIVEN that he had contested Grade 1 races on two of his previous three starts, it was slightly surprising that last year's winner was allowed to go off at 33-1 (easy to say now) and this is a race in which the odd huge priced winner does occur. *Splash Of Ginge* returned at the same price in 2014, whilst *Heathcote* was a 50-1 shot when winning in 2007. Since then, his stable-companion *Violet Dancer* won at 20-1, although it has been a mixed bag of results in recent years.

In the past nine years, five favourites (*Kalashnikov* was co-favourite in a very-open year, the other four were outright favourite) have been successful. Again, Ciel de Niege was less than a length away from making it four winning favourites-in-a-row last season.

KEY RACES

AS touched upon last year, five of the previous nine winners had contested a Grade 1 or Grade 2 on their previous start, and although he just missed out on that statistic, last year's winner had run in the Grade 1 Prix Renaud du Vivier at Auteuil on

his penultimate start. Two of the five – *Agrapart* and *Kalashnikov* – had run in the **Tolworth Novices' Hurdle** at Sandown the previous month.

The previous season's Grade 2 **Weatherbys Racing Bank Bumper** at Aintree has thrown up three winners in the past eight years. The three horses in question all ran well without winning, and although it is another race (from the abandoned Grand National fixture) which won't have an impact this season, it is worth keeping in mind that smart bumper form is clearly a good grounding for any novices lining up.

Indeed, Jamie Snowden's Thebannerkingrebel was sent off just 7-1 second-favourite for the Betfair in February, and he had finished runner-up in the Aintree bumper the previous April, when beaten just a length by McFabulous, who himself won a big handicap last spring (EBF Final). Thebannerkingrebel had won a Listed novice hurdle and ran well in a Grade 2 on his previous start, so certainly had the right kind of profile for this race. The point here being that Graded form in both bumpers and novice hurdle races is a positive, despite this not being an example which worked out positively.

TRAINERS TO NOTE

LOCAL trainer **Nicky Henderson** has won this race on five occasions, with the Seven Barrows team enjoying a red-hot period between 1998 and 2004, when they won the race four times in seven years. Since then, Henderson's sole winner in the past 14 years was *My Tent Or Yours*, who bolted up before going on to prove himself a top-class hurdler. Since that first victory in 1998, Henderson has run no fewer than 51 horses in the Betfair Hurdle, so strike-rate wise it isn't so impressive, and it is worth noting that his record stands at one winner from 35 runners during the past 14 years. He saddled two last year, one being Never Adapt who was tragically injured at the first flight. Henderson will, no doubt, continue to target the race, and his record with lightly-raced hurdlers is more noteworthy. All bar one of his winners (*Geos'* second win) had run eight times or less over hurdles, with *Landing Light* and *My Tent Or Yours* having had just the three starts. Therefore, pay more attention to the unexposed hurdlers which he runs.

As already touched upon, **Gary Moore** won the race three times between 2007 and 2015, and given the starting prices of all three, his level-stake profit in this race is huge. Going back to 1998, Moore has had 17 Betfair runners, and as well as his trio of winners, he has had another three finish in the first four. Backing them all blind would have yielded a profit of £70 to a level stake of £1.

Nigel Twiston-Davies had two runners in last season's renewal – with Sir Valentine shaping best in fourth – and he had won three of the previous six renewals. All three were novices, as was Flying Angel, who finished third in 2016, before winning the Imperial Cup on his next start. Pay healthy respect to any novice representing the Twiston-Davies camp.

Pic d'Orhy provided **Paul Nicholls** with a second win in the race in the past nine years, following on from *Zarkandar* in 2012. In between those two wins, Nicholls has been responsible for a further five placed horses (between second and fourth) and in total during the past decade, he has saddled 17 runners in the race.

Like Nicholls, **Philip Hobbs** saddled three runners last year, in a bid to end his poor run in the race. Responsible for four runners-up (Rooster Booster on three occasions and the aforementioned Cheltenian), Hobbs' record this century in the Betfair Hurdle now stands at 0/28.

Last year I also highlighted the poor recent record of Irish-trained horses in the race, since the victories of *Sprit Leader* (2003) and *Essex* (2005). **Willie Mullins** went close last year with runner-up Ciel de Niege (sent off 13-2 favourite), but his record – which spans back to 2002 – stands at 0/18, with several of his runners (as you would expect) sent off fairly prominently in the market. He has now been responsible for two outright beaten favourites, following on from Blazer (sent off at just 3-1) in 2016; both horses were owned by JP McManus.

Noel Meade is another Irish trainer who has had runners in recent seasons, although not to the same extent as Mullins. His record is 0/6, with his two runners during the past five years also sporting the McManus silks. It is clear – as highlighted earlier – that the leading owner likes to have runners in this race.

ROLL OF HONOUR

Year	Form	Winner	Age	Weight	OR	SP	Trainer	Runners	Last Race (No. of days)
2020	F6	Pic d'Orhy	5	11-5	146	33/1	P Nicholls	24	6th Ascot Hurdle (21)
2019*	111	Al Dancer	6	11-8	141	5/2F	N Twiston-Davies	14	1st Cheltenham Hurdle (64)
2018	112	Kalashnikov	5	11-5	141	8/1CF	A Murphy	24	2nd Gr.1 Tolworth Hurdle (35)
2017	232	Ballyandy	6	11-1	135	3/1F	N Twiston-Davies	16	2nd Gr.2 Sandown Nov. Hurdle (71)
2016	5213	Agrapart	5	10-5	137	16/1	N Williams	22	3rd Gr.1 Tolworth Hurdle (42)
2015	49322	Violet Dancer	5	10-9	132	20/1	G Moore	23	2nd Lingfield Maiden (17)
2014	24133	Splash of Ginge	6	10-3	134	33/1	N Twiston-Davies	20	3rd Gr.2 Leamington Hurdle (28)
2013	121	My Tent Or Yours	6	11-2	149	5/1F	N Henderson	21	1st Huntingdon Nov. Hurdle (29)
2012		Zarkandar	5	11-1	151	11/4F	P Nicholls	20	1st Gr.1 Anniversary Hurdle (316)
2011	1211	Recession Proof	5	10-8	134	12/1	J Quinn	15	1st Southwell Bumper (52)

LEADING TEN-YEAR GUIDES

The previous season's Weatherbys Racing Bank Bumper 3
(My Tent Or Yours 2nd, Ballyandy 4th, Al Dancer 4th)
Tolworth Novices' Hurdle 2 *(Agrapart 3rd, Kalashnikov 2nd)*
* Run at Ascot

EASY AS THAT - ONE OF THIS YEAR'S *LEADING PROSPECTS* WINS IN A CANTER AT MUSSELBURGH

ANOTHER OF THIS YEAR'S *LEADING PROSPECTS* - IMPERIAL ALCAZAR

Index